The International Yearbook of Environmental and Resource Economics 1997/1998

NEW HORIZONS IN ENVIRONMENTAL ECONOMICS

General Editor: Wallace E. Oates, *Professor of Economics, University of Maryland*

This important series is designed to make a significant contribution to the development of the principles and practices of environmental economics. It includes both theoretical and empirical work. International in scope, it addresses issues of current and future concern in both East and West and in developed and developing countries.

The main purpose of the series is to create a forum for the publication of high quality work and to show how economic analysis can make a contribution to understanding and resolving the environmental problems confronting the world in the late twentieth century.

Recent titles in the series include:

Climate Change, Transport and Environmental Policy
Empirical Applications in a Federal System
Edited by Stef Proost and John B. Braden

The Economics of Energy Policy in China
Implications for Global Climate Change
ZhongXiang Zhang

Advanced Principles in Environmental Policy
Anastasios Xepapadeas

Taxing Automobile Emissions for Pollution Control
Maureen Sevigny

Global Environmental Change and Agriculture
Assessing the Impacts
Edited by George Frisvold and Betsey Kuhn

Fiscal Policy and Environmental Welfare
Modelling Interjurisdictional Competition
Thorsten Bayindir-Upmann

The International Yearbook of Environmental and Resource Economics
1998/1999
A Survey of Current Issues
Edited by Tom Tietenberg and Henk Folmer

The Economic Approach to Environmental Policy
The Selected Essays of A. Myrick Freeman III
A. Myrick Freeman III

Economic Integration and the Environment
A Political–Economic Perspective
Rolf Bommer

Public Choice and Environmental Regulation
Tradable Permit Systems in the United States
and CO_2 Taxation in Europe
Gert Tingaard Svendsen

The International Yearbook of Environmental and Resource Economics 1997/1998

A Survey of Current Issues

Edited by

Henk Folmer

Professor of Economics, Wageningen Agricultural University and Professor of Environmental Economics, Tilburg University The Netherlands

Tom Tietenberg

Mitchell Family Professor of Economics, Colby College, USA

NEW HORIZONS IN ENVIRONMENTAL ECONOMICS SERIES

Edward Elgar
Cheltenham, UK • Northampton, MA, USA

Published by
Edward Elgar Publishing Limitied
8 Lansdown Place
Cheltenham
Glos GL50 2HU
UK

Edward Elgar Publishing, Inc.
6 Market Street
Northampton
Massachusetts 01060
USA

Paperback edition 1998

A catalogue record for this book
is available from the British Library

Library of Congress Cataloguing in Publication Data
The international yearbook of environmental and resource economics
    1997/1998: a survey of current issues / edited by Henk Folmer, Tom
    Tietenberg.
        (New horizons in environmental economics)
        Includes bibliographical references.
        1. Environmental economics. 2. Natural resources—Economic
    aspects. 3. Economic development—Environmental aspects.
    1. Folmer, Henk, 1945–   . II. Tietenberg, Thomas, H. III. Series.
    HC55.1575   1997
    338.4′73337—dc21   96–52727
                                                                              CIP

ISBN 1 85898 369 X (cased)
       1 85898 844 6 (paperback)

Printed and bound in Great Britain by
Biddles Ltd, Guildford and King's Lynn

Contents

Figures

Tables

Editorial Board

Contributors

David G. Abler is an Associate Professor of Agricultural Economics at the Pennsylvania State University. He holds a PhD in economics from the University of Chicago. His research interests include environmental policy design for agriculture, interactions between population growth and the environment, and environmental impacts of economic policies in developing countries.

Daniel W. Bromley is Anderson-Bascom Professor of applied economics at the University of Wisconsin-Madison, US. He has served as editor of the journal *Land Economics* since 1974. He is the author of: *Economic Interests and Institutions: The Conceptual Foundations of Public Policy* (1989) and *Environment and Economy: Property Rights and Public Policy* (1991). He has also edited *Making the Commons Work: Theory, Practice, and Policy* (1992); and *The Handbook of Environmental Economics* (1995). He is currently writing *Rousseau's Revenge: An Economic History of Private Property*.

Lawrence H. Goulder is Associate Professor of Economics and a Senior Fellow at the Institute for International Studies at Stanford University, US. His research examines the economic impacts of environmentally motivated tax reforms and other environmental regulations, often in a general equilibrium framework that accounts for interactions between environmental policies and other, pre-existing regulations or taxes. He has written numerous theoretical and empirical papers on these subjects and has developed applied environment–economy models for several US government agencies and international organizations.

John M. Hartwick has taught economics at Queen's University (Ontario) since 1969. His contributions to the economics of natural resources have been on 'green' national accounting and stock change valuation in the analysis of sustainable development. The second edition of his textbook with Nancy Olewiler (*The Economics of Natural Resource Use*) is in press.

Dominic Moran is currently Environmental Economic Advisor in the Economic Planning Unit, Kuala Lumpur, Malaysia and previously a Research Associate at the Centre for Social and Economic Research on the Global Environment at

University College London, UK. His main interests include the economics of nature conservation and biodiversity and the application of valuation methods. He holds MA and PhD degrees in economics from Manchester University and University College London respectively.

David Pearce is Professor of Environmental Economics at University College London, UK and Associate Director of the Centre for Social and Economic Research on the Global Environment. He is the author or editor of more than forty books mainly on environmental economics, holds the United Nations Global 500 award for services to the World Environment and was awarded the Gambrinus Prize for literature for *Blueprint for the Green Economy*.

James S. Shortle is Professor of Environmental and Natural Resource Economics in the Department of Agricultural Economics and Rural Sociology, Pennsylvania State University, US. He has conducted research on a range of environmental issues including nonpoint pollution control policy, environmental policies for agriculture, trade and the environment, agricultural productivity impacts of air pollution, and water resource impacts of climate change.

V. Kerry Smith is the Arts and Sciences Professor of Environmental Economics at Duke University, US and a University Fellow for the Quality of the Environment Division at Resources for the Future. He is a past President of the Southern Economic Association and the Association of Environmental and Resource Economists. His current research focuses on modelling how individuals deal with risks, investigating the development of recreation values for reducing marine pollution, measuring the trade consequences of environmental policy, incorporating nonmarket services into measures of GDP and calibrating nonmarket valuation methods. Dr Smith has served as editor of *Advances in Applied Microeconomics* and is associate editor for the *Journal of Risk and Uncertainty, Risk Analysis* and the *Review of Economics and Statistics*. His most recent book is a collection of new and published essays on non-market valuation entitled *Estimating Economic Values for Nature* (1996). He is currently completing work on another book, *The Economics of Environmental Risk*.

Alistair Ulph is Professor of Economics at the University of Southampton. He has published widely on a range of economic topics, but with an emphasis on resource and environmental economics, and labour economics. He served as economic assessor for a public enquiry into the Hinkley Point 'C' Nuclear Power Station, and has been a consultant on a range of projects for UK Government Departments, the European Commission, and ILO. His current research interests are trade and the environment, and the impact of environmental liabilities on financial markets.

Preface

As a discipline Environmental and Resource Economics has undergone a rapid evolution over the past three decades. Originally the literature focused on valuing environmental resources, designing policy instruments to correct externalities and providing for the optimal exploitation of resources. The relatively narrow focus of the field and the limited number of contributors made the task of keeping up with the literature relatively simple.

More recently, environmental and resource economics has broadened its focus by making connections with many other subdisciplines in economics as well as the natural and physical sciences. It has also attracted a much larger group of contributors. Thus the literature is exploding in terms of the number of topics addressed, the number of methodological approaches being applied and the sheer number of articles being written. Coupled with the high degree of specialization which characterizes modern academic life, this proliferation of topics and methodologies makes it impossible for anyone, even those who specialize in environmental and resource economics, to keep up with the developments in the field as a whole.

The editors have initiated *The International Yearbook of Environmental and Resource Economics: A Survey of Current Issues* to fill this niche. The *Yearbook* publishes state of the art papers by top specialists in their fields who have made substantial contributions to the area which they are surveying. Authors are invited by the editors, in consultation with members of the editorial board. Each paper is critically reviewed by the editors and by several members of the editorial board.

The editors would like to thank Wallace Oates for his help in getting the project started. We also owe a special debt of gratitude to Scott Barrett, Carlo Carraro, Per-Olov Johansson, Karl Gustav Löfgren, Wallace Oates, Steve Polasky, Alan Randall, Bob Solow and Olli Tahvonen for their assistance in editing this first collection of papers.

Henk Folmer
Tom Tietenberg

1. Property regimes in environmental economics

Daniel W. Bromley

PROPERTY ISSUES IN ENVIRONMENTAL ECONOMICS

The Early Interest in Environmental Property Rights

It would not be overstating things to assert that environmental problems are property rights problems. Pollution is simply the transmission beyond the recognized legal 'boundary' of the firm or the household of some quantity of matter (chemical compound, heat, smoke, garbage, noise, dust) that gives rise to costs for others. We call these effects 'externalities' precisely because the impacts on others are external to the unit that makes the decisions about resource allocation. By being external we understand that these economic effects transcend the domain over which the firm has socially sanctioned control. That is, pollutants transcend the property regime pertinent to the firm (or household), thus giving rise to the external costs at the core of externalities. The nominal boundary of the firm or the household – which is a legal notion – does not match the real boundary – which is a physical notion reflecting the space over which the physical effects (pollutants) travel.

But the importance of property regimes transcends pollution. Problems in fishery management, groundwater management, African grazing regimes, forestry, or the extraction of exhaustible resources, all arise because of the contentious nature of the property regimes pertinent to those environmental resources. Indeed, global climate change represents a property regime problem in a contemporary sense as well as in an intertemporal sense. That is, greenhouse gases represent pollution today, but allegedly alter global climate such that future generations may bear important costs not of their choosing. This is an intertemporal externality that may require a restructuring of the property regimes such that those living in the future acquire protection through altered rights structures (Bromley, 1989b).

One of the early illustrations of the importance of property regimes in environmental economics is found in the work of A.C. Pigou (1920). Pigou used the illustration of factory smoke harming clean laundry hung out to dry as an example of a 'social cost'. That is, the factory did not take into account the costs imposed on the owner of the laundry who must, following the increased prevalence of smoke with the Industrial Revolution, take extraordinary measures to keep clean linens from becoming dirty again. Pigou suggested a tax on the generator of smoke to reflect the 'external' costs borne by the laundry. While this account has been a valuable heuristic to explore the issue of pollution, there are several unexplored property issues in this famous example.

First, notice that the externality can be 'solved' immediately if one firm would but buy out the other. For instance, let the factory purchase the laundry – or the laundry purchase the factory – and suddenly the externality will have been internalized.[1] Once these two firms fall under a single owner then the 'efficient' solution will arise because one decision maker is balancing the two enterprises and making the correct decisions in the best interest of the joint enterprise. We see immediately that the 'externality' problem disappears once the property regime changes to combine two firms into one. The externality has been internalized to the new joint firm. The internalization occurs because the nominal boundary of the firm has now become coincidental with the real boundary of the firm. This solution is one possible outcome of the bargaining recommended by Coase (1960).

Second, note that there is another property rights lesson in the standard Pigovian story. Pigou assumed that the owner of the laundry had a right to clean air in which to dry linens. The other side of this presumed right to clean air for the laundry is the duty on the part of the factory not to emit smoke that would foul clean laundry. While it may be easy now to argue that the laundry should not have dirty air to contend with, it is not always obvious that this is so. For instance, what if the laundry moved into the immediate vicinity long after the factory had been in operation?[2] What if the factory was the source of most of the employment in the town, without which the laundry might not survive? We see that externality problems entail perceptions of 'rights' in a moral sense as well as in a legal sense. The Coasean response to Pigou was to argue that the rights should go to the most valuable use. In essence, while Pigou erred by regarding the smoke as the problem (rather than the unfortunate proximity of the two incompatible activities), Coase erred by stripping externality policy of any chance to consider that one use – even if of lower 'value' – may have some compelling moral claim (perhaps by being there first).[3]

Third, there is the important matter of so-called 'third-party' effects. We know that there are a large number of individuals who have an interest in factories and laundries, even if they have no immediate contact or involvement with either one. Some individuals want the air to be relatively free of smoke, while others might well see smoke as signs of 'progress'. The social costs of concern to Pigou did not encompass these third-party interests. Nor was Coase particularly concerned with those beyond the immediate parties to the externality. With

Coase's interest in bargaining, and his emphasis on low transaction costs, he saw most externality situations as fairly narrowly circumscribed. But it is essential to see that air quality is of concern to those beyond factories and laundries. Hence there are larger 'ownership' issues even in what may appear to be rather simple externality situations.

To address these issues, let us now turn our attention to the matter of property rights and property regimes.

Property Rights and Property Regimes

Before we can give clarity to the idea of property regimes in environmental policy, it is first necessary to understand the related ideas of rights and property rights.

To have a right is to have the capacity to call upon the collective power – some authority system – to stand behind one's interests. This authority system could be the government of a local village, or it could be a national government. Notice that rights can only have effect when there is some authority system that agrees to defend a right-holder's interest in a particular outcome. If I have a right, then it means that I can turn to the pertinent authority system to see that my interest is protected. The effective protection I gain from this authority is nothing other than a correlated duty or obligation for all others interested in my claim. A right is a triadic relationship that encompasses my interest, the outcome or object of my interest (whether a physical object or a stream of benefits), plus all others with conflicting interests, yet with a duty to respect my right. Rights are not relationships between me and an object, but are rather relationships between me and others with respect to that object. Rights only have empirical content when there is a social mechanism that gives duties to those interested in the particular outcome guaranteed to the right-holder.

When one has a right in something it means that the benefit stream arising from that situation is explicitly protected by some authority system. The authority system gives and takes away rights by its willingness – or unwillingness – to agree to protect one's claims in something. To have a property right, therefore, is to have secure control over a future benefit stream. And it is to know that the authority system will come to your defence when that control is threatened. The thing of value to you is the benefit stream and this benefit stream is the property interest that individuals seek to have protected with property rights.

The degree of protection afforded by a particular structure of property rights is always relative to other social concerns and priorities. I will discuss this in more detail later in this chapter, but for now we must recall that protection of the benefit stream associated with any particular asset is always relative to its social usefulness. Property rights in land are usually more secure than property rights in other assets, but this is not universally so across different cultures.

So 'property' is the stream of benefits, and rights to property offer varying degrees of security over that benefit stream. When I purchase a piece of land its price is a reflection of the present discounted value of all of its future benefit streams. By purchasing the land I am really purchasing the benefit stream. While land is sometimes called 'property', the property is, in fact, the benefit stream that I now own, and that I believe will be protected with the authority of some governance structure. If it would not be protected then my willingness to pay for it would be reduced in reflection of its less-secure status.

Before leaving this discussion of rights, it seems important to say a word about the rhetorical – as opposed to legal – aspect of the term 'right'. There are two dimensions to this rhetorical idea of a right, and they both get invoked at various times. For instance, individuals will assert that they have a 'right' to smoke in some location – say in an airplane. When used in this sense, the term 'right' is being used as a persuasive device to buttress a self-serving argument. Those who use this language know that this phrasing is much stronger than merely claiming that they wish to smoke. In addition, they confuse the traditional practice of smoking in public places with the legal right to do so. The owners of factories, with a long tradition of disposing of their waste in nearby rivers, have been known to assert that they have a 'right' to continue to do so. In this instance, the long use of a particular practice – smoking in public places, disposing of industrial wastes in rivers – is taken as proof of its propriety. There is, or so some would like to argue, a compelling moral authority in tradition.

This argument is particularly prominent in environmental disputes. The human and ecological ramifications of many traditional industrial practices are of rather recent origin. When efforts are made to modify such practices, those who will be thereby disadvantaged will invoke that long tradition to suggest that they have a 'right' to do those things now discovered to be harmful. Farmers will insist they have a right to spray poisonous chemicals on their crops. Industrial managers will insist they have a right to dispose of their waste products as they have been doing for the past 75 years. Suburban residents will claim they have a right to burn the leaves from their ample yards. While the confusion of tradition for a right certainly has no grounding in law, it can often be used in the political arena to put on the defensive those who desire a change in the status quo. 'Rights talk' has some heft in such debates (Glendon, 1991).

The idea of a right can also be used to suggest something much more compelling than mere tradition. In fundamental terms, a right is often associated with some moral position. We see this in the area of so-called human rights. Here the term 'right' is used to suggest some inherent virtues and capacities associated with being human that transcend legal and political strictures that are the creation of some government. The related domain of discourse about the 'rights of nature' appeals to this moral element. This line of attack is then used, in a rhetorical sense, to persuade others that nature should be protected. As with the previous category of rights talk, it is much more compelling to couch one's interests in terms of rights. Given the alternatives of fighting to have nature protected because we prefer that outcome, or arguing that nature should be protected because nature has 'rights', the choice is quite obvious.

We see, therefore, that the idea of rights has both a rhetorical element and a legal element; rights are both prescriptive (normative) and descriptive. These two domains are clearly interdependent. After all, the law is simply a manifestation of the normative realm of human associations. What at one time is expressed as an 'ought' or a 'should' becomes, through the legislative process, a 'must' in a subsequent time. Rights are simply the socially sanctioned and enforced normative elements of civil society. Property rights extend that legal force to the realm of objects and benefit streams.

It is now time to explore alternative property rights arrangements. In what follows I will use the term resource-management regime to denote these possible property rights structures. A resource-management regime is a constellation of legal correlates that defines the relationship of individuals to one another with respect to that particular environmental resource. Property relations between two or more individuals (or groups) are defined by recognizing that one party has an interest that is protected by a right if and only if all others have a duty. When one has a right one has the expectation that their claims will be respected by those with duty. And, when necessary, the state is available to compel compliance.

There are four broad types of management regimes worthy of attention by environmental economists: (1) state-property regimes; (2) private-property regimes; (3) common-property regimes; and (4) non-property regimes (open access).

State-property regimes
These are when ownership and control over natural resource use and management rests in the hands of the state through various government agencies. Individuals and groups may use the natural resources, but only with the approval of the administrative agency responsible for carrying out the wishes of the larger political community. National forests, national parks and military reservations are examples of state-property regimes. The state may either directly manage and control the use of state-owned natural resources through government agencies, or it may lease the natural resource to groups or individuals – for example, timber companies, livestock producers – who are thus given usufruct rights for a specified period of time. That is, state-property regimes remove most discretion from the user, and generally do not convey long-term expectations to the immediate users. However, state-property regimes, by their very nature, convey secure expectations for many others. That is, national parks and forest preserves ensure that the resources under such management regimes will be conserved for future generations. To be successful, such regimes require

governmental structures and functions that can match policy pronouncements with meaningful administrative capacity.

Resource degradation in state-property regimes will arise when the administrative reach of the management agency is insufficient to control the behaviours of those authorized to use the resource. This can happen because of an absence of knowledge about proper use, or it can arise because of inadequate funding to make timely enforcement decisions. Resource degradation also occurs in such property regimes when political processes are not sufficiently robust to resist pressures from those allowed to use natural resources.

Where governments are weak, and their legitimacy is easily undermined, there is a tendency for resource degradation to arise from the inability of the government to confront powerful commercial interests which exploit natural resources under state property regimes. Timber concessions in the developing countries represent a typical form of this practice. It takes a secure government to stand up to those who are making large economic gains from the use of those natural resources the government has said it owns. Unfortunately, such governments are also likely to be ineffective in regulating the use of privately held natural resources.

Private-property regimes
The most familiar property regime is that of private property. Here the range of discretion open to the owner(s) is fairly extensive and will include the right to control, the right to transfer, the right to use, and several other aspects signifying relative autonomy for the owner. Note that private property does not necessarily mean individual property; corporate property is private property administered by a group. Similarly, marital property is often the joint property of the spouses. Nor does private property imply absolute control for the owner. An owner is always faced with a number of strictures and obligations in the use of private land and its related natural resources (Christman, 1994). But given the ubiquity of private property, and given the presumptions that accompany this particular property regime, it is necessary to elaborate on some aspects of private property.

As with any property regime, the case for private-property regimes ultimately rests on judgements concerning social utility. Becker (1977) notes that any property regime must be understood at three levels: (1) the general level; (2) the particular level; and (3) the specific level. A general argument for private property in the abstract is difficult to refute. Even at a particular level, one can argue that land is often best suited to a regime of private property. However, at the specific level, the issue may not be so clear. To argue that pasture land in the valleys of Switzerland is best managed as private property is not to say that the Swiss summer pastures at 3000 meters elevation are best managed as private property. Indeed, the Swiss have answered this institutional question by creating common-property regimes over the high mountain pastures (Netting, 1976). Should we conclude from this that the Swiss fail to understand the efficiency attributes of private property? Or should we conclude that the Swiss, like mountain people the world over, see something in private-property regimes that is not well suited to ecological and social situations in the higher Alps? Efficiency does not drive institutional choice but rather flows from it (Bromley, 1989a, 1991).

There is a presumption among some economists that private-property regimes are the only ones in which proper care of natural resources will occur (Alchian and Demsetz, 1973; Barzel, 1989; Buchanan, 1962, 1972, 1973; Coase, 1960; Demsetz, 1967; Furubotn and Pejovich, 1974; North and Thomas, 1977). The idea in this literature is that only an individual owner can make the proper management decisions and that when governments get in the way (as in state-property regimes), or when there is a group of co-owners (as in common-property regimes), then the natural resource will inevitably be destroyed. This presumption needs to be addressed at three levels.

At the first level, the argument will often be advanced that economic efficiency results when individual decision-makers hold exclusive rights over the use of an asset (a natural resource). This proposition follows from the assumptions of economic theory in which efficiency results when decision makers have perfect information, all resources are divisible and mobile, and decision makers are unable to influence prices in factor or product markets. Notice that efficiency is defined as the outcome that will occur in situations in which these assumptions hold, and therefore actions taken under these circumstances are, by definition, efficient actions.

On this logic, advocates of individualized control over environmental resources argue that thoroughgoing private property, and the absence of governmental environmental regulations, will ensure the proper use and care of environmental resources.[4] In response to this argument, Talbot Page (1977) has shown that careful management by an informed owner can result in the destruction of living resources if the time rate of growth of the resource is less than the rate of time preference of the owner. Beyond the domain of living resources, there is the widespread loss of valuable top soil from privately owned farms. The question becomes, if private property contains the proper incentives for wise natural resource management, why does one find extreme problems of soil erosion in agriculture? Don't farmers care if valuable top soil is washing away? If private property ownership is so conducive to conservation, how does one explain the horrors of the 'Dust Bowl' in America during the early part of the 20th century?

At the second level, the above arguments suggest that the choices of private owners are efficient, and that alone is sufficient justification for their social legitimacy. Yet this claim assumes away externality problems and hence often confuses efficient outcomes with socially preferred outcomes. The defenders of individualized control over environmental resources suggest that what owners of assets want is identical with what others in society want. Or, it will be suggested that the only thing that matters in environmental policy is what the owners of privately held assets want.

In practical terms the argument often gets advanced as follows. If a mining company is treating the landscape in a way that offends a large number of residents in a particular region, ownership bestows on the mining company the 'right' to do as it wishes. If those who are offended wish for other outcomes for the landscape then they must be prepared to buy out the mining company. We see this line of argument dominating the recent interest in 'takings' law.

For the moment, the obvious conflict is between private interests and collective interest. The private-property advocates suggest that such ownership protects the decision maker from social pressure concerning how the resource is used. However, the content of 'ownership' itself is a social construct and if private owners are allowed to create social costs for others with impunity then that very content will certainly be re-examined in the legislatures and the courts (Bromley, 1991, 1993; Christman, 1994; Sax, 1983).

Finally, we come to the third level at which the efficacy of private property must be addressed; we now concern ourselves with the practical side of the matter. Specifically, it is not possible to turn the world's fisheries over to a single private owner. Nor can one individual 'own' the earth's atmosphere and manage it as the private-property advocates suggest. It would obviously be technically and administratively difficult for a single party to own the high seas or the global atmosphere.

So we see that private-property regimes for environmental resources can be expected to operate under rather limited circumstances. If there are no socially relevant off-site effects from decisions made by individual owners, and if the private owner correctly takes into account the interests of the future, then individualized control of environmental resources will conduce to social efficiency. If those assumptions do not hold, then it is hard to sustain an argument that individualized control will lead to socially preferred resource decisions. This can be seen by recognizing that the more complete is the individualization of control over environmental resources, the more possibilities there are for external effects. This leads us back to an earlier point; that much environmental policy is driven by those many instances in which the nominal boundary of decision-making units does not coincide with the real boundary of such units. Indeed, recognition of this fact in many social settings has produced the third type of resource management regime – common property.

Common-property regimes
There has been much confusion in the environmental literature over common-property resources. Scott Gordon's use of the term 'common property' to

describe the open-access fishery, and Garrett Hardin's 'tragedy of the commons', both set environmental economics off on an unfortunate path. The matter has been set right over the past decade and it is now well understood that Gordon and Hardin had open-access resources in mind, not common property (Bromley, 1991; Ciriacy-Wantrup and Bishop, 1975).

At the most fundamental level, common property is similar to private property in the sense that non-owners are excluded from use and decision making. Along with this exclusionary similarity, we also find that each of the co-owners in a common-property regime has rights and duties inside the regime. A true common-property regime requires the same thing as private property – exclusion of non-owners. While we know that property-owning groups vary in nature, size, and internal structure across a broad spectrum, they are all social units with definite membership and boundaries, with certain common interests, with at least some interaction among members, with some common cultural norms, and with their own endogenous authority systems. Tribal groups or subgroups, subvillages, neighbourhoods, small transhumant groups, kin systems, or extended families are all possible examples of meaningful authority systems. In many societies, these groupings hold customary ownership of certain natural resources such as farmland, grazing land, and water sources (Netting, 1976; McKean, 1992; Wade, 1992).

It has been previously noted that an essential component of any property regime is an authority system able to ensure that the expectations of rights-holders are met through the effective enforcement of duties on others. Compliance, protected and reinforced by an authority system, is a necessary condition for the viability of any property regime. Private property would not work without the requisite authority system that makes certain the rights and duties are adhered to. The same requirements exist for common property and for state property. Without authority there can be no property. When the authority system breaks down, the coherent management of natural resource use can no longer exist. Under these circumstances, any property regime – private, common, state – degenerates into open access.

A common-property regime entails exchange rights, entitlements over the distribution of net economic surplus accruing to the group, a management subsystem, and authority mechanisms as necessary components of the enforcement system. When any part of this complex system is undermined, the entire system malfunctions and ceases to operate as a property regime. It is indeed the management subsystem, with its authority mechanisms and ability to enforce operating rules and system-maintenance provisions, that ensures the particular property regime is adhered to, and that its systemic integrity (or system equilibrium) is well protected. This, in principle, is not different from the ways in which the other property regimes operate as authority systems. For instance, in private-property regimes the owner also relies on the authority of the state and its coercive power to assure compliance and hence to prevent intrusion by non-owners. If this (or other) authority would not be exercised, even private property would collapse and become an open-access regime.

Resource degradation in common-property regimes will usually arise for two reasons. The first is a breakdown in compliance with group rules by the members of the regime. This will often happen because of an increase in co-owners through population growth within the group. If economic opportunities beyond the boundaries of the regime are disappearing, then this disintegration in compliance with the rules of the regime may be difficult to prevent. If spreading privatization in the surrounding area precludes seasonal adaptation to fluctuating resource conditions – a problem of particular importance in semi-arid grazing regimes – then overuse of a local resource may be necessary for survival by members of the group. This problem represents a form of disintegration of the internal coherence of the property regime.

Secondly, if the government holds common property in low esteem – that is, if the state disregards the interests of those segments of the population largely dependent upon common-property regimes – then external threats to the regime will not receive the same governmental response as would a threat to private property. The willingness of the modern state to legitimize and protect different property regimes is partly explained by the state's perception of the importance of the citizens holding different types of property rights. If pastoralists are regarded as politically marginal – a not uncommon occurrence in many parts of the world – then the property regimes central to pastoralism will be only indifferently protected against threat from others. If those threatening pastoralist property regimes – sedentary agriculturalists, for example – happen to enjoy more favour from the state, then the protection of rangelands under common property against encroachments for cultivation will be haphazard at best. This represents the disintegration of external legitimacy of the property regime.

Individuals have rights and obligations in situations of common property, just as in private property situations. The difference between private and common property is not to be found in the nature of the rights and duties as much as it is in the number to which inclusion or exclusion applies. The difference is also in the unwillingness of the group to evict redundant individuals when that eviction will almost certainly relegate the evicted to severe deprivation. In a sense, the group of co-owners in a common-property regime agrees to lower its own standard of living rather than to single out particular members for disinheritance.

Finally, there is the presumption that common-property regimes are quaint remnants of some bygone era in which life was 'solitary, poor, nasty, brutish, and short', to quote from that renowned pessimist Thomas Hobbes. But of course contemporary Swiss farmers hardly seem to fit the Hobbesian mould in their management of common pastures in the Swiss highlands (Netting, 1976; Stevenson, 1991). Nor is it obvious that the co-owners of country clubs, tennis clubs, or condominium apartments fall under the Hobbesian indictment. And of course the contemporary Japanese manage to do just fine with their common-property regimes (the *Iriaichi*) (McKean, 1992). Common-property regimes are not quite the horrible failures – or settings for conflict and resource destruction – often attributed to them. Of course they are not all wonders of wise resource management either. The evaluation of common-property regimes, as with all resource-management regimes, must be undertaken with objectivity and their purpose clearly in mind. Indeed much of the so-called 'tragedy of the commons' is properly attributable to open-access regimes.

Non-property or open-access regimes

These are devoid of any property rights – they are unowned resources (*res nullius*). To return to the earlier discussion of legal relations, open-access regimes allow individuals or groups to make use of scarce resources without regard for the interests of others who may also seek to make use of the same resources. Under open access, the first individual to make use becomes the beneficiary of the benefit stream arising from the resource. There are no property rights in open access, there is only the rule of first capture. Unlike property regimes where individuals and groups have both rights and duties, open-access regimes are fundamentally situations of *no law*. Everybody's access is nobody's property; a resource under an open-access regime belongs to the party to first exercise control over it. The investment in (or improvement of) natural resources under open-access regimes must first focus on this institutional dimension. If property and management arrangements are not spelled out in clear detail, and then if there are investments such as improved tree species or range revegetation, the institutional vacuum of open access ensures that use rates will eventually deplete the asset and the investments will have been for naught.

Most environmental problems can be traced to a property regime that approaches that of open access. Pollution occurs because the ownership of the medium – air or water – is in doubt. Fish are over-harvested because there are no limits on who may harvest fish. Groundwater is over-extracted because there are no institutional arrangements controlling pumping. The same applies to oil pools, certain forested areas, and some grazing areas.

Open access results from the absence, or the breakdown, of a management and authority system whose purpose is to introduce and enforce a set of norms of behaviour among participants with respect to that particular natural resource. When valuable natural resources are available to the first party to effect capture, it is either because those natural resources have never before been incorporated into a regulated social system, or because they have become open-access resources through institutional failures that have undermined former collective or individual management regimes.

The solution to many environmental problems will usually start with addressing the problems of open access. When air pollution regulations set new ambient air standards, a formerly open access resource comes under the legal structure of a state-property regime. Now an agency will specify the legislative intent as to what constitutes 'clean', and it will develop a set of administrative rules and procedures to make sure that the intentions of the legislative process are realized. We may say the same thing about water pollution. If firms were, at one time, free to dump their industrial wastes into rivers, then they were making use of an open-access resource. The advent of strict water-quality standards represents a fundamental shift in the property arrangements over water. Now, industry must recognize others with an interest in water quality. These others, when the regulatory process has been completed, will have acquired a 'right' to cleaner water, and industry will have acquired a 'duty' not to contaminate water bodies below some declared ambient standard.

The fact that there may be a permit-trading system introduced to facilitate efficiency in achieving the new ambient standard does not obviate the fact that a regulatory action had previously redefined the property regime with respect to water resources. The instruments chosen – quantity restrictions on each plant's emissions versus marketable permits – are simply implementation refinements incorporated into a new legal relationship.

We now turn to a discussion of some familiar property regimes in environmental economics.

PROPERTY REGIMES IN ENVIRONMENTAL ECONOMICS

An early area of interest among economists focused on management problems associated with the extraction of valuable resources from so-called common pools. The circumstances here are such that the users of the resource are jointly linked by the physical characteristics of the resource. Unlike a piece of land that can be physically demarcated, individualization of these common pool resources is impossible. Therefore, the basic problem arises from the inherent jointness of production when more than one decision maker undertakes extraction decisions that hold economic implications for others using the same pool. Early analytical attention focused on the externalities inherent in such joint extraction. These externalities were manifest in two distinct ways.

First, the extraction activities of one user render the resources less available for the $n-1$ other users. In traditional terms, extraction costs for $n-1$ users of the common pool are affected by the extraction decisions of the one producer. But of course all n producers are pursuing their own independent extraction programmes and so the externality in this case is reciprocal in nature; all producers affect the per-unit extraction costs of all other producers. Each producer also affects the market price of others extracting the same commodity – the more total production, presumably, the lower must be the market-clearing price. But this interdependence, working through the price system, is a pecuniary effect and therefore not one to be condemned since it does not qualify as an externality.[5] However, the physical interdependence among the n extractors is a problem of economic significance. An inefficiency arises because of the interconnected yet independent management decisions of the n firms extracting from the common pool.

This inefficiency leads to a second form of economic problem of an intertemporal nature. That is, with a number of producers independently deciding the level of extraction, the long-run sustainability of the natural resource is threatened. Since forbearance by one producer will not be rewarded with a more abundant resource in the future, no individual has an incentive to exercise restraint.

Consider the oil pool with n individual firms undertaking independent pumping activity. An inefficiency is introduced because the performance of any single well is reduced by the pumping actions of the remainder which reduce the effective pressure of the pool. That is, the inherent pressure in the oil pool itself allows each pump to work more effectively than is possible under reduced pressure. With multiple pumpers, this pressure for any single well is reduced and so the extraction costs of each are increased. But of course the demand for oil does not necessarily coincide with the imperatives for pumping and so another inefficiency arises. Because such common pool resources are not fully appropriable until captured by a firm, each producer has an incentive to pump more than can be sold at the moment to prevent others from acquiring a property interest in the oil. We call these fugacious resources to indicate that they are 'fugitive' until reduced to the possession of an individual firm (Ostrom, 1990).

The solution to the joint pumping externality is found in what we know as the 'unitized pool'. Here, all pumpers are required to join together to make sure that aggregate pumping from the pool is pro-rated among them in an efficient manner. We see a similar phenomenon in the pumping of groundwater. However, here there is a somewhat more complicated economic process at work. Specifically, groundwater resources are often a substitute for surface water resources. The property regimes pertinent to both water resources are often quite distinct and this difference leads to problems in the management of both.

There are two general means whereby owners of land acquire property rights to water. One, called the riparian doctrine, bestows rights in water by virtue of proximity. We see this doctrine at work in the eastern United States where streams and rivers have a somewhat reliable and steady flow. Individuals, cities, and industries acquire rights to water that is contiguous to land. Hence the term 'riparian'. This same doctrine applies, in most settings, to the water beneath a piece of land. To own the land is to have a presumptive property right to the water that lies beneath that land. In general, the earliest riparian user retains the presumptive right to the water but must usually act with consideration for downstream riparian right-holders.

The other mechanism is known as the prior appropriation doctrine. In the arid western regions of the United States, where irrigable land is often at some distance from the intermittent flow of streams and rivers, individuals who first appropriated the water and applied it to land – often at some considerable distance from the water – acquired the water right. Hence the term 'prior appropriation'. In these cases, the water right attaches to the land to which it was first applied. And the right endures as long as the water is put to 'beneficial' use.

The economic issue here is that groundwater is often seen as a substitute for surface water resources. Because groundwater property regimes are often less well-developed than those for surface water, groundwater resources are usually seen as freely available for exploitation. As with the oil pool, multiple users can impose external costs on each other. And, unrestricted extraction by a group of water users can lead to efficiency problems over time. The resource issues that concern surface and groundwater problems have been addressed through models of the conjunctive use of water. The first step in these models is to understand the nature of the property regime over groundwater (Provencher, 1993, 1995; Provencher and Burt, 1993). Once the institutional structure is understood, it is possible to address the policy response to solve the misallocation problem.

On the subject of open-access resources, there is a long tradition of economics research concerning the fishery. While the fishery entails many of the common pool problems associated with the oil pool and groundwater resources, an additional critical dimension is present. These models must incorporate the fact that, unlike water and oil, fish populations are driven by biological phenomena. This means that fisheries research must be truly multi-disciplinary in nature.

The relevant work on fisheries started in the mid-1950s with seminal articles by H. Scott Gordon (1954) and Anthony Scott (1955). Gordon was the first economist to understand and explore the important implications associated with the common pool aspects of fisheries. He developed a simple model to illustrate that unlimited access to fish stocks will drive a fishery beyond the level of maximum sustainable yield. Indeed, open access usually results in a level of total fishing effort in a fishery that is far in excess of that which would prevail under proper institutional structures. As with oil pools and groundwater, the 'sole owner' emerged as the analytical metaphor of choice (Scott, 1955). With a sole owner controlling entry into, and fishing power within, the fishery, economic efficiency could be restored. Of course an economically efficient fishery is not necessarily a biologically sustainable fishery and so the conjunction of biology and economics is required to develop coherent fisheries policy over the long run (Anderson, 1976, 1985, 1986, 1995; Conrad, 1989, 1995; Rettig, 1995).

Considerable progress has been made recently in fisheries policy. The early notion that the high-seas fishery was a common property resource has now been corrected to reflect the general understanding that it is an open-access resource. The United Nations Convention on the Law of the Sea (1982) extended exclusive economic zones out to 200 miles beyond coastal states. In doing so, this additional territory was converted from an open-access regime to one of state property. Under the new property regime, individual coastal nations control entry of fishing vessels into these waters, as well as quotas and fishing gear. The new institutional regime in coastal fisheries has established the necessary ingredient of a functioning property regime as opposed to a free-for-all. While the Convention has not been ratified by enough nation states to gain the full force hoped for, many of its provisions, including the 200-mile economic zone, have been followed in practice (Rettig, 1995).

Once the high seas have been converted from open-access to some form of state property, then nations can implement various schemes to apportion fishing pressure. One of those schemes gaining recent popularity is individual transferable quotas (ITQs). Under these regimes, fishers may trade (buy and sell) opportunities to participate in the harvest of the predetermined total allowable catch. This introduction of a market for permits into a regulated regime regarding total catch allows for the realization of important efficiency properties (Anderson, 1995; Townsend, 1992).

Turning from fisheries to grazing regimes, the same theoretical approaches apply. In general terms, it is well to recall that common property is similar to private property for the group of co-owners because non-owners are excluded from use and decision making. These group property regimes are compatible with individual use of one or another segment of the resources held by the group in common. For instance, in customary tenure systems over much of Africa, the ownership of certain farmland may be vested in a group. The group's leaders then allocate use rights on portions of the land to various individuals or families. As long as those individuals cultivate their plot, no other person may use it or benefit from its produce. But note that the cultivator holds use rights only (usufruct) and is unable to alienate or transfer either the ownership or the use of that land to another individual. Sometimes there will be provisions for permission to be granted by those in a position of authority, but the decision is a collective one as opposed to an individual one. Once the current user ceases to put the land to 'good use', the usufruct reverts to the jurisdiction of the corporate ownership of the group. Contrary to regimes of state ownership, the customary common-property regimes in sub-Saharan Africa are usually characterized by group-corporate ownership with management authority vested in the respective group or its leaders (Swallow and Bromley, 1995; Van den Brink, et. al. 1995).

A functioning common-property regime is one in which the behaviours of all members of the group are subject to accepted rules, and there is a mechanism for dealing with deviant behaviours. Enforcement is rarely perfect, but we need to understand the important difference between the concept of common-property regimes and their specific operation. It is worth noting that in many African settings, conformity with group norms at the local level is often an effective sanction against antisocial behaviour. Therefore, we can say that viable common-property regimes will usually have a built-in structure of economic and non-economic incentives that encourage compliance with existing conventions and institutions. Where those sanctions and incentives have become inoperative or dysfunctional – usually because of pressures and forces beyond the control of the group, or because of internal processes that the groups were unable to master – resource degradation has resulted. But in a social setting in which individual conformity to group norms is an important part of daily life, common-property regimes may have a cultural context compatible with – indeed vital for – effective performance.

Note that the best land in most settings has already been privatized and the worst has been left in the public domain either as state property, common property, or open access. It is not legitimate to ask of common-property regimes that they manage highly variable and low-productivity resources, and also to adapt and adjust to severe internal and external pressures, when conditions beyond the bounds of that common-property regime preclude the adaptation to those internal and external pressures. That is, the internal pressure of population growth may be impossible to resolve if traditional adaptation mechanisms – hiving off for instance – are precluded by increased population growth beyond the confines of the common-property regime under study.

Likewise, in many settings private property and associated fences are encroaching on common-property regimes thus preventing the traditional movements of people and their livestock. In these circumstances, it is hardly legitimate to blame the common-property regime for increased use caused by encroachment. Private-property regimes appear to be stable and adaptive because they have the social and legal sanction to exclude excess population, and effectively to resist, through the power of the state, unwanted intrusions. These powers have often been eroded for common-property regimes. To see the exclusionary aspect of private property, consider the effects of primogeniture. The dispossession of younger sons (to say nothing of all daughters) is regarded as a costless social process and therefore it looks as though private property is robust and adaptable. Private property in such a setting may work for the oldest son; but those with no rights in the estate may be harder to convince.

Turning to grazing issues in North America, the vast arid regions of the United States provide a striking contrast to the situation in sub-Saharan Africa. Prior to governmental action, much of the land in the arid west was freely available to cattle and sheep ranchers who behaved as we might expect in terms of open-access resources. The range was seriously overgrazed. With the establishment of the US Forest Service, and then the Grazing Service (later to become the Bureau of Land Management), the open-access character of America's rangelands was converted into a state-property regime. Today it is managed in a way that is not too different from how fisheries are managed under the new coastal regulations; a group of users and government officials make decisions about resource use.

The forest lands in the United States have undergone a similar transformation. When the nation was young, the forested areas, just as the rangelands, were open-access resources available to whomever was the first to use them. Today, forested areas are either private-property resources or they are state-property resources. This same holds in most of the industrialized countries of the world.

In the tropics it is much less common to find large tracts of private forest land. Most forested areas are state-property regimes with harvesting concessions granted to logging firms. Indeed these contracts often form the basis of illicit revenues to government officials charged with issuing and monitoring logging activities.

We turn now to a discussion of property regimes pertinent to genetic stocks and biological resources.[6] The exact meaning of a 'genetic resource' is not necessarily obvious. At one level, since each individual species is a unique genetic complex, each species is a genetic resource. Yet the process of natural evolution is one in which individual species may disappear and so one cannot hope to establish a property regime in which each species is said to have a right to exist. At the same time, an encompassing perspective of ecology would suggest that a large number of genetic resources must be preserved to maintain the necessary biodiversity.

One step beyond this sweeping view is that we might seek to create property regimes that will allow for the protection of a wide variety of genetic resources in particular settings. Under this strategy we may stand some chance of having saved those individual species which will someday acquire extraordinary value. This broad spectrum approach can be viewed as part of a two-stage process driven by a strategy in which we seek to minimize the probability of maximum losses from the disappearance of potentially valuable genetic resources.

The broad spectrum approach gains its legitimacy from the fact that genetic resources – as with all natural resources – become valuable as tastes and preferences change, as new knowledge and technology offer up new alternatives, and as new scarcities arise. The broad spectrum approach has its conceptual analogue in portfolio analysis in which one seeks an investment strategy with minimally correlated risks among its constituent parts. The appropriate property regime for broad spectrum resource policies would focus on habitat as opposed to individual species.

With respect to broad spectrum issues, certain habitats offer genetic richness of current and potential value. The task is to inventory such habitats to find those harbouring the desired variety and concentration of genetic resources. One cannot, of course, know exactly which genetic resources deserve absolute protection and so the challenge is to select habitats most likely to contain resources of future value. Some of these will derive from currently known valuable stocks, while others will necessarily be speculative.

Along with the broad spectrum approach one needs to contemplate property regimes for protecting individual species. This is, by its very nature, a complex challenge since individual species do not exist in isolation but rather occupy a specific niche in a particular ecosystem. Therefore, one needs focused property regimes that complement broad spectrum policies with *compact niche* policies in which a very few closely related members of an ecosystem become the focus of policy attention. Note that this is not a single species policy but is, instead, a focused policy on specific niches in particular ecosystems. The proximate predators and prey of the object of attention must become part of the management – and hence property – regime. Notice that a property regime is as a management regime. Property rights cannot be meaningfully regarded as anything other than policy instruments, the use of which result in certain desired behaviours on the part of members of society.

The compact niche approach starts with the obvious species of significance. The 'endangered species' approach is a compact niche policy. Here the strategy is to focus on single species and then to determine the minimum necessary habitat conditions that will assure survival of the species. The key to successful property regimes for protecting genetic resources will be to avoid the temptation to claim that all species are inherently valuable and worthy of protection. That strategy will be so confrontational to many citizens and governments that meaningful progress will be impeded. A more carefully crafted strategy is called for.

Any property regime for managing genetic resources will fail if it is not understood to be part of an authority system whose ultimate purpose is to enforce rules of behaviour for individuals. All of the abundant literature on property rights assumes perfect compliance with the new institutional structure. In the absence of compliance, the most highly articulated property regime is nothing, and it is certainly no deterrence to those whose interests are at odds with the new entitlement structure. This obvious fact is frequently overlooked. Indeed the acknowledged failures of many national governments in natural resource management stem from the non-trivial gap between the promulgation and pronouncement of new rules, and the enforcement of those rules (Bromley, 1991). When a government declares that it henceforth prohibits, say, lumbering and then fails to enforce that new prohibition, the end result is worse than if nothing had been proclaimed in the first instance.

By announcing a ban on lumbering, and then by failing to act on that declaration, the government sends a signal to all that it is powerless to enforce what it declares. Note that policy is a combination of intentions, rules and enforcement. The first two in the absence of the third simply leads to abuse of the new rules, bribes if certain individuals are apprehended, and cynicism. Governments without the resolve – or the means – to enforce what they proclaim in the interest of environmental policy are creating the conditions for further destruction of scarce and valuable resources.

Property rights and property regimes are crafted to provide rights and duties with respect to valuable, or possibly valuable, genetic complexes. This protection, however, must be accompanied by a collective determination of the value of the subjects of these new rights, and the sense that this value exceeds the perceived losses borne by those with newly acquired duties. This reinforces the point that property rights are instrumental variables. That is, if the core of property is the external acknowledgement (social recognition) of the legitimacy of that particular claim by the 'owner', then it follows necessarily that property claims failing to win this external acknowledgement will not be recognized as legitimate by those forced to forswear interest in the benefit stream. Put more bluntly, if the collective fails to admit the social usefulness of a particular property claim, then that property claim is delegitimized because it is regarded as non-instrumental (Sax, 1983).

The continuing struggle to protect genetic resources must be grounded in the need to convince a large number of people that they have a duty to endow those to follow in the future with a wealth of genetic resources. Only through this collective recognition of rights and duties will it be possible to pass on that endowment with a maximum of compliance, and hence with a 'tolerable' expenditure of financial resources devoted to the task of enforcement.

The management of biological resources is currently undergoing some reconsideration of the proper institutional arrangements. The norm throughout the world has been to create state-property regimes in the form of national parks and national wilderness areas. In the United States, parks and wilderness areas are administered by the National Park Service. The great wildlife parks of east and southern Africa represent another example of state-property regimes in the service of conservation and preservation. Such reserves are always under pressure from those uses, and users, who may have been displaced. In America there is mounting pressure to allow drilling for oil in some wilderness areas in Alaska. In the tropical countries, those who have been evicted from parks are now making renewed claims to be allowed to graze their livestock in such areas. While the international conservation community has long been opposed to such ideas, there are signs that the reincorporation of people and their animals into large wildlife preserves may actually facilitate improved conservation policies and outcomes. These innovative programmes are often known as community-based conservation initiatives.

Community-based conservation (CBC) is concerned with inducing certain behaviours among individuals and groups closest to particular ecosystems in order to enhance the long-run sustainable management of those ecosystems. The economic dimension of CBC is concerned with the search for new institutional arrangements that will align the interests of those local people with the interests of non-local – and often distant – individuals and groups seeking sustainable management of particular ecosystems. In essence, we seek new resource management regimes in which the interests of those living in such regimes coincide with the interests of those living elsewhere who seek wildlife preservation.

When the relatively rich in the industrialized north are able to enjoy the benefits of biodiversity conservation at a low individual cost, while that conservation restricts the choice domain of poor individuals in the tropics where a particular ecosystem has attracted international attention, then incentive problems abound. The interests of local people whose active cooperation is a necessary condition for the survival of a particular ecosystem are discounted relative to the interests of those who care for the ecosystem but not for the welfare of those whose economic well-being is linked to the fate of that local ecosystem.

Incentive compatibility is established when local inhabitants acquire an economic interest in the long-run viability of the ecosystem of such importance to those situated elsewhere. Note that the interests of the locals need not be identical to those of the international conservation community. Sustained conservation of local resources requires only that the local stake in conservation becomes somewhat greater than the previous interest in resource-use patterns deemed inimical to conservation. Recall that such ecosystems represent benefit streams to both parties – those in the industrialized north who seek to preserve biodiversity, and those who must make a living among this genetic resource. Local inhabitants acquire an interest in the new resource management regime when they gain a stake in a benefit stream arising from that regime. The secret here is to adjust the property regime so that local people living in proximity to valuable biological resources become agents of preservation rather than agents of destruction.

The world's genetic resources are under constant threat from a range of land-use changes and economic pressures. This threat is the more serious because of the failure of existing institutional arrangements to guide and control individual and group behaviours with respect to these genetic resources. Recent international efforts, including the 1992 'Earth Summit', suggest that many of the world's leaders are prepared to make a commitment to the preservation of biodiversity. New policy initiatives with respect to biodiversity conservation are being pursued on several fronts. These policy initiatives must be understood as but part of a larger institutional transformation necessary to affect the way in which local people use and manage genetic resources.

The fundamental problem in biological conservation is to understand the critical interrelation between the interests of individuals, groups, and national governments as those interests drive behaviours with serious implications for the world's genetic resources. The various property regimes imply differential prospects for gains and losses to various agents in the system. If the destruction of biological resources is of no consequence to the responsible party, then there is no incentive to encourage greater care in preventing such damages. On the other hand, if the legal regime shifts so that parties responsible for resource destruction are also financially responsible for compensating those harmed by said damages, then the economic incentives have shifted dramatically as the potentially responsible party now contemplates the financial implications of expected compensation payments.

PROPERTY RIGHTS AND CONTEMPORARY POLICY PROBLEMS

The foregoing discussion highlights a rich tradition in environmental economics – a tradition in which property rights issues are implicit, if not explicit, in every policy debate. I will close with a brief discussion of two contemporary environmental issues in which property rights are at the centre of the dispute. The first issue concerns our view of what should be done for those who will come after us (future generations). This is the externality problem in an intertemporal sense. The other issue concerns the perceptions that current landowners have about the nature and extent of their property rights. We can immediately see the connection between these two issues.

The Endangered Species Act (ESA) in the United States seeks to restrict the destruction of habitat that is considered essential for the survival of certain species. The ESA represents an institutional overlay on top of the private property regime that ordinarily defines land ownership. As such it accomplishes what urban zoning has long done – redefine the choice domain of individual landowners. With respect to biological resources, the ESA represents the 'compact niche' approach discussed previously.

The ESA also exists out of regard for the future. In essence, the law is predicated on the idea that those living in the future have 'rights' with respect to certain species – the bald eagle, the northern spotted owl, and other protected species. By preventing those now living from destroying habitat crucial to the survival of such species, the law has redefined the legal relations between those of us living in the present, and those who will come after us. It is a mistake, however, to conclude from this that 'nature has rights'. Rather, those living in the future have acquired rights with respect to certain species. And those of us living now have acquired duties to make sure that certain species survive (Bromley, 1991).

This intertemporal legal structure is necessary for the simple reason that those of us living in the present stand as dictators over the endowment that will be passed on to future generations. The Coasean solution to externality problems – of much charm to those who favour individual bargaining over externalities – fails absolutely across time. After all, future generations are not able to bargain with the present generation, and so the vaunted assumption of zero transaction costs in a Coasean world is violated. It is impossible to suppose that bargaining across generations has any prospect of informing the correct choice.

The only solution to such problems is to redefine the domains of choice for those living now such that the probable interests of the future are considered. I say 'probable' because we can never precisely know what the interests of the future will be; we can only guess. And so we guess in terms of what we assume the future might value – bald eagles and northern spotted owls. The 'intertemporal bargaining' problem is solved by creating a new rights regime in which the future acquires rights, and we who are now living incur some new obligations (duties) toward those who will follow.

This is precisely where the matter of 'takings' enters the picture. There is a growing backlash to many environmental regulations, but especially toward those that impact the presumed extent of ownership of land. This opposition is located, in a general sense, in various 'property rights' groups. These groups rely on an aside in the Fifth Amendment to the US Constitution that states that the government may not take property for public use without paying just compensation. We see that the struggle then comes down to three ideas: (1) what is 'property'? (2) what does it mean to 'take'? and (3) what constitutes 'public use'? Volumes have been written on this matter and it is impossible to do justice here to the debate. But a few brief comments will suggest the contours of the controversy.

One view starts with the idea that individuals possess, through natural law, inalienable property rights in their labour. When they use their labour to acquire or improve land, they thereby acquire inalienable rights over that land. Any action by government that diminishes the value of that land constitutes – to this group – a 'takings' that must be compensated. This view relies on the dyadic conception of an individual standing tall against Leviathan (government). John Locke figures prominently in the philosophical underpinnings of this view. In essence, this particular view sees landed property rights as an indissoluble barrier against a tyrannical government. In contemporary disputes the most forceful advocate of this position is probably Richard Epstein (1985).

The other view suggests that rights (and hence property rights) cannot be located in natural law but rather flow from the consensus of the political community we know as the state. To use an unpleasant example, if there were such a thing as 'natural rights', slavery would not have been possible. But in fact we know that slavery flourished, in various forms, for several thousand years. It was not until nation states acted against slavery – often grudgingly and only at the relentless urging of abolitionist forces – that slavery as an institution was largely eliminated. Had human-beings possessed 'natural rights', human history would have been much different, and much more pleasant.

This side of the 'takings' debate argues that rights are properly seen as triadic relations that define two parties to a dispute, and the one force that can resolve such disputes – the state. To return to the slavery example, the dispute here was not simply between some slave owner and the government of the day. Rather the struggle was between two human-beings – one legally defined as an owner, the other legally defined as a slave. Notice that the owner regarded the slave as his 'property' and argued against the abolition of slavery in the United States on the grounds that valuable property was being taken without compensation. To the plantation owner, the slave was, in essence, not different from a piece of machinery. It was not until the coercive power of the state was used to abolish those two legal categories (owner, slave) that slavery was eliminated. We see clearly that the triadic model is a more powerful heuristic than is the dyadic approach favoured by the so-called 'property rights' advocates.

In the environmental area, 'takings' arises in the same triadic form. Landowners, and those who care about endangered species, are locked in a struggle over who has rights to define how habitat may be used – and whether compensation must be paid to a landowner when the imperatives of habitat preservation alter the owner's plans for the land. A view that runs counter to that espoused by the 'property rights' advocates suggests that regulations such as the Endangered Species Act do not 'take' property rights because the landowner never had a right to use land in ways that are at odds with accepted social norms. Nuisance law concerns precisely this issue. In essence, there is no compensation called for because there was no property right there in the first place. The new regulations did not 'take' something the landowner ever had (Bromley, 1993).

There is, of course, a precedent for this view in the environmental arena. Various legislative initiatives over the past several decades have prevented landowners (factories, farmers) from discharging their wastes into the air and nearby bodies of water. Clearly these regulations have altered the value of the newly regulated business enterprise and hence 'took' some economic value from the owners. But the genesis of the regulatory action must be understood to reside in the presumed collective desire to reduce unwanted social costs. Once such social costs have been stopped, one might well ask why the erstwhile perpetrators of those costs should now be compensated? To compensate them is to suggest that they had a 'right' to impose such costs on others.

In essence, this issue concerns fundamental moral arguments that transcend environmental policy. As suggested at the outset, the idea of rights – the operational conception of rights – entails legal, rhetorical, and moral components. These components are joined in the area of environmental policy precisely because the environment represents a moral domain. While a number of efforts persist to assign monetary values to parts of it (or to activities associated with the natural environment), these efforts – useful though they are – will be unlikely to trump the larger moral dimension of the natural environment (Vatn and Bromley, 1994). And that is precisely why property rights are at the core of environmental policy.

CONCLUSIONS

I have argued here that environmental policy is about property rights. As the world around us continues to evolve technologically and socially, new institutional arrangements also evolve. Property rights are part of the institutional set-up of any society, and so property rights evolve as well. This is disturbing to those who imagine, in some rather wistful way, that there could be just a few constants in this world. They wish for property rights to be defined once and for all, or not to change unless those who will thereby lose are compensated. But such arguments beg the fundamental question in all policy. That is, why should those who seek a change in the status quo institutional set-up be made to buy out those who would lose?

Economists have a ready answer to that rhetorical question. Compensation is called for to make sure that the move is Pareto safe. Unfortunately, this argument still begs the question of what rights are (were) present in the status quo institutional set-up. The so-called 'property rights' school would like to suggest that the status quo is inviolate and must be compensated whenever a change occurs. But of course today's status quo is probably different from yesterday's status quo – and where does this infinite regress stop?

Were the North American Indians compensated when their land was taken by European settlers? Many descendants of those same European settlers are now pleased to argue that their property rights are somehow sacred. But by what sort of conjuring do they reach this conclusion? Did the relevant world only start after the Indians were subjugated, resettled on reservations, or killed? Or, in the area of environmental quality, were the rivers of America or Europe chemically contaminated before the advent of modern industry? To argue that 'property rights' protect industry and agriculture from uncompensated regulations is to be very selective about the timeframe that one uses to define the status quo. Property rights are the essence of environmental policy, and hence environmental policy will always be contentious.

NOTES

1. This easy solution assumes that the only entity to suffer costs from the smoke is the laundry. Others may also find the smoke harmful, in which case the easy answer may, in reality, be unrealistic.
2. This is called the problem of 'coming to nuisance'. The courts deal with such problems in ways that will often appear to be in the interest of both efficiency and fairness. In a famous case, a residential development came rather too close to a malodorous cattle-feeding facility. Land may have been cheap for the developer, but houses did not sell as well as he had hoped. He brought suit against the cattle company on grounds of creating harm (nuisance). Since the housing developer 'came to the nuisance', the court found sympathy for the developer, but not too much sympathy. The cattle company was forced to move but the housing developer was forced to pay for the move. See *Spur Industries, Inc.* v *Del E. Webb Development Company* 494 P (2d) 701 (1972).
3. These issues are explored in more detail in Vatn and Bromley (forthcoming).
4. This view is often known as 'free-market environmentalism'.
5. This category of interdependence qualifies as a 'Pareto irrelevant externality' since it is not a source of correctable inefficiency.
6. Some of this discussion is modified from parts of Bromley (1994).

REFERENCES

Alchian, A. and H. Demsetz (1973), 'The Property Rights Paradigm', *Journal of Economic History*, **13**, 16–27.

Anderson, L.G. (1976), 'The Relationship Between Firm and Fishery in Common Property Fisheries', *Land Economics*, **52**, 180–91.

Anderson, L.G. (1985), 'Potential Economic Benefits from Gear Restrictions and License Limitation in Fisheries Regulation', *Land Economics*, **61**, 409–18.

Anderson, L.G. (1986), *The Economics of Fisheries Management*, Baltimore, Md.: Johns Hopkins University Press.

Anderson, L.G. (1995), 'Privatizing Open Access Fisheries: Individual Transferable Quotas', in D.W. Bromley (ed.), *The Handbook of Environmental Economics*, Oxford: Blackwell Publishers, pp. 453–74.

Barzel, Y. (1989), *Economic Analysis of Property Rights*, Cambridge: Cambridge University Press.

Becker, L. (1977), *Property Rights*, London: Routledge and Kegan Paul.

Bromley, D.W. (1989a), 'Property Relations and Economic Development: The Other Land Reform', *World Development*, **17**(6), 867–77.

Bromley, D.W. (1989b), 'Entitlements, Missing Markets, and Environmental Uncertainty', *Journal of Environmental Economics and Management*, **17**(2), 181–94, September.

Bromley, D.W. (1991), *Environment and Economy: Property Rights and Public Policy*, Oxford: Blackwell Publishers.

Bromley, D.W. (1993), 'Regulatory Takings: Coherent Concept or Logical Contradiction?', *Vermont Law Review*, **17**(3), 647–82.

Bromley, D.W. (1994), 'Economic Dimensions of Community-Based Conservation', in D. Western, R.M. Wright and S.C. Strum (eds), *Natural Connections: Perspectives in Community-Based Conservation*, Washington, DC: Island Press, chapter 19.

Buchanan, J.M. (1962), 'Politics, Policy, and Pigovian Margins', *Economica*, **29**, 17–28.

Buchanan, J.M. (1972), 'Politics, Property, and the Law: An Alternative Explanation of Miller *et al.* v. Schoene', *Journal of Law and Economics*, **15**, 439–52.

Buchanan, J.M. (1973), 'The Coase Theorem and the Theory of the State', *Natural Resources Journal*, **13**, 579–84.

Christman, J. (1994), *The Myth of Property*, New York: Oxford University Press.

Ciriacy-Wantrup, S.V. and R.C. Bishop (1975), 'Common Property as a Concept in Natural Resource Policy', *Natural Resources Journal*, **15**, 713–27.

Coase, R.H. (1960), 'The Problem of Social Cost', *Journal of Law and Economics*, **3**, 1–44.

Conrad, J.M. (1989), 'Bioeconomics and the Bowhead Whale', *Journal of Political Economy*, **97**(4), 974–87.

Conrad, J.M. (1995), 'Bioeconomic Models of the Fishery', in D.W. Bromley (ed.), *The Handbook of Environmental Economics*, Oxford: Blackwell Publishers, pp. 405–32.

Demsetz, H. (1967), 'Toward a Theory of Property Rights', *American Economic Review*, **57**, 347–59.

Epstein, R.A. (1985), *Takings: Private Property and the Power of Eminent Domain*, Cambridge, MA: Harvard University Press.

Furubotn, E. and S. Pejovich (eds) (1974), *The Economics of Property Rights*, Cambridge, MA: Ballinger.

Glendon, M.A. (1991), *Rights Talk*, New York: The Free Press.

Gordon, H.S. (1954), 'The Economic Theory of a Common Property Resource: The Fishery', *Journal of Political Economy*, **62**, 124–42.

McKean, M.A. (1992), 'Management of Traditional Common Lands (Iriaichi) in Japan', in D.W. Bromley *et al.* (eds), *Making the Commons Work*, San Francisco: ICS Press, pp. 63–98.

Netting, R. (1976), 'What Alpine Peasants Have in Common: Observations On Communal Tenure in a Swiss Village', *Human Ecology*, **4**, 135–46.

North, D.C. and R.P. Thomas (1977), 'The First Economic Revolution', *Economic History Review*, **30**, 229–41.

Ostrom, E. (1990), *Governing the Commons*, Cambridge: Cambridge University Press.

Page, T. (1977), *Conservation and Economic Efficiency*, Baltimore, Md.: Johns Hopkins University Press.

Pigou, A.C. (1920), *The Economics of Welfare*, London: Macmillan.

Provencher, R.W. (1993), 'A Private Property Rights Regime to Replenish a Groundwater Aquifer', *Land Economics*, **69**, 325–40.

Provencher, R.W. (1995), 'Issues in the Conjunctive Use of Surface and Groundwater', in D.W. Bromley (ed.), *The Handbook of Environmental Economics*, Oxford: Blackwell Publishers, pp. 503–20.

Provencher, R.W. and D. Burt (1993), 'The Externalities Associated With the Common Property Exploitation of Groundwater', *Journal of Environmental Economics and Management*, **24**, 139–58.

Rettig, R.B. (1995), 'Management Regimes in Ocean Fisheries', in D.W. Bromley (ed.), *The Handbook of Environmental Economics*, Oxford: Blackwell Publishers, pp. 433–52.

Sax, J. (1983), 'Some Thoughts on the Decline of Private Property', *Washington Law Review*, **58**, 481–96.

Scott, A. (1955), 'The Fishery: The Objective of Sole Ownership', *Journal of Political Economy*, **63**, 116–24.

Stevenson, G.G. (1991), *Common Property Economics*, Cambridge: Cambridge University Press.

Swallow, B. and D.W. Bromley (1995), 'Institutions, Governance, and Common Property Regimes for African Rangelands', *Environmental and Resource Economics*, **6**, 99–118.

Townsend, R. (1992), 'A Fractional Licensing Program for Fisheries', *Land Economics* **68**(2), 185–90.

Van den Brink, R., D.W. Bromley, and J.-P. Chavas (1995), 'The Economics of Cain and Abel: Agro-Pastoral Property Rights in the Sahel', *Journal of Development Studies*, **31**(3), 373–99, February.

Vatn, A. and D.W. Bromley (1994), 'Choices Without Prices Without Apologies', *Journal of Environmental Economics and Management*, **26**(2), 129–48.

Vatn, A. and D.W. Bromley (forthcoming), 'Externalities: A Market Model Failure', *Environmental and Resource Economics*.

Wade, R. (1992), 'Common-Property Resource Management in South Indian Villages', in D.W. Bromley *et al.* (eds), *Making the Commons Work*, San Francisco: ICS Press, pp. 207–28.

2. Environmental taxation in a second-best world

Lawrence H. Goulder[1]

INTRODUCTION

At least since Pigou (1938), economists have recognized the potential of taxes to deal with environmental problems and other market failures associated with externalities. Taxes are a mechanism for 'getting the prices right', that is, for helping prices better approximate marginal social cost. In many, though not all, circumstances, environmental economists tend to favour taxes over other forms of environmental regulation, because often taxes impose less severe information requirements, involve lower administrative costs, or exert more effective economic incentives than the alternatives.

From Pigou's work emerged a fundamental, 'Pigovian' principle asserting that the optimal environmental tax rate is equal to the marginal environmental damage from pollution. This principle has become a central tenet in environmental economics. It works well in a first-best setting where no other taxes are present. However, as Sandmo (1975) showed more than two decades ago, the principle requires modification in realistic cases where governments require more revenues than can be obtained through Pigovian taxation alone. Sandmo's analysis revealed that in these cases, environmental and ordinary taxes need to be examined together. Despite this finding, until recently most analyses have disregarded the rest of the tax system. Existing distortionary taxes – including income, payroll, and sales taxes – are usually omitted from the analysis. Typical analyses consider only one inefficiency – that posed by an environmental externality – and indicate how environmental taxes might eliminate or reduce that inefficiency.

The omission is important. Recent research refines and extends Sandmo's general result, showing that one cannot effectively fathom optimal environmental tax rates or evaluate the impacts of incremental or marginal reforms without paying attention to the magnitudes and types of existing, distortionary taxes. As this chapter will show, this is the case for two reasons. First, taxes interact. The gross[2] costs of new, environmentally motivated taxes depend critically on the marginal rates of existing, distortionary taxes. Second, the presence of prior distortionary taxes introduces opportunities to use revenues from new environmental taxes to finance cuts in existing taxes. Consider a tax reform in which an environmental tax is introduced and its revenues are used to finance reductions in the income tax. The overall gross cost of this revenue-neutral package depends not only on the costs attributable to the environmental tax itself but also on certain efficiency benefits (avoided costs) associate with the reduction in income tax rates.[3]

Some recent investigations show that attention to the connections with other taxes can make more than a slight difference to one's assessment of the impacts of a new environmental tax initiative. Indeed, in some cases, the sign of the net benefits – gross benefits from environmental improvement minus gross costs of achieving pollution reductions – can be reversed when second-best issues are taken into account.

These findings are highly relevant to current policy debates about environmental taxes. There has been substantial controversy, for example, about the advisability of a carbon tax to reduce the rate of accumulation of carbon dioxide and thereby lower the expected future damages from climate change. In this debate, a key question is whether the costs of a carbon tax might be significantly reduced or even eliminated if the revenues from this tax are devoted to cuts in existing income taxes. The possibility of a zero-cost carbon tax is obviously attractive to policy analysts who are concerned about the spectre of global climate change but are frustrated by the uncertainties as to the likely benefits (avoided environmental damages) from a carbon tax. If a revenue-neutral carbon tax involves zero cost, then one can comfortably support such a tax on efficiency grounds despite the uncertainties about benefits: it suffices simply to know the sign of the benefits – to know that they are positive. Thus, understanding the impacts of environmental taxes in the presence of other taxes bears importantly on current environmental policy debates. Such understanding is relevant not only to marginal or incremental reforms but also to discussions of optimal environmental taxation. Again in the area of carbon taxes, there has been a great deal of discussion as to whether possibilities of revenue-recycling might substantially raise the optimal carbon tax. Recent theoretical and numerical work has shed considerable light on this issue, in some cases yielding results contrary to one's initial intuition.

This chapter describes recent developments in the theoretical and empirical assessment of environmental taxation in a second-best setting where other, distortionary taxes are present. The next section investigates 'marginal' tax reforms – marginal in the sense that the rest of the tax system is not optimized as part of the reform, or in the sense that one is not concerned with the optimality of the rate chosen for the environmental tax. A key issue here is the circumstances under which revenue-neutral environmental reforms might have zero gross cost. The third section examines optimal environmental taxation in this second-best setting. It describes how the Pigovian principle of environmental taxation is no longer valid under these circumstances, and offers an alternative formulation for second-best optimal taxation. The final section draws conclusions and indicates areas where further theoretical and empirical work in second-best environmental taxation might have large pay-offs.

MARGINAL ENVIRONMENTAL REFORMS AND THE 'DOUBLE DIVIDEND'[4]

There has been a great deal of discussion in recent years about 'green tax reform', that is, a reorienting of the tax system to place more emphasis on pollution taxes (taxes on 'bads') and less emphasis on ordinary labour or capital taxes (taxes on 'goods' like labour effort or savings). In this connection, some analysts have claimed that a swapping of environmental taxes for income taxes might offer a 'double dividend': not only (1) improve the environment, but also (2) reduce certain non-environment-related costs of the tax system.[5] Many have taken the view that the case for environmental taxes is strengthened by the recognition that these taxes not only enhance (or reduce deterioration of) environmental quality but also improve the functioning of factor markets.

Is this the case? It's important, at the outset, to distinguish various interpretations of the 'double dividend'. The term has been used in very different ways, which has caused confusion. To begin with, we can distinguish a 'weak' and 'strong' form of the double dividend:[6]

- *Weak form:* By using revenues from the environmental tax to finance reductions in marginal rates of an existing distortionary tax, one achieves cost savings relative to the case where the tax revenues are returned to taxpayers in lump-sum fashion.
- *Strong form:* The revenue-neutral substitution of the environmental tax for typical or representative distortionary taxes involves a zero or negative gross cost.

The Weak Form

These forms differ in their claims about the costs of revenue-neutral environmental tax policies. Let 'gross cost' refer to the reduction in individual welfare (in wealth equivalents) of a given tax initiative, abstracting from the welfare effect from changes in environmental quality.[7] Let $C(t_E, \Delta T_L)$ denote the gross cost of the new environmental tax t_E in combination with lump-sum tax reductions ΔT_L sufficient to make the policy revenue-neutral. Similarly, let

$C(t_E, \Delta t_X)$ denote the gross cost of the new tax t_E accompanied by cuts in the distortionary tax Δt_X sufficient to achieve revenue-neutrality. The weak double-dividend claim is that:

$$C(t_E, \Delta t_X) < C(t_E, \Delta T_L) \tag{2.1}$$

that is, the gross cost is lower when revenues are replaced through cuts in the distortionary tax than when revenues are replaced lump-sum. Under this proposition, the 'second dividend' is the lower distortionary cost in the former case (left-hand side) relative to the cost in the latter case (right-hand side).

The weak double dividend claim is relatively uncontroversial. This is fortunate, because the key assumption on which it depends is relatively innocuous. This claim can be shown to be equivalent to the claim that replacing, at the margin, a lump-sum tax by a distortionary tax entails a positive welfare cost (apart from environmental considerations).[8] This latter claim is not difficult to uphold, since the idea that swapping a distortionary tax for a lump-sum tax has a positive welfare cost is part of the usual definition of 'distortionary'. So long as the tax t_X deserves its title as a distortionary tax, it will have a positive efficiency cost and the weak double-dividend claim will hold.[9]

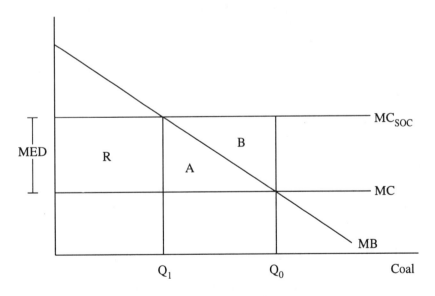

Figure 2.1 Typical first-best, partial eqilibrium framework for analysing efficiency effects of environmental taxes

The weak form can be related to the elements of Figure 2.1 which offers the typical partial equilibrium and first-best framework for analysing welfare effects of an environmental tax.[10] MC denotes the private marginal costs of producing the given commodity, which in this example is coal. MC_{soc} represents the social marginal cost curve, incorporating the marginal external damage (marginal external cost), MED. MB represents the marginal benefit (demand) curve. If a tax is imposed on coal equal to the marginal external damage, social and private marginal costs become aligned. The usual textbook analysis regards the welfare gain as area B.[11] This is the value of the environmental improvement (A + B) minus the gross costs of the tax (A).[12]

In the first-best, partial equilibrium analysis, no efficiency impacts are associated with the tax revenue, R. Implicitly, it is assumed that R is transferred costlessly from those who pay the coal tax to the government and back (in lump-sum fashion) to the private sector. The weak notion of the double dividend recognizes the fact that this 'recycling' of the revenues (R) may indeed have efficiency consequences. In particular, using the revenues to cut existing distortionary taxes can help reduce the overall (gross) distortionary costs of the tax system.

If area A in Figure 2.1 were to represent the gross costs when revenues are returned in lump-sum fashion, then the costs would be less than A when revenues are returned through cuts in distortionary taxes.[13] But other critical cost considerations are obscured by the first-best, partial equilibrium framework embodied in Figure 2.1. In particular, when other taxes (such as income taxes) are present, area A is not a good indicator of the gross costs of the tax on coal. Although the weak double dividend notion correctly claims that rebating revenues through cuts in distortionary taxes reduces gross costs relative to their level under lump-sum replacement, the reference level from which the reduction occurs is generally quite different from that suggested by area A in the diagram. We return to this issue below.

The Strong Form

The stronger double-dividend notion involves assertions about the *sign* of the gross cost of a revenue-neutral policy in which an environmental tax replaces (some of) an existing distortionary tax. The assertion is:

$$C(t_E, \Delta t_X) < 0. \qquad (2.2)$$

The assertion here is that swapping an environmental tax for a distortionary tax involves a negative gross cost. For any given distortionary tax (t_X) involved in the tax swap, condition (2.2) is stronger than (2.1) assuming $C(t_E, \Delta T_L) > 0$.

One can decompose the overall gross cost $C(t_E, \Delta t_X)$ into that which is 'directly attributable' to the environmental tax and that which is 'directly attributable' to the reduction in the distortionary tax.[14] The strong double dividend claim is that the first cost – the cost resulting from the environmental tax – is smaller in absolute magnitude than the second cost – the cost associated with the cut in the distortionary tax. In other words, when the taxes are scaled to imply the same revenue impact, the environmental tax introduces a smaller cost than an equal-revenue change in the distortionary tax.

It is important to keep in mind what is meant by 'costs'. As mentioned, costs (C) are a measure of the policy-induced changes in individual welfare (abstracting from welfare effects associated with policy-related changes in environmental quality). In models that examine these costs, welfare depends directly on individual consumption of goods and services and enjoyment of leisure. Measured this way, the economic cost can differ in sign and magnitude from changes in important macroeconomic variables such as GNP or the growth of GNP. The question whether a given revenue-neutral tax swap entails positive costs is different from the question whether the swap entails a reduction in GNP or its growth rate.

Much of the debate about the potential for environmental tax reform revolves around whether this strong form holds. If one exploits possibilities for using environmental tax revenues to cut other taxes, might many environmental tax initiatives become zero-cost options? In the rest of this section, we concentrate on this double-dividend notion.

A Central Result

An important theoretical investigation of this issue was provided by Bovenberg and de Mooij (1992, 1994a). These authors develop a simple general equilibrium model with one primary factor of production – labour – and three produced commodities – a 'clean' consumption good, a 'dirty' consumption good, and a public good (non-rival in consumption). Production exhibits constant returns to scale, and the rates of transformation between the three produced commodities are constant and equal to unity. Environmental quality is negatively related to aggregate production of the dirty consumption good. A representative household derives utility from leisure, from consumption of the three produced goods, and from environmental quality. The two private goods and leisure are weakly separable from the public good and environmental quality in the utility function.

Bovenberg and de Mooij begin with the situation where the only tax is a labour income tax with a constant marginal tax rate. They then consider the effects of a revenue-neutral policy change in which a tax is imposed on the dirty consumption commodity and the revenues are devoted to a reduction in the labour tax rate. The commodity tax is non-infinitesimal.[15] The strong double dividend claim is that this policy would yield an increase in non-environment-related welfare, that is, in the utility from the composite of consumption and leisure enjoyed by the representative household. These authors obtain analytical solutions indicating that this claim is substantiated if and only if the uncompensated wage elasticity of labour supply is negative, that is, if and only if the labour supply function is backward-bending. Most empirical studies of labour supply yield positive values for the uncompensated elasticity (see, for example, Hausman (1985)); thus, the Bovenberg–de Mooij results tend to reject the double dividend proposition in its strong form.

What lies behind the Bovenberg–de Mooij result? There are two key components. First, the tax on the environmentally harmful consumption good lowers the after-tax wage and generates distortions in the *labour* market, and these labour market distortions are at least as great in magnitude as the labour market distortions from a labour tax increment of equal revenue yield. Hence, the revenue-neutral swap in which the environmental tax replaces (some of) the labour tax leads to no reduction (and usually an increase) in labour market distortions. Second, the tax on the environmentally damaging commodity induces changes in the commodity market – 'distorting' the choice among alternative commodities.[16] These two distortionary effects – in labour and commodity markets – imply that, apart from environmental considerations, the revenue-neutral combination of an environmental tax and reduction in labour tax involves a reduction in the non-environmental component of welfare. In fact, the distortions in the commodity and labour markets are connected. To the extent that the environmentally motivated commodity tax leads households to substitute other commodities for the taxed commodity, there is a reduction in the gross revenue yield of the tax. This limits the extent to which the environmental tax can finance a reduction in the labour tax, and augments the overall gross cost of the tax initiative.

Intuition for this result is as follows. Consider a static model in which there is one labour market (no labour heterogeneity). Let Case 1 refer to the situation where there is just one produced commodity. Suppose that initially there is a tax on labour but no commodity tax. Under these circumstances the commodity tax (even an infinitesimal one) produces a non-infinitesimal excess burden. This occurs because, under the circumstances just described, the introduction of a commodity tax is formally identical to an increase in the labour tax. It reduces the real wage in precisely the same way an increase in a labour tax would.[17] Now suppose, in contrast to this first case, that there are many distinct produced commodities. As before, suppose that the initial situation involves only a tax on labour. Now consider (Case 2) the effect of introducing a uniform but small tax on *all* commodities, and (Case 3) the effect of introducing a small tax on just *one* of the commodities. Case 2 is formally similar to Case 1; it will generate non-infinitesimal excess burdens because this tax is equivalent to an increase in the wage tax.[18] Case 3 is relevant to the imposition of an environmental tax on one commodity. Bovenberg and de Mooij show analytically that, for a given revenue yield, the excess burden in Case 3 is non-infinitesimal and is in fact larger than in Case 1 or 2. The reason is that Case 3 generates the same, or larger, labour market distortion as in the other cases and a larger distortion in the commodity markets.

These results indicate that there are *two* important omissions in Figure 2.1. They work in opposite directions. First (as emphasized by the weak double dividend claim), the revenues R can be used to reduce gross distortionary costs. This suggests that the partial equilibrium analysis would overstate the cost of the environmental tax initiative. At the same time, the presence of other (labour) taxes implies that, for any given use of the tax revenues, the gross distortion from the environmental tax will be larger than implied by Figure 2.1. This implies the opposite bias in the partial equilibrium analysis. Bovenberg and de Mooij show that the latter effect is larger in magnitude than the former: overall, the presence of prior taxes implies higher gross costs from the environmental tax – even when revenues are recycled through cuts in the distortionary tax. These two effects are schematized in Figure 2.2. Adopting terminology similar to that introduced by Parry (1995a), I call the former effect the *revenue-recycling effect* and the latter the *tax-interaction effect*.[19] Using a different analytical approach, Parry obtains results that conform to those of Bovenberg and de Mooij, showing that the tax interaction effect is of greater magnitude than the revenue-recycling effect under plausible values for parameters.[20]

Earlier analyses of revenue-neutral environmental taxes emphasized the revenue-recycling effect and did not recognize the tax-interaction effect. These

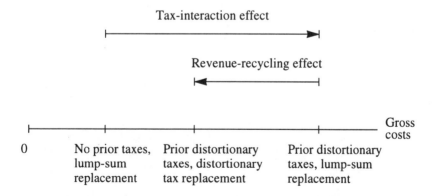

Figure 2.2   Gross costs of an environmental tax under alternative initial conditions and recycling methods

analyses suggested that the strong double dividend was inevitable. An important contribution of Bovenberg–de Mooij, Parry, and others is to call attention to the tax-interaction effect and its implications for the costs of revenue-neutral environmental tax reforms. A related and important lesson from this work is that partial equilibrium analyses of the gross costs of environmental taxes can be highly misleading. This research shows that environmental taxes importantly affect resource use in markets other than the market in which the tax is applied – with significant implications for gross costs. These general equilibrium impacts are especially important if there are prior taxes in 'other' markets such as the labour market.

How General are these Results? Further Considerations

The analytical results from Bovenberg–de Mooij and Parry stem from simplified models. What are the key simplifying assumptions of these models, and to what extent are these simplifications critical to the results?

Capital
One important simplification in the above models is that they involve only one primary factor of production. How would consideration of a second factor – capital – affect the results?

Including capital introduces the possibility of a third effect in addition to the revenue-recycling and tax-interaction effects previously discussed. This is the *tax-shifting effect* – the shifting of the burden of taxation from one factor to another.

Bovenberg and Goulder (1995) show that the tax-shifting effect can help reduce the gross costs of revenue-neutral environmental policies, or expand these costs, depending on initial conditions. In some circumstances the tax-shifting effect not only works in favour of the (strong) double dividend, but indeed can be strong enough to produce the double dividend. Bovenberg and Goulder find, in particular, that to support the double dividend, the following two conditions must obtain:

1. In the initial (*status quo ante*) situation, the relative taxation of capital and labour must be inefficient in the sense that the marginal excess burden of labour and capital taxes are not equal.
2. The revenue-neutral combination of environmental tax and cut in other (e.g. income) tax must shift the burden from the hitherto overtaxed factor of production to the previously undertaxed factor of production.

Under these circumstances, the environmental tax initiative ends up improving the relative taxation of labour and capital: 'green' tax reform serves a 'traditional' tax reform function. If the efficiency gain associated with the improved relative tax treatment of capital and labour is large enough, it can offset the gross costs that would otherwise result from the tax-interaction effect (net of the revenue-recycling effect): the double dividend arises after all.

Empirical studies of US taxes tend to indicate that capital taxes have higher marginal excess burdens than do labour taxes (see Ballard, Shoven and Whalley (1985) and Jorgenson and Yun (1990)). Under these circumstances, an environmental tax reform would produce a 'favourable' tax-shifting effect to the extent that the environmental tax itself tends to put a disproportionate burden on labour, and the revenues from the tax are recycled in ways that tend to reduce capital taxes more than labour taxes. Bovenberg and Goulder (1995) show that a tax on consumer purchases of gasoline, with revenues devoted to cuts in capital income taxes, meets these conditions, and is thus an exceptionally good candidate for an initiative that would yield the double dividend. Although these conditions work in favour of the double dividend, they do not guarantee it will arise. In numerical simulations Bovenberg and Goulder find that, under plausible parameter values, the tax-shifting effect generally is not strong enough to offset the tax-interaction effect (net of revenue-recycling effect) and produce the double dividend. Only under extreme assumptions about savings elasticities (which imply very large initial differences in marginal excess burdens of capital and labour taxes) does the double dividend arise.

Pre-existing subsidies
Prior subsidies clearly offer scope for the strong double dividend. For example, a carbon tax can serve to undo prior subsidies on fossil fuels and thereby reduce or eliminate the gross distortionary costs in fuels markets. Shah and Larsen (1992) emphasize this point in considering the potential for carbon taxes in developing countries.

Intermediate inputs
The simplest models disregard intermediate inputs. However, in Bovenberg and Goulder (1995), the Bovenberg–de Mooij model is extended to incorporate intermediate inputs, and the results above prevail in the extended model. Bovenberg and Goulder analyse the effects of environmentally motivated taxes on 'dirty' intermediate goods and on 'dirty' consumption goods. In each case, the strong double dividend claim fails to materialize when the uncompensated wage elasticity of labour supply is positive. The economic basis for the result in the case of the intermediate good tax is the same as that provided above for the commodity (consumer good) tax. Similar results are obtained in Bovenberg and de Mooij (1994b).

Emissions taxes
The analytical models discussed above consider taxes on commodities (consumer goods or intermediate inputs) whose production or use generates pollution. Other

things equal (abstracting from monitoring costs, etc.), it is most efficient to tax the source of the externality, that is, emissions. Relative to commodity taxes, emissions taxes can yield higher *overall* efficiency gains. But the results concerning the double dividend are not changed. One can think of emissions as another intermediate input. As with taxes imposed on an ordinary intermediate input, emissions taxes alter the mix of all intermediate inputs and 'distort' factor markets. The same mechanisms as discussed earlier indicate that emissions taxes will involve larger gross costs per dollar of revenue than the income (labour) taxes they replace. Whether they are more or less attractive in terms of gross costs than intermediate input taxes depends on the production technology. It may seem counter-intuitive that emissions taxes do not automatically fare better than ordinary input taxes in terms of the double dividend. It helps to keep in mind that the issue here is *gross*, not *net* costs, and thus that the advantages along the environmental dimension do not apply in this context. Once we take the environmental dimension into account, the 'targeting' of emissions taxes gives them an advantage (abstracting from monitoring and enforcement issues) over taxes on ordinary inputs or commodities. But note that the same feature that makes emissions taxes attractive in terms of overall efficiency – their ability to induce larger emissions reductions per dollar of revenue than ordinary intermediate input taxes – curtails their attractiveness in terms of gross costs. Narrowness implies larger gross distortions.

Exhaustible resources and decreasing returns

To this point we have only considered taxes on produced goods. In assessing the gross costs, we needed to consider the distortions produced in the markets for the factors that produced these goods. In particular, in examining the costs of a tax on fossil fuels, we regarded fossil fuels as produced intermediate goods and attended to the related distortions in the markets for labour and capital.

Of course, natural stocks of fossil fuels are primary resources, not produced goods. They are exhaustible resources whose reserves are given by nature.[21] The essential scarcity of natural resource stocks gives rise to scarcity rents. A basic result from the literature on the taxation of natural resources is that a constant tax on these rents does not alter the intertemporal allocation of these resources and has no efficiency cost.[22] This suggests that an environmentally motivated tax on, say, fossil fuels, might not have a significant (gross) efficiency cost after all, given the exhaustible nature of these fuels. If this were the case, then swapping a tax on these fuels for ordinary income taxes might be a negative cost option, upholding the double dividend claim in its strong form.

Should the previous results be discarded because they derive from models that ignored exhaustible resources? Not necessarily. It should be recognized that in most cases, the environmentally motivated taxes under actual consideration are not taxes on scarcity rents. The base of a carbon tax, for example, is not the scarcity rent but rather the quantity of fuel purchased (since carbon combustion and the amount of CO_2 emitted are functions of the quantity of fuel consumed). In contrast with a tax on pure rent, the tax on fuel output affects intertemporal choice and introduces a gross efficiency cost.[23] Despite the exhaustible nature of fossil fuels, a carbon tax does not attain the non-distortionary ideal.

Of course, this does not entirely disprove the significance of exhaustibility to the double dividend issue. Even if the environmental taxes in question are related to fuel output rather than rent, it is possible that the gross efficiency costs of these taxes might be considerably lower when these 'outputs' are extracted exhaustible resources. To continue with the fossil fuels example, *extracted* fossil fuels are the product of several primary factor inputs: natural resource stocks (fuels in the ground), capital and labour. The gross efficiency cost from taxes on these fuels will be a weighted average of the gross efficiency cost generated by the tax in the exhaustible resource market, the capital market, and the labour market.[24] To discern this efficiency cost, one would need to know the extent to which the tax is borne by each of these factors and the marginal efficiency cost associated with reductions in scarcity rents, the return to capital, and the wage. This information is not easy to obtain, to say the least. Ascertaining the marginal efficiency cost in the resource market alone is exceedingly difficult. Despite these difficulties, further empirical work aimed at gauging these magnitudes might be of considerable value.

Environmental taxes and unemployment
A number of authors have examined the possibility of a double dividend in situations where rigid wages or other institutional factors imply significant involuntary unemployment. Space limitations preclude a detailed assessment of these studies here. The presence of involuntary unemployment does not usually help the case for the double dividend as defined here, although it can under particular formulations of labour market imperfections (see, for example, Bovenberg and van der Ploeg (1993, 1994, 1996), and Sörensen, Pedersen and Neilsen (1994)).

It is worth noting that the 'dividends' we consider here are measured in terms of changes in welfare. In Europe, there has been intense discussion about an 'employment dividend' from environmental taxes. (See, for example, Carraro and Siniscalco (1995), and Carraro, Geleotti, and Gallo (1994).) In general, it is less difficult to obtain the second dividend when it is defined in terms of employment rather then welfare. A revenue-neutral environmental reform that causes demand to shift from capital-intensive to labour-intensive industries stands a good chance of generating the employment dividend. There may be considerable political appeal to such policies, but it should be kept in mind that the employment dividend does not usually imply a gross (exclusive of environmental effects) efficiency gain.

It is also worth noting that the thrust of the analytical work goes against the initially compelling idea that an environmental tax combined with a reduction in labour taxes reduces the overall tax burden on labour. The research described above rejects this idea. Environmental taxes are *implicit* factor taxes, so that the swapping of an environmental tax for a labour tax can easily fail to reduce labour's tax burden. Indeed, Bovenberg and de Mooij make clear that, since the environmental tax is a less efficient revenue-raising device than a labour tax (because its base is narrower), a revenue-neutral combination of environmental tax and cut in labour tax can easily raise the effective tax burden on labour.

A general theme

A number of other issues might be invoked that bear on the possibility of a double dividend. For example, for a country with monopsony power in fuels markets, an environmentally motivated tax on fossil fuels could produce terms of trade gains that offset some or perhaps all of the gross costs of the environmental tax.[25]

With the exception of the terms-of-trade case, to enjoy the strong double dividend there must be a pre-existing inefficiency in the tax system along non-environmental dimensions. We noted above, for example, that the strong double dividend could arise if the environmental tax served to undo prior inefficiencies in the relative taxation of labour and capital. In this case the strong double dividend presumes a need, based on non-environmental considerations, for factor tax reform. It is reasonable to ask why these inefficiencies cannot be addressed directly (through changes in factor tax rates) rather than through an environmental tax. It seems more natural to address these inefficiencies directly as part of general tax reform than indirectly as part of environmental policy.

But political considerations might warrant the indirect approach. By permitting coalitions of those interested in factor tax reform and those interested in environmental improvement, a revenue-neutral policy that achieves both might have more backing than 'pure' factor tax reform or 'pure' environmental policies. One can certainly imagine circumstances where this is the case. Whether it applies in the real world is a difficult empirical issue that deserves close analysis.

Numerical Findings

This section presents some numerical results applicable to the double dividend issue. Here I consider only the results that bear on the strong double dividend notion defined above: the issue under investigation is the gross costs (non-environment-related welfare costs) of revenue-neutral tax swaps. As mentioned earlier, some other studies define reductions in unemployment or increased profits as additional 'dividends' from green taxes. I do not report results from these studies here because I do not have the information necessary to combine the reported changes in unemployment, profits, and other economic variables into the more general welfare notion expressed by 'gross costs'.[26]

Table 2.1 presents results from five numerical models. These are the Goulder and Jorgenson–Wilcoxen intertemporal general equilibrium models of the US, the DRI and LINK econometric macroeconomic models of the US, and the Shah–Larsen partial equilibrium model, which has been applied to five countries, including the US.[27] The results in Table 2.1 are for the revenue-neutral combination of an environmental tax (usually a carbon tax) and reduction in the personal income tax, except in cases where this combination was not available. I have focused on the case where revenues are returned through cuts in the personal income tax because this tax seems 'typical' and 'representative'; hence this case is relevant to the strong double dividend claim.

All welfare changes abstract from changes in welfare associated with improvements in environmental quality (reductions in greenhouse gas emissions). Thus they correspond to the gross cost concept discussed above. In the Goulder and Jorgenson–Wilcoxen models, welfare changes are reported in terms of the equivalent variation; in the Shah–Larsen model, the changes are based on the compensating variation.[28] In the DRI and LINK macroeconomic models, the percentage change in aggregate real consumption substitutes for a utility-based welfare measure.[29]

In most cases, the revenue-neutral green tax swap involves a reduction in welfare, that is, entails positive gross costs. This militates against the strong double dividend claim. Results from the Jorgenson–Wilcoxen model, however, support the strong double dividend notion. To what might the differences in results be attributed? A thorough examination of the differences in structure of these models, and an extensive test of how these differences account for differences in model outcomes, is beyond the scope of this chapter. However, one potential explanation lies in the differences between the Jorgenson–Wilcoxen and Goulder models in the marginal excess burden (MEB) of capital taxation.[30] The interest elasticity of saving is higher in the Jorgenson–Wilcoxen model than in the Goulder model. In addition, the Jorgenson–Wilcoxen model assumes that capital is fully mobile across sectors, while the Goulder model includes adjustment costs, which limit the speed at which capital can be reallocated and lower the elasticity of capital demand. Thus, elasticities of capital supply and capital demand are higher in the Jorgenson–Wilcoxen model; correspondingly, the marginal excess burden of capital taxation is considerably higher in the Jorgenson–Wilcoxen model than in the Goulder model, and the difference in the marginal excess burdens of capital and of labour is larger. In the Goulder model, the difference in MEBs per dollar is $0.10;[31] the difference in the Jorgenson–Wilcoxen model appears to be considerably higher.[32] As indicated in the previous section, a large deviation in the MEBs on capital and labour taxes works in favour of the strong double dividend (particularly if the burden of the environmental tax falls on labour). This helps explain why, in the Jorgenson–Wilcoxen model, a revenue-neutral combination of carbon tax and

Table 2.1 Comparative numerical results

Model	Reference	Country	Type of environmental tax	Form of revenue replacement	Welfare change	Results Change in real GNP (%) period 1	period 2
DRI	Shackleton et al. (forthcoming)	US	Phased-in carbon tax[a]	Personal tax cut	-0.39[b]	0.00	-0.76
Goulder	Goulder (1995b)	US	$25/ton carbon tax	Personal tax cut	-0.33[c]	-0.15	-0.22
Goulder	Goulder (1994)	US	Fossil fuel Btu tax	Personal tax cut	-0.28[c]	-0.09	-0.18
Jorgenson–Wilcoxen	Shackleton et al. (forthcoming)	US	Phased-in carbon tax[a]	Labour tax cut	1.01[d]	0.03	-0.41
Jorgenson–Wilcoxen	Shackleton et al. (forthcoming)	US	Phased-in carbon tax[a]	Capital tax cut	0.19[d]	0.20	0.95
LINK	Shackleton et al. (forthcoming)	US	Phased-in carbon tax[a]	Personal tax cut	-0.51[b]	0.00	-0.35
Shah–Larsen	Shah and Larsen (1992)	US	$10/ton	Personal tax cut	-1049[e]	-0.020[f]	—
Shah–Larsen	Shah and Larsen (1992)	India	$10/ton	Personal tax cut	-129	-0.060	—

	Country	Carbon tax	Policy			
Shah–Larsen (1992)	Indonesia	$10/ton	Personal tax cut	−4	−0.005	—
Shah–Larsen (1992)	Japan	$10/ton	Personal tax cut	−269	−0.008	—
Shah–Larsen (1992)	Pakistan	$10/ton	Personal tax cut	−23	−0.070	—

Notes:

(a) Beginning at $15/ton in 1990 (period 1), growing at 5% annually to $39.80 per ton in 2010 (period 21), and remaining at that level thereafter.
(b) Percentage change in the present value of consumption; the model does not allow for utility-based welfare measures.
(c) Welfare cost per dollar of tax revenue, as measured by the equivalent variation.
(d) Equivalent variation as a percentage of benchmark private wealth.
(e) Compensating variation in levels (US$m).
(f) Percentage change in GDP (not GNP). This is a one-period model.

reduction in *capital* tax involves negative gross costs (that is, a positive change in gross welfare). It is more difficult to account for the fact that substituting a carbon tax for a *labour* tax involves negative gross costs in the model.

Table 2.1 also includes GNP impacts. These are included simply because they may be of interest. As mentioned above, conceptually they bear no systematic relationship to welfare impacts. Indeed, in some of the numerical simulations the GNP and welfare changes are of opposite sign.

Like the theoretical results, the numerical outcomes in Table 2.1 tend to weigh against the strong double dividend claim. But there is less than perfect agreement among the numerical results. Discerning the sources of differences in results across models is difficult and frustrating, in large part because of the lack of relevant information on simulation outcomes and parameters. Relatively few studies have performed the type of analysis that exposes the channels underlying the overall impacts. There is a need for more systematic sensitivity analysis, as well as closer investigations of how structural aspects of tax policies (type of tax base, narrowness of tax base, uniformity of tax rates, etc.) influence the outcomes. In addition, key behavioural parameters need to be reported. Serious attention to these issues will help explain differences in results and, one hopes, lead to a greater consensus on likely policy impacts.

OPTIMAL ENVIRONMENTAL TAXATION

Beyond the Pigovian Rule

The standard partial equilibrium, first-best approach to optimal environmental taxation was suggested by Figure 2.1. The figure indicates that welfare is maximized when the Pigovian principle is followed, that is, when the environmental tax rate is set equal to the marginal environmental damage (MED) from pollution. This principle implicitly assumes that the marginal gross cost (or marginal abatement cost) associated with a given tax rate is equal to the tax rate. Thus, when the tax rate is set equal to the MED, gross costs and environmental benefits are equated at the margin, assuring optimality.

In the presence of other taxes, gross costs are no longer equal to the tax rate. Whether they are greater or less than the tax rate depends on the tax-interaction and revenue-recycling effects discussed earlier. The previous discussion indicated that, most often, the tax-interaction effect is larger in absolute magnitude than the revenue-recycling effect. This implies that the gross costs of an environmental tax are larger in a second-best setting than in the first-best case, and implies that the optimal environmental tax rate is less than the rate given by the Pigovian principle.

This problem is analysed formally by Bovenberg and van der Ploeg (1994) and Parry (1995a). Bovenberg and van der Ploeg consider the following optimal tax problem. The government wishes to maximize the well-being of a representative household, where utility is expressed by:

$$U = U(V(C, D, \ell); G; E) \qquad (2.3)$$

where C and D are a 'clean' and 'dirty' consumption good, ℓ is leisure (equal to 1 minus the fixed labour time endowment), G is a non-rival (public) good provided by the government, and E is the quality of the environment. The subutility function V is increasing in its arguments, C, D, and ℓ. U is increasing in V, G, and E. C and D and G are produced with labour, and the marginal rate of transformation between these goods is linear. Environmental quality is a decreasing function of the quantity produced of the dirty consumption good. The government can employ taxes on labour and on each of the consumption goods.

The optimal tax problem is to obtain the vector of tax rates that maximizes the utility of the household subject to the household and government budget constraints and the specified technology.[33] In the case where C and D are separable from ℓ in V, the solution involves a positive tax on labour,[34] no taxes on the clean consumption good C, and an environmental tax t on the dirty consumption good given by:

$$t^* = MED/\mu \qquad (2.4)$$

where μ is the marginal cost of public funds.[35] In Bovenberg and van der Ploeg's model, μ is greater than unity if and only if the uncompensated elasticity of labour supply is positive. In this case, the optimal tax rate is less than the MED. Estimates for the marginal cost of public funds in the US tend to range between 1.1 and 1.6,[36] suggesting that the optimal environmental tax rate is significantly below the MED.

Equation (2.4) is consistent with the idea that the gross costs of environmental taxes are larger in the presence of other distortionary taxes than in a first-best setting. As discussed by Bovenberg and van der Ploeg, environmental quality can be viewed as a good that the public sector provides by obtaining public revenues with the environmental tax. The higher the value of μ, the higher is the cost of providing environmental quality. Thus, the optimal amount of environmental quality is lower, as is the optimal tax rate, t^*.

Bovenberg and van der Ploeg's analysis has been extended to consider more complicated cases, including the case where C and D are not separable from leisure, and the case where pollution has adverse impacts on production (in addition to direct utility impacts). These cases lead to modified formulas for the optimal environmental tax. But the general result remains: in a second-best setting, the costs of environmental taxes are larger, and thus the optimal environmental tax is lower than in a first-best world, other things being equal.[37,38]

Policy Implications

These issues are highly relevant to considerations of the optimal carbon tax. Nordhaus (1993) calculates the optimal carbon tax in the case where revenues are returned lump sum, and compares that with the optimal tax when revenues are returned through cuts in distortionary taxes. In the former case, the optimal tax begins at about $5 per ton, while in the latter case it begins at $59 per ton! This seems to contradict the notion, indicated by the optimal tax formula above, that second-best considerations should *reduce* the optimal tax rate. It turns out, however, that although Nordhaus's experiments attend to the revenue-replacement effect, they do not capture the tax-interaction effect because the model did not include pre-existing taxes. Including pre-existing taxes in the benchmark data would likely reverse the Nordhaus results. In this connection, simulations by Bovenberg and Goulder (1996) indicate that the optimal carbon tax declines with the level of pre-existing taxes.

In real-world situations, it may be difficult to apply the tax formulas by Bovenberg–van der Ploeg and Parry, for two reasons. First, policymakers may be constrained in terms of the range of instruments that can be employed to optimize the tax system. In many cases one does not have the privilege of optimizing the entire tax system, but rather is concerned with optimizing the environmental tax alone. If the rest of the tax system is suboptimal (in an efficiency sense), there is no single marginal cost of public funds: a symptom of a suboptimal tax system is that the marginal cost of public funds differs depending on how public funds are raised, that is, which tax is incremented. Technically, the optimal environmental tax rate will be equal to the MED divided by a weighted average of the marginal costs of public funds from different taxes, but the weights are not easily fathomed.

A second complication is that policymakers may be constrained in the ways they use the revenues from environmental taxes. In general, it pays to devote the revenues to cuts in existing distortionary taxes; this exploits the revenue-recycling effect. If revenues are returned in lump-sum fashion, the net benefits (environmental benefits minus gross costs) of an environmental tax initiative may fall considerably short of the maximum, even if the environmental tax rate is at the value prescribed by equation (2.4).[39] In this connection, Bovenberg and Goulder (1996) have shown that when revenues are returned in lump-sum fashion, *any* positive carbon tax reduces welfare if the marginal environmental benefits from carbon abatement fall short of $50 per ton! Suboptimal use of revenues can have dramatic welfare consequences.

These issues have important implications for the choice between revenue-raising (RR) and other, non-revenue-raising (NRR) instruments for environmental protection. With an analytical model, Parry (1995b) compares the gross costs of RR and NRR instruments that achieve a given level of pollution abatement. He finds that NRR instruments (such as quotas or grandfathered tradeable permits) produce the same tax-interaction effect as is generated by RR instruments (taxes). At the same time, he demonstrates that only RR instruments enjoy the (cost-reducing) revenue-recyling effect. Parry shows that the absence of the revenue-recyling effect is a significant disadvantage of NRR policies. Indeed, NRR policies can cause *reductions* in welfare if the marginal environmental benefits from pollution reduction are not above a certain threshold. Goulder, Parry and Burtraw (1996) obtain similar results using a family of analytically and numerically solved models. Their analytical model indicates that, under reasonable assumptions for parameters, any reduction in pollution through an NRR policy reduces welfare when marginal environmental benefits do not exceed 30 per cent of marginal production cost. These studies, along with the previously mentioned carbon tax study by Bovenberg and Goulder (1996), attest to the significance of the revenue-recycling effect.

CONCLUSIONS

Economists are accustomed to determining optimal environmental tax rates or evaluating the impacts of incremental environmental tax reforms in a partial equilibrium framework. Recent work has made clear, however, that such a framework can be seriously inadequate in a second-best world where other, distortionary taxes are present. A key insight from this work is that environmental taxes are not simply taxes on polluting activities: *they are implicit taxes on primary factors of production* – labour, capital, and (as applicable) stocks of natural resources. This insight has powerful implications for environmental tax policy. It implies that an environmental tax will 'distort' factor markets much as explicit factor taxes do, and that the magnitude of the distortion rises the higher the marginal rates of pre-existing factor taxes are.

The connections between environmental taxes and other taxes are expressed by the tax-interaction effect. Because of this effect, revenue-neutral environmental tax reforms generally will involve positive gross costs, even when revenues from the environmental taxes are devoted to cuts in marginal rates of existing distortionary taxes. Revenue-recycling tends to offset some, but not all, of the gross costs of environmental taxes: the double dividend (in its strong form) does not materialize. Swapping environmental taxes for existing factor taxes (particularly labour taxes) may actually raise the overall tax burden on labour.

The tax-interaction effect implies that environmental taxes are more costly in a second-best setting than in a first-best setting. This means that the optimal environmental tax rate is generally less than the marginal environmental damage from pollution. The optimal environmental tax rate is a smaller fraction of the marginal damages, the higher the marginal cost of public funds is. Higher pre-existing tax rates imply higher marginal costs of public funds.

Although second-best considerations tend to imply greater costs of environmental taxes, they do not vitiate the case for environmental tax reform. Even if revenue-neutral swaps of environmental taxes for ordinary income taxes involve positive gross costs, they may be warranted on overall efficiency grounds: the gross benefits associated with the policy's improvement of the environment may outweigh – perhaps vastly outweigh – the gross costs. Even if the lunch is not free, it may be worth buying.

All of these considerations underscore the importance of gaining better information on the environment-related *benefits* associated with environmental taxes. The efforts to find a double dividend stemmed in part from the hope that, in the face of uncertainties about magnitudes of environmental benefits, the costs of revenue-neutral environmental taxes could be shown to be zero or negative, so that uncertainties about benefits wouldn't matter. This has proved to be a false hope. It makes it all the more important to obtain useful information as to the magnitudes of environmental benefits from these reforms.

Similarly, we need good information on marginal environmental damages (or, equivalently, marginal environmental benefits from pollution reductions) in order to put optimal environmental tax principles to work. We tend to have much better information nowadays on the denominator of the optimal tax formula (the marginal cost of public funds) than on the numerator (the marginal environmental damages). Recognizing tax interactions and other second-best connections is of little value in the absence of reliable information about environmental benefits. The science of estimating environmental benefits is imperfect, but even imperfect new information could be extremely useful for environmental policy-making.

NOTES

1. I am grateful to the editors and two referees for very helpful comments on earlier drafts of this chapter.
2. The qualifier 'gross' is included here to make clear that we refer to costs before netting out the benefits associated with policy-induced improvements to the environment. The next section offers a more precise definition of gross cost.
3. This idea was advanced several decades ago by Tullock (1967) and Kneese and Bower (1968) and somewhat more recently by Nichols (1984). Terkla (1984) appears to have been the first to perform a numerical assessment of the efficiency benefits associated with devoting environmental tax revenues to cuts in existing taxes.
4. This section borrows from Goulder (1995a).

5. Pearce (1991) appears to have coined the term. For general discussions of the double dividend issue, see, for example, Pezzey (1992), Repetto *et al.* (1992), Poterba (1993), Bovenberg (1996), Oates (1991, 1994) and Goulder (1995a).

6. One could also define (as in Goulder (1995a)) an intermediate form, which asserts that there exists some distortionary tax such that the revenue-neutral substitution of the environmental tax for this tax involves a zero or negative gross cost. While the strong form claims zero or negative gross costs arise in typical cases, the intermediate form is simply claiming the possibility of finding some case where this occurs. Most of the discussion about the strong form applies to the intermediate form as well.

7. I emphasize efficiency issues here, and thus I define gross costs in welfare terms. These costs are most easily defined with respect to a representative individual whose overall utility U can be defined by $U(u_1(E), u_2(G))$, where u_1 is utility from environmental quality *(E)* and u_2 is utility from 'ordinary' goods and services *(G)*. Policy initiatives generally lead to changes in both u_1 and u_2. Gross benefits are the wealth equivalent (as measured, for example, by the equivalent variation) of the change in u_1; gross costs are the negative of the wealth equivalent of the change in u_2.

8. This can be shown as follows. Consider the two post-reform situations associated with equation (2.1). One (associated with the left-hand side) involves a reduction in a distortionary tax; the other (associated with the right-hand side) involves a lump-sum tax reduction. The two post-reform situations are alike in other important respects: they involve the same tax revenue and all other tax rates (including t_E) are the same. One can write the levels of welfare associated with the two post-reform situations as $W(t_E, t_X', T_L)$ and $W(t_E, t_X, T_L')$, where $t_X' = t_X + \Delta t_X$ and $T_L' = T_L + \Delta T_L$. (Note that $\Delta t_X < 0$, $\Delta T_L < 0$.) The weak double dividend assertion is equivalent to the assertion that $W(t_E, t_X', T_L) > W(t_E, t_X, T_L')$. This, however, is equivalent to the assertion that the gross efficiency cost of raising the distortionary tax from t_X' to t_X, where the change is financed through a reduction in lump-sum taxes from T_L to T_L', is positive. Thus, the weak double dividend claim is upheld so long as the distortionary tax considered has a positive gross efficiency cost or excess burden.

9. Two clarifications are in order here. First, it should be kept in mind that this discussion only considers *efficiency* costs and benefits from environmental tax initiatives: distributional concerns are ignored. When distributional impacts are taken into account, it is no longer guaranteed that the social costs of a revenue-neutral environmental tax initiative are lower when revenues are recycled through cuts in distortionary taxes than when they are recycled in lump-sum fashion. For an exploration of these issues, see Proost and van Regemorter (1996).

    Second, it is interesting to consider whether the weak double dividend notion is upheld in the case where t_X is negative in the *status quo ante*. Starting from a negative value (or subsidy), a further reduction in this tax (financed through lump-sum taxes) may be efficiency-worsening. Under these circumstances, if a new environmental tax is employed to finance reductions in a 'distortionary' tax whose value is already negative, the weak double-dividend will not obtain. This does not contradict the claims in the text. In the situation described here, the key requirement of the weak double-dividend notion – that the tax t_X have a positive marginal excess burden – is missing.

10. In this example, the tax is a strict Pigovian tax in that it applies to a commodity with which pollution is associated rather than directly to pollution emissions. The basic lessons apply to emissions taxes as well.

11. In the case with non-constant private marginal costs or non-constant marginal external costs, the presentation is slightly more complicated, but the results are essentially the same.

12. The environmental economics literature often refers to *abatement costs*. These are usually defined in a way that corresponds, in Figure 2.1, to the entire area below the MB curve (including the area below the MC curve) over the interval from Q_0 to Q_1. Gross costs are smaller than abatement costs because they net out the avoided expenditure on polluting inputs. In Figure 2.1, this avoided expenditure is the area under the MC curve from Q_0 to Q_1.

13. Of course, the government could waste the revenues – for example, by applying them to government projects with benefit-cost ratios below one. In this case the gross costs will be greater than A. In this chapter I do not consider which use of revenues is most likely; I leave that to political scientists.

14. Since taxes interact, the attribution of the cost of the revenue-neutral policy change into 'direct' effects of t_E and 'direct' effects of Δt_X is not automatic. A reasonable decomposition is to split $C(t_E, \Delta t_X)$ into $C(t_E, \Delta T_{L1})$ and $C(\Delta t_X, \Delta T_{L2})$, where ΔT_{L1} and ΔT_{L2} are the lump-sum tax changes necessary to make the component changes t_E and Δt_X revenue-neutral.

15. Alternatively, the tax is incremental but superimposed on an existing non-infinitesimal tax on the dirty consumption commodity.

16. It should be kept in mind that we are concerned with distortions in the gross sense – abstracting from environmental considerations. One can measure gross distortions by the extent to which resource allocation departs from what would be the efficient allocation if there were no concern for environmental quality. Once we take account of the environmental dimension, environmental taxes have the potential to improve, rather than distort, resource allocation.

17. The after-tax real wage is (1) the after-tax nominal wage divided by (2) the gross of tax price of consumption. Income taxes directly affect the after-tax real wage by reducing (1), whereas energy taxes directly influence this wage by raising (2).

18. A uniform commodity tax does not avoid distorting the commodity market in all circumstances. A sufficient set of conditions for its optimality is that commodity consumption be separable from leisure in utility and that the utility function be homothetic. See Bovenberg and de Mooij (1994a).

19. Parry terms these the 'revenue effect' and 'interdependency effect'.

20. Figure 2.2 shows that to uphold the strong double dividend claim, the magnitude of the revenue-recycling effect must in fact be *larger* than that of the tax-interaction effect – by enough to bring the gross costs to zero. In Bovenberg–de Mooij and Parry's analyses, since the tax-interaction effect is larger than the revenue-recycling effect, environmental taxes not only involve positive gross costs, but larger gross costs than would result from the same tax in a first-best setting where there are no pre-existing taxes and where revenues are returned lump-sum.

21. *Known* reserves, of course, are endogenous, a function of exploration activity. This does not alter the main points discussed here.

22. See, for example, Sweeney (1977, 1993) and Dasgupta and Heal (1979). It may be noted that under these circumstances the environmental tax does not yield any environmental benefits.

23. This is the case because, in general, the present value of the tax payment per unit of fuel is not constant through time. On this see, for example, Sweeney (1977).

24. Whether the strong double dividend arises depends on whether the government has already taxed fixed-factor rents. In a model with three factors of production – labour, resources, and a fixed factor, Bovenberg and van der Ploeg (1993) show analytically that a tax on a 'dirty' consumption commodity fails to yield a double dividend (in the strong sense) if all the rents from the fixed factor are already taxed. On the other hand, if fixed factor rents are not taxed, the same type of tax offers the double dividend. In the latter case the commodity tax proxies for the tax on fixed factor rents, and enjoys much of its efficiency potential.

25. For further discussion of this issue, see Goulder (1995a).

26. Nor do I consider the evidence for the weak double dividend notion. As mentioned earlier, there is virtually unanimous numerical support for this notion, so a weighing of this evidence seems unnecessary.

27. For a more detailed description of these models, see Goulder (1995b), Jorgenson and Wilcoxen (1990, 1994), Shackleton *et al.* (forthcoming), and Shah and Larsen (1992). The Shah–Larsen model is by far the simplest of the five models, in part because it takes pre-tax factor prices as given. Despite its simplicity, the model addresses interactions between commodity and factor markets and thus incorporates some of the major efficiency connections discussed earlier.

28. The equivalent variation is the lump-sum change in wealth which, under the 'business-as-usual' or base case, would leave the household as well off as in the policy-change case. Thus a positive equivalent variation indicates that the policy is welfare-improving. The compensating variation is the lump-sum change in wealth which, in the policy-change scenario, would cause the household to be as well off as in the base case. In reporting the Shah–Larsen results I adopt the convention of multiplying the compensating variation by –1, so that a positive number in the table signifies a welfare improvement here as well.

29. The demand functions in these models are not derived from an explicit utility function. Hence they do not yield utility-based measures.

30. Of the five models in Table 2.1, these two are the most similar and allow for the most straightforward comparisons.
31. The MEBs per dollar are $0.22 and $0.12 for the tax on individual capital and individual labour income, respectively, for central values of parameters.
32. This assumption is based on reported values in Jorgenson and Yun (1990). The Jorgenson–Yun and Jorgenson–Wilcoxen models have some similarities in structure and parameters, but there are important differences as well. Marginal excess burden numbers from the Jorgenson–Wilcoxen model were not yet available.
33. This problem is a generalization of that considered by Ramsey in that the technology is more general and the level of government spending (or tax revenue) is determined as part of the optimization problem.
34. Strictly speaking, the tax on labour is positive only if household preferences for the public good require a level of tax revenue that exceeds what would be provided by Pigovian taxation alone. If households require less tax revenue than would be provided by Pigovian taxation, the optimum involves a subsidy to labour and an environmental tax on D.
35. The marginal cost of public funds (MCPF) is the welfare loss (in monetary equivalents) associated with the reduction in private consumption associated with a unit increase in public revenue. An MCPF of unity means that there is no excess burden from taxation, that is, that raising an additional dollar of public revenue costs the private sector exactly one dollar in terms of foregone consumption.
36. See Ballard, Shoven, and Whalley (1985), Browning (1987) and Jorgenson and Yun (1990).
37. In the more general case where C and D are not separable from leisure, the optimal tax on D is expressed by $t^* = t^R + MED/\mu$. The second term on the right-hand side is the environmental component of the tax on D, and is identical to the right-hand side of equation (2.4). The first term (t^R) on the right-hand side is the 'Ramsey' component of the tax on D. It is the differentiation in taxation between C and D that derives from traditional 'Ramsey' optimal tax considerations, specifically, the fact that C and D are not equally complementary to leisure. (These considerations indicate that it is best to impose higher taxes on goods that are relatively strong complements to leisure, which cannot be taxed directly.) In both this extended expression and in the simpler expression (2.4), the tax on D that stems from strictly environmental considerations is equal to the MED divided by the marginal cost of public funds.
    In the case where pollution causes damage to production, environmental quality is effectively an input into the production process. Bovenberg (1996) considers this case and derives the following formula for the optimal tax on the polluting activity: $t^* = MED_U/\mu + MED_P$, where MED_U is the direct marginal environmental damage of pollution stemming from changes in E in the utility function (it is the same as MED in equation (2.4)), and MED_P represents the marginal damage that pollution imposes on production.
38. Optimal tax analysis has also been applied to the case where industrial market structure is not perfectly competitive. Several papers in Carraro *et al.* (1996) address this issue. In a setting with imperfect competition, there is a second source of deviation between the optimal tax rate and the marginal environmental damage. Environmental taxes can indirectly offset or exacerbate resource misallocations attributable to imperfect competition. Thus, the optimal environmental tax rate in a setting with imperfect competition takes account of these effects.
39. This occurs when the marginal rates of existing distortionary taxes are too high; revenue-neutrality should have been obtained through cuts in these rates rather than through lump-sum tax reductions.

REFERENCES

Ballard, C.L., J.B. Shoven and J. Whalley (1985), 'General Equilibrium Computations of the Marginal Welfare Costs of Taxes in the U.S.', *American Economic Review*, **75** (1), 128–38.

Bovenberg, A.L. (1996), 'Environmental Policy, Distortionary Labor Taxation, and Employment: Pollution Taxes and the Double Dividend', in C. Carraro, Y. Katsoulacos and A. Xepapadeas (eds), *Environmental Policy and Market Structure*, Dordrecht and Boston: Kluwer Academic Publishers.

Bovenberg, A.L. and R.A. de Mooij (1994), 'Environmental Taxation and Labor Market Distortions', *European Journal of Political Economy*, **10**(4), December, 655–83.

Bovenberg, A.L. and R.A. de Mooij (1994a), 'Environmental Levies and Distortionary Taxation', *American Economic Review*, **84**(4), 1085–9.

Bovenberg, A.L. and R.A. de Mooij (1994b), 'Environmental Tax Reform and Endogenous Growth', working paper, Tilburg University (forthcoming in *Journal of Public Economics*).

Bovenberg, A.L. and L.H. Goulder (1995), 'Costs of Environmental Taxation in the Presence of Other Taxes: General Equilibrium Analyses', working paper, Stanford University, June.

Bovenberg, A.L. and L.H. Goulder (1996), 'Optimal Environmental Taxation in the Presence of Other Taxes: General Equilibrium Analyses', *American Economic Review*, **86**(4), 985–1000.

Bovenberg, A.L. and F. van der Ploeg (1993), 'Consequences of Environmental Tax Reform for Involuntary Unemployment and Welfare', working paper, Tilburg University, September.

Bovenberg, A.L. and F. van der Ploeg (1994), 'Environmental Policy, Public Finance and the Labour Market in a Second-Best World', *Journal of Public Economics*, **55**(3), 349–90.

Bovenberg, A.L. and F. van der Ploeg (1996), 'Optimal Taxation, Public Goods and Environmental Policy with Involuntary Unemployment', *Journal of Public Economics*, **62**(1–2), 59–83.

Browning, E.K. (1987), 'On the Marginal Welfare Cost of Taxation', *American Economic Review*, **77**(1), 11–23.

Carraro, C., M. Geleotti and M. Gallo (1994), 'Environmental Taxation and Unemployment: Some Evidence on the Double Dividend Hypothesis in Europe', working paper, GRETA Econometrics, May.

Carraro, C. and D. Siniscalco (eds) (1996), *Environmental Fiscal Reform and Unemployment*, Dordrecht, Boston and London: Kluwer Academic Publishers.

Carraro, C., Y. Katsoulacos and A. Xepapadeas (eds) (1996), *Environmental Policy and Market Structure*, Dordrecht and Boston: Kluwer Academic Publishers.

Dasgupta, P.S. and G.M. Heal (1979), *Economic Theory and Exhaustible Resources*, Cambridge: Cambridge University Press.

Goulder, L.H. (1994), 'Energy Taxes: Traditional Efficiency Effects and Environmental Implications', in J.M. Poterba (ed.), *Tax Policy and the Economy 8*, Cambridge, Mass.: MIT Press.

Goulder, L.H. (1995a), 'Environmental Taxation and the "Double Dividend": A Reader's Guide', *International Tax and Public Finance*, **2**(2), 157–83.

Goulder, L.H. (1995b), 'Effects of Carbon Taxes in an Economy with Prior Tax Distortions: An Intertemporal General Equilibrium Analysis', *Journal of Environmental Economics and Management*, **29**(3), 271–97.

Goulder, L.H., I.W.H. Parry and D. Burtraw (1996), 'Revenue-Raising vs. Other Approaches to Environmental Protection: The Critical Significance of Pre-existing Tax Distortions', NBER working paper No. 5641, June.

Hausman, J.A. (1985), 'Taxes and Labor Supply', in A.J. Auerbach and M.S. Feldstein (eds), *Handbook of Public Economics*, Vol. 1, Amsterdam: North-Holland.

Jorgenson, D.W. and P.J. Wilcoxen (1990), 'Environmental Regulation and U.S. Economic Growth', *The Rand Journal of Economics*, **21**(2), 314–40.

Jorgenson, D.W. and P.J. Wilcoxen (1994), 'Reducing U.S. Carbon Emissions: An Econometric General Equilibrium Assessment', in D. Gaskins and J. Weyant (eds), *Reducing Global Carbon Dioxide Emissions: Costs and Policy Options*, Stanford, CA: Stanford University Press.

Jorgenson, D.W. and K.-Y. Yun (1990), *Tax Policy and the Cost of Capital*, Oxford: Oxford University Press.

Kneese, A.V. and B.T. Bower (1968), *Managing Water Quality: Economics, Technology, Institutions*, Baltimore, Md.: Johns Hopkins Press.

Nichols, A.L. (1984), *Targeting Economic Incentives for Environmental Protection*, Cambridge, Mass.: MIT Press.

Nordhaus, W.D. (1993), 'Optimal Greenhouse-Gas Reductions and Tax Policy in the "DICE" Model', *American Economic Review*, **83**(2) (papers and proceedings), 313–17.

Oates, W.E. (1991), 'Pollution Charges as a Source of Public Revenues', Resources for the Future Discussion Paper QE92-05, Resources for the Future, Washington, DC, November.

Oates, W.E. (1994), 'Green taxes: Can We Protect the Environment and Improve the Tax System at the Same Time?', *Southern Economic Journal*, **61**(4), 914–22.

Parry, I.W.H. (1995a), 'Pollution Taxes and Revenue Recycling', *Journal of Environmental Economics and Management*, **29**(3), S64–S77.

Parry, I.W.H. (1995b), 'Environmental Policy and the Tax System', working paper, Resources for the Future, Washington, DC.

Pearce, D.W. (1991), 'The Role of Carbon Taxes in Adjusting to Global Warming', *Economic Journal*, **101**, 938–48.

Pezzey, J. (1992), 'Some Interactions between Environmental Policy and Public Finance', working paper, University of Bristol, June.

Pigou, A.C. (1938), *The Economics of Welfare*, 4th edn, London: Weidenfeld and Nicolson.

Poterba, J.M. (1993), 'Global Warming: A Public Finance Perspective', *Journal of Economic Perspectives*, **7**(4), 47–63.

Proost, S. and D. van Regemorter (1996), 'The Double Dividend Hypothesis, the Environmental Benefits and the International Coordination of Tax Recycling', in C. Carraro and D. Siniscalco (eds), *Environmental Fiscal Reform and Unemployment*, Dordrecht, Boston and London: Kluwer Academic Publishers, 171–91.

Repetto, R., R.C. Dower, R. Jenkins, and J. Geoghegan (1992), *Green Fees: How a Tax Shift Can Work for the Environment and the Economy*, Washington, DC: World Resources Institute.

Sandmo, A. (1975), 'Optimal Taxation in the Presence of Externalities', *Swedish Journal of Economics*, 77.

Shackleton, R. *et al.* (forthcoming), 'The Efficiency Value of Carbon Tax Revenues', in D. Gaskins and J. Weyant (eds), *Reducing Global Carbon Dioxide Emissions: Costs and Policy Options*, Stanford, CA: Stanford University Press.

Shah, A. and B. Larsen (1992), 'Carbon Taxes, the Greenhouse Effect and Developing Countries', World Bank Policy Research Working Paper Series No. 957, The World Bank, Washington, DC.

Sörensen, P.B., L.H. Pedersen and S.B. Nielsen (1994), 'Taxation, Pollution, Unemployment and Growth: Could There Be a "Triple Dividend" from a Green Tax

Reform?', working paper, Economic Policy Research Unit, Copenhagen Business School.

Sweeney, J.L. (1977), 'Economics of Depletable Resources: Market Forces and Intertemporal Bias', *The Review of Economic Studies*, **44**(1), 125–42.

Sweeney, J.L. (1993), 'Economic Theory of Depletable Resources: An Introduction', in A.V. Kneese and J.L. Sweeney (eds), *Handbook of Natural Resource and Energy Economics*, Vol. 3, New York: North Holland.

Terkla, D. (1984), 'The Efficiency Value of Effluent Tax Revenues', *Journal of Environmental Economics and Management*, **11**, 107–23.

Tullock, G. (1967), 'Excess Benefit', *Water Resources Research*, **3**(2), Second Quarter, 643–4.

3. National wealth, constant consumption and sustainable development[1]

John M. Hartwick[1]

We consider models with constant consumption paths and relate them to paths of national wealth. Open economy considerations are examined as well as an overlapping generations formulation. After taking up constant consumption in partial equilibrium models, we turn to general equilibrium. Other approaches to sustainability are noted.

INTRODUCTION

Sustainable development for an economy is a future without noticeable decline. The future state of the economy at any date is like the current state in a welfare sense, or better. Today's economic activity is sustained or improved upon. For renewable resources such as fertile fields, forests and fish stocks, it is not too difficult to imagine using them on a sustainable basis. But for depletable stocks such as oil pools, coal deposits and the like, it is difficult to imagine what a sustainable pattern of use means. The simplest approach to these resources is to view them as providing a bridge to a future renewable supply – an age of hydrocarbon depletion preceding an age of solar power and fusion power. Sustainable use of depletable stocks becomes linked to the development of substitute sources. One anticipates that technical progress will make future renewable substitute sources available at moderate costs. The bounty of past technical progress seems to assure us of future additional large dividends. We will not be caught out. In fact technical progress seems to have resulted in the substitution of labour and produced capital for a considerable amount of the pure natural resource content in commodities in the 20th century. In certain respects, technology has been overcoming fundamental scarcities. However, energy use still relies heavily on depletable stocks. But maybe fusion power plants and solar collector farms will be the capital that substitutes for primary fossil fuels in energy use in the future. Perhaps fossil fuels will occupy an increasingly smaller fraction of the price of energy in the future. This is the view that underlies our approach below.

We enquire about sustainable development in a stylized economy that is substituting away from fossil fuels. Finite oil stocks are being depleted by oil use essential to current production. Sustainability takes the form of the requirement that consumption does not decline in the future. With a constant population in the economy, constant consumption implies no decline in future welfare. Toward the end, we reflect on this criterion and report on alternatives. A virtue of the constant consumption approach to sustainability is that it involves the net investment zero property which has been exploited in measuring sustainability by Pearce and Atkinson (1993).

We keep empirical implementability in mind in our presentation. This leads us into new topics involving the discreteness of time in applications and terms of trade effects in measurements for open economies. We have recent results to report on these topics. We also report recent results on the market realizability of constant consumption paths (Long, Mitra, Sorger, 1995). We open with a partial equilibrium analysis, a simple framework in which basic results emerge without technical complications. We emphasize throughout, the connections between constant consumption paths and value of national capital or national wealth paths. Some observers have linked sustainability to maintaining capital intact and we keep this interesting notion in mind. We report on recent results in this area.[2]

A constant consumption path is, in a framework of depleting essential stocks, a benchmark case. One asks in such situations: 'What would an economy be like which could maintain consumption constant indefinitely while essential stocks were being depleted?'. The essential quality is the zero net investment property or the covering off of the current value of stock decline for depleting stocks with a current augmentation in the value of producible stocks. There is a link between a reasonable goal (non-declining consumption) and a menu of actions (what savings-investment strategy should the nation pursue). There are numerous assumptions required for constant consumption to emerge from a policy of zero net investment. For example, in the very long run, different forms of flows from stocks must be sufficiently substitutable in production. We take these matters up below. What policy prescriptions emerge from an understanding of constant consumption paths? Current national well-being gets linked to current natural stock depletion via the zero net investment property of constant consumption paths. One answer to the question, 'Is current economic development sustainable in our economy?', is 'Yes if we are covering off the value of natural stock decline with investment in other forms of capital'.

It is natural to associate the term stationary state with a situation in which consumption remains constant indefinitely. And steady states seem inadequate compared with expanding states and quite rosy compared with declining states. Technical change is usually identified with an expanding economy. Constant consumption paths have usually been examined in cases with no technical progress. In this sense the analysis of constant consumption paths is an exercise in caution. Can we contemplate sustainability without the 'crutch' of technical progress? But if technical progress is the essential engine of economic progress, we are missing the protagonist in our drama if we concentrate on the analysis of economies displaying constant consumption behaviour. Weitzman (1995) implies this position. Those who believe in unbounded technical progress will find the concentration on stationary-state analysis of limited relevance.

Once one espouses the view that the normal state of economic development is one of expansion, one is confronted with the question of the appropriate rate of expansion. The carrying capacity of the environment, broadly defined, becomes an element to be reckoned with. In no time, one is obliged to evaluate the appropriate current 'sacrifice' for future enjoyment. What is the correct trade-off of current consumption for future consumption, of current oil conservation for future oil use? These questions are often lumped under the economics of discounting. Any definition of sustainable development involves implicitly, the trading-off consumption today for consumption tomorrow and thus implies a revealed time preference on the part of the definer. Constant consumption paths are associated with zero as the social discount rate and infinity as the coefficient of risk aversion in utility (Dasgupta and Heal, 1979, p. 307). Thus in linking sustainable development to a constant consumption path we are 'saying something' about social intertemporal choice. Clearly, a constant consumption framework is implicitly prudential. Some people may consider the implicit social choice framework restrictive or unrealistic. However, once our position is set out at the beginning, we are free to move on to the analysis of its implications.

Sustainability seems impossible with large and growing populations. We are pessimistic about maintaining eco-system and atmospheric functions and high worldwide, per capita energy consumption in a world of net population increase. Though fertility is obviously linked to family economic well-being, we do not take up this question here.

THE OIL REPUBLIC (OR) MODEL: PARTIAL EQUILIBRIUM

The nation lives off proceeds from oil sales $pq(t)$, and investment income $rH(t)$. p is the world price of oil and r is the world interest rate. Out of this income stream it finances investment abroad $\dot{H}(t)$, plus oil extraction costs $C(q(t))$ and consumption $Y(t)$ of oil owners. (Oil workers finance their consumption out of their wage income which is part of costs $C(q(t))$.) The question of interest is what is the consumption path $(Y(t))$ corresponding to different investment 'formulas'. Oil extraction is governed by the $r\%$ rule (dynamic efficiency condition)

$$\frac{d[p - C_q(q(t))]}{dt} = [p - C_q(q(t))]r$$

This condition characterizes paths over which oil wealth is maximized (see National Accounting, p. 69). There is an old tradition that recommends that owners of a declining asset, such as a machine in regular use, set aside an amount in a sinking fund so that a new asset can be acquired at the desired replacement date. One sets aside depreciation[3] or the decline in value of the asset at each date in the sinking fund. Determining the value of this depreciation is difficult unless there is a thick market for different vintages of the asset. The owner usually makes do with a rule of thumb in determining how much to set aside in the sinking fund each year. For our case, the durable asset is the oil in the ground S(t) and its value V(S(t)) is its discounted future profit stream, under an optimal depletion programme. That is

$$V(S(t)) = \int_t^T [pq^*(v) - C(q^*(v))]e^{-r(v-t)}dv$$

where [q*(t)] is an optimal or profit maximizing extraction programme. This is a programme that satisfies the r% rule or dynamic efficiency. Thus the decline in value $\dot{V}(S(t))$ can be determined precisely for this oil stock or this durable asset (see Appendix I).[4] The amount to set aside in the sinking fund is readily calculable. It turns out that

$$\dot{V}(S(t)) = -[p - C_q(q(t))]q(t)$$

or the decline in value is dynamic or Hotelling rent. This is the product of a stock change $\dot{S}(t)$ (= $-q(t)$) and a marginal value $p - C_q(q(t))$. Depreciation of assets generally assumes this expression, namely stock change times marginal value of a unit of stock. Green national accounting involves estimating such values of reductions in natural stocks (see the section below). It turns out that for our oil republic, this allocation of income to a sinking fund of size H(t), a bank account abroad paying r% per period, will leave consumption by oil owners constant over time. The sinking fund approach does lead to a fund at exhaustion date T of value V(S(T)), sufficient to buy a new oil deposit identical to the original deposit, but also leads to a constant flow of net income to finance consumption by oil owners. Investing rents abroad from oil extracted is thus a policy that implies a constant consumption path for oil owners. This latter result is a variant of the Solow–Hartwick Rule: in a closed economy, the investment of oil rents in new produced machine capital results in a constant consumption path. Matters are simpler in our model of the oil republic because the world oil price p is constant and the world interest rate r is constant. In the Solow (1974) model, taken up below, these two prices are endogenous and are always changing, in a systematic fashion, over time. The result for the oil republic here is that under efficiency in oil extraction and the investing of rents from oil extracted and sold, aggregate consumption Y(t) remains constant. Let us establish this formally. Now

$$Y(t) = pq(t) - C(q(t)) - \dot{H}(t) + rH(t)$$

and

$$\dot{Y}(t) = [p - C_q(q(t))]\dot{q}(t) - \ddot{H}(t) + r\dot{H}(t)$$

and

$$\ddot{H}(t) = [p - C_q(q(t))]\dot{q}(t) + q(t)d[p - C_q(q(t))]/dt.$$

Recall that investment $\dot{H}(t) = ([p - C_q(q(t))]q(t)$. Use $\ddot{H}(t)$ in the expression for $\dot{Y}$ and we have

$$\dot{Y} = -q(t)d[p - (C_q(t))]/dt + r\dot{H}(t)$$

$$= -q(t)[p - C_q(q(t))]r + r\dot{H}(t) \text{ (using the efficiency condition)}$$
$$= 0 \qquad\qquad\qquad\qquad\text{ (using the definition of } \dot{H}(t)).$$

Solow (1974) labelled a path with per capita consumption constant as one exhibiting intergenerational equity. If such a path can be maintained indefinitely, it is a sustainable path. Thus if the number of claimants to oil income remain constant, investing resource rents yields a sustainable path. When the oil is exhausted at date T, an optimized value, there is a fund H(T) abroad whose interest, rH(T), equals the constant consumption value Y(t) observed before date T. Hence there is no change in living standards when the oil runs out. The investing of oil rents yields a sustainable consumption path.

A different view of sustainability suggests consuming in such a way that capital is left intact. Though this notion is attractive, it does seem to favour capital over human welfare. Our approach above involved investing in H(t) an amount equal to the value of the decline in the value of the oil stock, $\dot{V}(S(t))$. This resembles building up one capital stock, namely H(t), to balance off the value of the decline in another. It is true in this model that capital value H(t) + V(S(t)) is remaining constant over time because the change in capital value is $\dot{H}(t) + \dot{V}(S(t))$, which is zero under investing resource rents.

This constancy of total capital value $H(t) + V(S(t))$ and the earlier constancy in consumption $Y(t)$ are not coincidental. Consumption in this model is an interest flow from capital value or wealth. Recall that $Y(t) = rH(t) + [pq(t) - C(q(t))] - \dot{H}(t)$ where $\dot{H}(t) = [p - C_q(q(t))]q(t)$. In Appendix I we decomposed $pq(t) - C(q(t))$ into the sum $\dot{H}(t) + rV(\dot{S}(t))$. Hence $Y(t) = rH(t) + rV(S(t))$ or *consumption is interest on total capital value* and consumption, total capital value and the interest rate are constant under dynamic efficiency in oil extraction or use and the investing of rents on current oil extraction. A central aspect of this result is that interest on capital value is being drawn off as consumption. Hence capital value cannot increase by interest accumulation. Furthermore *net investment*, $\dot{H} + \dot{S}$. $[p - C_q(q(t))]$, is zero at each date. Hence capital value is not being increased by investment. Hence total capital value is remaining constant. This is in the tradition of sinking fund economics. One sets aside income sufficient to replace worn out capital in the future. Capital value remains constant under a strict application of this strategy.

APPLYING THE MEASURE OF SUSTAINABILITY

Pearce and Atkinson (1993) set out to estimate our implicit measure of sustainability, namely the value of net investment, $\dot{K} + [p - C_q(q(t))] \dot{S}$, for a group of countries. $\dot{K}$ is net investment in new machines, buildings, roads, etc. The idea is that if net investment is positive, consumption will be increasing because the economy will be more productive next period, and so on. The economy is on a *super-sustainable path with net investment positive*. With net investment zero, the economy is on a sustainable path. With net investment negative, the economy is on a non-sustainable path. There will be less capital in the future and 'productivity' and consumption will decline.[5] We should emphasize that this is a local-in-time measure of the sustainability of a country's economic course or position.[6] One has to consider long-term availabilities of different types of capital and how they substitute for each other in production in the long run in a global picture of sustainability. We will address the long-run perspective below.

The two aspects of applying the measure of sustainability we take up here are (a) an increasing price of oil facing the small open economy doing the exporting and (b) the difficulty of applying the measure, derived in a continuous time framework, to data based on periods in discrete time. First, in applications one is dealing with economies trading with other countries. As an exporter, the country faces a *world price path* for oil. This complicates matters because the exporter is receiving a terms of trade improvement, period by period as its export good earns more relative to the cost of its import good, with its constant world price. The imported good is the consumption good, represented by $Y(t)$. To maintain constant consumption the oil republic need not invest so much abroad. It can consume more currently, relative to the state when its export good was not facing a rising world price. It turns out that constant consumption can be maintained if investment abroad, $\dot{H}(t)$, is reduced to rents, $[p(t) - C_q(q(t))]q(t)$, *minus* the cumulative terms of trade effect, $\int_t^T q(v)\dot{p}(v)e^{-(v-t)r}dv$ where T is still the date of exhaustion of the oil republic's oil deposit (Vincent, Panayotou and Hartwick, 1995). Needless to say, the cumulative terms of trade effect would be difficult to estimate since it is based on the unknown future path of export prices.[7] Current production is also based on an 'estimate' of this path as well. Theory draws heavily on the assumption of perfect foresight by rational agents. Extraction is done correctly because future prices and interest rates are anticipated correctly under the assumption of perfect foresight.

The second matter in applications involves the discreteness of data, usually based on periods as years. Even in the stationary case of unchanging prices, technology, and the interest rate (the autonomous case), the discreteness of time results in subtle wedges that are not present in the continuous time formulation. In discrete time, the efficiency condition (r% rule) is

$$[p - C_q(q(t + 1))] - [p - C_q(q(t))] = [p - C_q(q(t))]r,$$

and the investing of resource rents takes the form

$$H(t + 1) - H(t) = [p - C_q(q(t))]q(t).$$

If one calculates $Y(t + 1) - Y(t)$, one ends up with $C(q(t)) - C(q(t + 1)) = [q(t) - q(t + 1)] C_q(q(t + 1))$, which is approximately[8] the triangle, $1/2 [q(t) - q(t + 1)][C_q(q(t)) - C_q(q(t + 1))]$, a positive amount. Thus in discrete time, dynamic efficiency and the investing of resource rents do not imply consumption constant, only approximately constant. This species of index number problem should not pose serious problems for proceeding to measure sustainability with net investment and discrete time, but one should be aware of the bias involved.

SUMMARY

We have observed how the economic depreciation of an oil stock, the investment of rents from oil extracted, and efficient extraction paths are associated with constant consumption or net surplus and constant wealth or capital value. Moreover, constant consumption turns out to be the interest flow from the constant wealth. Current net investment, the difference between investment out of oil income and the disinvestment (decline in value) of the oil stock, turns out to be a useful measure of an economy's sustainability. We noted some difficulties in implementing this measure, one dealing with the discrete nature of available data and the other with the price-takingness of most exporters of natural resource based products. Our framework was partial equilibrium. We now turn to a general equilibrium rendering (the Solow (1974) framework) and re-examine our issues and results above.

GENERAL EQUILIBRIUM

The Solow (1974) model is a general equilibrium version of our OR model above. Oil price and the interest rate are endogenous. Solow (1974), Cass and Mitra (1991) and others were interested in the case of oil being essential to world production and conditions under which the economy and specifically consumption could be maintained positive and constant *indefinitely*. In the OR model, the oil was treated as running out for the exporter in question but the economy or consumption at least went on indefinitely. In the general equilibrium model, there will be asymptotic depletion of the finite stock of oil. Oil will be an input to production forever but in dwindling amounts. The sum of the quantities of all oil extracted and used in production will be finite. This is discussed in more detail below. We can continue to consider our oil extractor as a trading nation. In return for oil exports, it receives the composite consumption-investment good produced abroad. Output abroad is $Q(t) = F(K(t), R(t), N(t))$ where $F(.)$ is constant returns to scale and the inputs are substitutable, $K(t)$ is the services of machine capital $K(t)$, $R(t)$ is the flow of oil from stock $S(t)$, $(R(t) = -\dot{S}(t))$, and $N(t)$ is a flow of labour services from a labour force. $N(t)$ is assumed to be constant.

Dynamic efficiency in oil extraction requires $dF_R(t)/dt = F_K(t)F_R(t)$ where F_x is a partial derivative. Thus $F_R(t)$ and $F_K(t)$ are the marginal products of oil and capital respectively. Since the price of composite good Q is unity, $F_R(t)$ is the price of oil and $F_K(t)$ is the rental rate on capital and the interest rate. The dynamic efficiency condition is thus an r% rule where $F_K(t)$ plays the role of the interest rate r.

The oil exporter invests oil rents $R(t)F_R(t)$ abroad in machine capital.[9]

$$\dot{K}(t) = R(t)F_R(t).$$

Its income from abroad is $K(t)F_K(t)$. Abroad $Q(t)$ is produced, oil is imported and $N(t)F_N(t)$ is income left for consumption abroad. Under constant returns, $Q(t) = K(t)F_K(t) + R(t)F_R(t) + N(t)F_N(t)$. The central result is that *aggregate consumption* $Q(t) - \dot{K}(t) = C(t)$ is constant. To see this, we differentiate $\dot{K}(t)$ and $C(t)$ to obtain

$$\ddot{K}(t) = R(t)\dot{F}_R(t) + F_R(t)\dot{R}(t)$$

and

$$\dot{C}(t) = F_K(t)\,\dot{K}(t) + F_R(t)\,\dot{R}(t) + F_N(t)\,\dot{N}(t) - \ddot{K}(t)$$

$$= F_K(t)R(t)F_R(t) - R(t)\dot{F}_R(t)$$

(since $\dot{N}(t) = 0$ and substituting for $\dot{K}(t)$ and $\ddot{K}(t)$

$$= 0$$

using the dynamic efficiency condition. It follows from constant returns to scale that the constant aggregate consumption level[10] is $K(t)F_K(t) + N(t)F_N(t)$. In the special and central[11] case of F(.) Cobb–Douglas, the oil exporter's consumption will be $K(t)F_K(t)$, a constant, and the oil importer's consumption will be $N(t)F_N(t)$, also constant. In this special case, the positive terms of trade effect enjoyed by the oil exporter because the export price $F_R(t)$ is increasing relative to the import price (unity) is exactly offset by the decline in rental or interest rate $F_K(t)$ over time so that the exporter's consumption level remains constant, and this level is exactly the interest on its $K(t)$, held abroad.

Consumption as an interest flow from capital or wealth is an idea that has been around for some time. Solow (1986) took it up in the context of the framework of the investing of resource rents.[12] We will take a different approach, following Hartwick (1996). We consider ourselves in a closed economy, in a general equilibrium setting. We are interested in the nature of the above general result: constant aggregate consumption $C(t)$ is labour income $N(t)F_N(t)$ plus interest on machine stock $K(t)$. Part of consumption is an interest flow. Suppose the labour services $N(t)$ flowed from human capital stock $Z(t)$ as in $\dot{Z}(t) = mZ(t) - N(t)$, where m is a positive constant. $mZ(t) - N(t)$ is improvement in one's human capital in non-labouring time. The dynamic efficiency condition for the use of this stock is $m + \dot{F}_N(t) = F_K(t)F_N(t)$. m is referred to as the own rate of interest on stock $Z(t)$. If we expand investment to $\dot{K} + \dot{S}(t)F_R(t) + \dot{Z}(t)F_N(t) = 0$, i.e., net investment zero, we obtain $\dot{C}(t) = 0$. (The steps are the same as those we used above when we establish $\dot{C} = 0$ for the simpler case.)

The new result is that under constant returns to scale we obtain the constant $C(t)$ as a vector product of values of capital stocks and own rates of interest. That is, we obtain

$$C = K(t)F_K(t) + Z(t)F_N(t)m$$

where $(K(t), Z(t)F_N(t))$ is the vector of dollar-valued capital stocks and $(F_K(t),$ m) is the vector of own interest rates.[13] The own interest rate on the oil stock is zero since it produces no flow of services in its incarnation as a stock, *per se.* This result should not be confused with the notion of a steady-state fish harvest as being an interest flow from the natural stock since in the result above, $K(t)$ and $F_K(t)$ will be changing over time. The above result is a generalized 'steady-state' result.

Net investment zero at each date implies that the initial 'capital' is remaining constant. That is

$$\Omega(t) = \Omega_0 + \int_0^t [\dot{K}(v) + F_R(v)\,\dot{S}(v) + F_N(v)\,\dot{Z}(v)]\,dv$$

a constant capital stock, where Ω_0 is the initial value at date zero and the term in square brackets is net investment, equal to zero. In this case $d\Omega(t)/dt = 0$, under net investment zero. From this view, constant consumption $C(t)$ can be viewed as a flow associated with constant capital Ω_0, the initial endowment.[14] This idea was put forth in Solow (1986) and the wealth concept in $\Omega(t)$ was appealed to in Hartwick's (1994) new look at Weitzman (1976).

MARKET REALIZATION AS AN OVERLAPPING GENERATIONS MODEL

Following Solow (1974), we have been vague about the details of the mechanics of a constant population and who owns what stocks at what dates. Long, Mitra and Sorger (1995) decided to be precise about these details. They introduced finite, two-period lives for people and specific ownership arrangements for stocks.

At each date there is a younger generation, labouring, investing in machine capital K and consuming, and an older generation, only consuming and with its consumption financed from income derived from capital rentals from K and rents from oil sales, R. Labour is treated as a pure flow and human capital is ignored. If one accepts a continuous time setting for the moment and a Cobb–Douglas constant returns production function, one simply separates aggregate output and expenditure into two parts, young and old. Then, consumption C^Y of the young is

$$C^Y = N(t)F_N(t) - \dot{K}(t)$$

and consumption C^E of the older is

$$C^E = K(t)F_K(t) + R(t)F_R(t).$$

We know that the combination of the two groups is an aggregate constant consumption scenario when $\dot{K} = K(t)F_R(t)$. A subtlety is that for C^Y positive, $N(t)F_N(t) - \dot{K}(t)$ must be positive or the share of labour in production must exceed the share of oil rents. This becomes a new feasibility condition for the existence of the overlapping generations realization. Long, Mitra and Sorger (1995) investigated the implementation of such an equilibrium when the younger generation must *purchase* the stocks of machines $K(t)$ and remaining oil $S(t)$ from the older generation. Their central result was that this is not possible. The cost of acquisition, namely $K(t) + F_R(t)S(t)$, eventually exceeds labour income, $N(t)F_N(t)$. (This is not hard to see for the Cobb–Douglas case, since $N(t)F_N(t)$ and $\dot{K}(t)$ will both be constant shares of output, and $K(t)$ grows without bound.) They proposed a tax-transfer scheme to enable the younger generation to acquire the stocks from the older generation. Clearly, setting $T(t) = \theta(t) = K(t) + F_R(t)S(t)$ will work. Then

$$C^Y = N(t)F_N(t) - \dot{K}(t) + \theta(t) - K(t) - F_R(t)S(t)$$

and

$$C^E = K(t)F_K(t) + R(t)F_R(t) + K(t) + F_R(t)S(t) - T(t).$$

Then we have the result that a market realization of the Solow (1974) model requires transfers between generations. If the share of labour is less than the share of oil income, transfers must exceed the value of the stocks in order for the younger generation to have a non-negative consumption.

A complication in the overlapping generations framework is the common and plausible assumption of discrete time. Long, Mitra and Sorger (1995) was set in discrete time. We ask the simple question: how does the Solow model appear and work in discrete time. We separate the matter of discrete time from the matter of transfers between generations. A central subtlety is that the discrete time dynamic efficiency condition is

$$F_R(t + 1) - F_R(t) = F_R(t)F_K(t + 1).$$

Familiarity with continuous-time models conditioned us to expect $F_K(t)$ on the right-hand side. It turns out that in order to 'compensate' for this fact ($F_K(t+1)$ where $F_K(t)$ was expected) the savings-investment rule must be

$$K(t + 1) - K(t) = R(t)F_R(t - 1).$$

Table 3.1   Simulation of Solow (1974) with distinct periods

Iteration	K	R	C (N = 1000)
0	1001	.01	
1	1014.561953	.009646776622	42.1967412
82	2121.278687	.002154602715	41.896116
83	2135.003562	.002126691033	41.894353
100	2368.462528	.001724402400	41.867490
101	2382.202824	.001704374934	41.866074
102	2395.943885	.001684693264	41.864673
103	2409.685701	.001665349491	41.863289
199	3745.279227	.0006846661943	41.777334
200	3759.068429	.0006796215158	41.776766
201	3772.857941	.0006746322756	41.776201
300	5153.069319	.0003604525135	41.735045
301	5166.881641	.0003585193234	41.734745
302	5180.694128	.0003566016213	41.734446
400	6534.998574	.0002236989176	41.711278
401	6548.823943	.0002227520717	41.711090
402	6562.649414	.0002218112176	41.710905
500	7917.983840	.0001521907813	41.695806
501	7931.817721	.0001516588262	41.695678
502	7945.651672	.0001511296526	41.695552

Experience with continuous-time models leads one to expect $F_R(t)$ on the right-hand side. We must invest less than rents $R(t)F_R(t)$ because $F_K(t-1)$ will be lower than $F_K(t)$. Under constant returns to scale, $Q(t) = K(t)F_K(t) + R(t)F_R(t) + N(t)F_N(t)$ and $C(t) = Q(t) - [K(t+1) - K(t)]$. Routine substitution yields

$$C(t+1) - C(t) = [F_K(t+1) - F_K(t)]K(t+1) + [F_R(t+1) - F_R(t)]R(t+1) + [F_N(t+1) - F_N(t)]N(t+1).$$

In the Cobb–Douglas case, $F_K(t+1) - F_K(t)$ approaches zero for large t and $R(t)$ approaches zero for large t. For $N(t)$ constant, $F_N(t+1) - F_N(t)$ approaches zero for large t. Note that $F_K(t+1) - F_K(t)$ and $F_R(t+1) - F_R(t)$ are opposite in sign. Hence, $C(t+1) - C(t)$ approaches zero for large t for the case of the Cobb–Douglas production function[15] (see also Dasgupta and Mitra, 1983). We report an example in Table 3.1. The production function is $K^{1/2}R^{1/4}N^{1/4}$. Initial values were $K_{-1} = 1000$, $K_0 = 1001$, $R_0 = 0.01$, $N_0 = 1000$ and N was held constant. After one 'iteration', $K_1 = 1014.561953$, $R_1 = .009646776622$ and consumption $C = 42.1967412$. After 502 iterations, C was 41.695552 with $\Delta C = .000126$, K was 7945.651672 with $\Delta K = 13.833951$ and R was 0.0001511296526. ΔK was approaching a positive constant from below and C was approaching a positive constant from above. R was approaching 0 from above. Considerable probing was carried out, including backward recursions. The model was stable. Discrete time introduces a regular asymptotic approach to the constant consumption configuration. In continuous time, the model 'jumps to' the constant consumption path at time zero. In all runs, the asymptotic value of C was approached *from above*. If policymakers moved directly (at a time zero) to the investing of resource rents, and the economy were Cobb–Douglas as in our example, the consumption level would decline to its positive asymptote. For other specifications of the production function, we conjecture that cycles could be present as constant consumption is or is not approached. For the Cobb–Douglas case in continuous time, we know that constant consumption is feasible over infinite time. This key property should reappear asymptotically in discrete time, as we suggest above. See also the numerical example with a Cobb–Douglas production function in Long, Mitra and Sorger. Summarizing, a market realization of the Solow (1974) model involves essential intergenerational transfers (a form of government-imposed altruism) and subtleties of discrete time dynamics *vis-à-vis* continuous time dynamics.

OPEN ECONOMY FORMULATIONS

Suppose the world economy comprises distinct, price-taking countries trading oil flows. Does investing local oil rents achieve a constant consumption in each country? Asheim (1986) discovered, 'no'. There are 'extra' positive terms of trade effects for oil exporters and negative terms of trade effects for oil importers. Hartwick (1995) presented weights on own country oil rents which yielded constant consumption in each country in a system of trading countries. The weights can be thought of as offsetting or neutralizing the terms of trade effects.

Consider a closed world economy of the Solow (1974) type. Now split the economy into two countries, identical except that country 1 has a small amount more of the oil stock. Thus the two countries will have identical economies from a production standpoint. Country 1 will export a small amount of oil to country 2 and 2 will export some of its composite produced good in return. Let $\gamma_i(t)$ be the fraction of country i's resource rents invested in its machine capital. There is constant returns to scale in production. Then

$$\dot{K}_i(t) = \gamma_i(t)R_i(t)F_R(t). \qquad (i = 1,2).$$

Prices will be the same for all inputs and outputs in each country. $F_R(t)$ is the world oil price. γ_i will exceed 1 for the oil importer and be less than unity for the oil exporter. $\varepsilon(t)$ is oil exports from country 1.

Then

$$C_1(t) = F[K_1(t), R_1(t) - \varepsilon(t), N_1(t)] - \gamma_1(t)R_1(t)F_R(t) + \varepsilon(t)F_R(t)$$

and

$$C_2(t) = F[K_2(t), R_2(t) + \varepsilon(t), N_2(t)] - \gamma_2(t)R_2(t)F_R(t) - \varepsilon(t)F_R(t).$$

$R_i(t) = -\dot{S}_i(t)$ in each country and $R_1(t) - \varepsilon(t) = R_2(t) + \varepsilon(t)$ under constant returns to scale, free trade and dynamic efficiency in extraction. That is $dF_R(t)/dt = F_K(t)F_R(t)$.

Differentiation of $\dot{K}_i(t)$ and $C_i(t)$ with respect to time and substitution in the expression for $\dot{C}_i(t)$ yields[16]

$$\dot{C}_1(t) = F_R(t)d[(1-\gamma_1(t))R_1(t)]/dt$$

and

$$\dot{C}_2(t) = F_R(t)d[(1-\gamma_2(t))R_2(t)]/dt$$

or

$$\frac{\dot{\Delta}_1(R_1)}{\varepsilon(t)} = F_K(t) = -\frac{\dot{\Delta}_2(R_2)}{\varepsilon(t)}$$

for $\Delta_i(R_i) = (1-\gamma_i(t))R_i(t)$. For the case $\gamma_i = 1$, we have that $\dot{C}_1(t) = \varepsilon(t)\,\dot{F}_R(t) = -\dot{C}_2(t)$ or the motion of consumption is the terms of trade effect $\varepsilon(t)\,\dot{F}_R$. In the closed economy Solow model, the motion of rental rate $F_K(t)$ exactly offset the motion of $F_R(t)$, but in the two economy model, trade breaks this balancing of price effects. We need a wedge in each country on the investing of own resource rents in order to restore constant consumption in each country. Clearly the oil importer will experience a lower level of consumption relative to the exporter. However, when the two country model is sandwiched together, the familiar single closed economy will be recreated.

We argued earlier that open economy effects were important to consider when one was doing empirical analysis of net investment in a country or region because no economy is entirely closed to trade. Investing resource rents or zero net investment needs adjusting as a criterion of local in time sustainability. We have seen the nature of adjustments for some central cases. In brief, terms of trade effects of rising exhaustible resource prices must be taken into account in the calculation of zero net investment.

NATIONAL ACCOUNTING

There are two quite distinct aspects to green accounting. The first is accounting for pollution, congestion, etc. by mechanisms in which prices reflect full social costs – private costs plus external costs. This aspect of green accounting has been kept high on the agenda for improving accounting since at least the time of Pigou's work, starting in the 1920s. The second aspect is accounting for the using up of natural capital in current economic activity. A straightforward case is, say, the running down of oil stocks by the use of oil in current production. We will dwell on this latter issue here.

Depreciation is the general term for the decline in value of a capital good from use. Economic depreciation is the decline in value associated with a capital good when the good is being used (depleted) in a way which maximizes capital value over the longer term. (Keynes referred to economic depreciation as user cost.) 'Depreciation' appears as the difference between gross national product (GNP) and net national product (NNP). In particular, the 'capital consumption allowance' is the part of GNP which is set aside to replace or maintain capital in an economy. This concept of national income (NNP) dates from Hicks who recommended that 'income' be defined as the amount of current product left over (for prospective consumption) after capital has been maintained intact. That is, NNP is what is left from GNP after capital has been maintained intact, after its wear and tear from current use over the year has been replaced. Green national accounting applies this Hicksian notion to natural capital such as oil stocks, in addition to conventional capital (machine, structure and infrastructure capital). The idea is simply to expand the 'capital consumption allowance' to include terms representing declines or losses in value of natural stocks as they are depleted by current usage. One is figuratively replacing used-up natural capital with investment in other kinds of capital.[17]

It is worth noting that this dimension of greening the national accounts is directly in the mainstream of national accounting theory and practice. The innovation is the idea of replacing decline in capital value from use with an allocation not directly tied to the capital stock in question. The decline in the value of oil stocks, for example, is 'accounted for' by a new item in the 'capital consumption allowance'. The effect is to lower measured 'national income' or NNP because the 'capital consumption allowance'is expanded to include the decline in value of natural capital in addition to the value of the decline in person-made capital. The two tricky parts in this greening of the accounts are (a) obtaining valid and accessible measures of the current decline in the value of natural stocks, and (b) delimiting which natural stocks to include. For example, should the decline in the stock measuring biodiversity be included in natural stocks? If a stock's decline, other things being the same, reduces the value of current production and the stock is in turn affected by current economic activity then it is a candidate for inclusion in an expanded capital consumption allowance.

One can obtain valid measures of natural stock value decline from an understanding of the economy as a dynamic general equilibrium system (Hartwick, 1990; and Mäler, 1991). The principle is that stock i's decline in value is measured by its net physical diminution multiplied by the marginal value of a unit of stock. This concept is in fact economic depreciation. Marginal value generally takes the form of market price minus marginal extraction cost of the current 'harvest'. The relevant prices and quantities are observable in principle. With non-marketed natural inputs such as abatement services of air and water, one must develop proxies for stock decline and the marginal value of current output. However, if we sense that we are free-riding on the natural environment and degrading it in the process, we must take account of our impacts in our calculation of the true cost of what we produce. A green national accounts is designed to do this full costing based on economic principles and accepted practice. We turn to the derivation of expressions for NNP and economic depreciation. Consider the case of a closed economy with a constant labour force N in which output $Q(t)$ ($= F(K(t), R(t), N)$) involves the services of capital from stock $K(t)$, and of oil $R(t)$ from stock $S(t)$. That is, $R(t) = -\dot{S}(t)$. Net investment $\dot{K}(t)$ competes with aggregate consumption $C(t)$ in current output, i.e.,

$$\dot{K}(t) = F(K(t), R(t), N) - C(t). \tag{3.1}$$

Under optimal savings[18] (the marginal value of a unit of $Q(t)$ in current consumption equals the marginal value of a unit of $Q(t)$ in investment), paths $C(t)$, $K(t)$, and $R(t)$ satisfy maximization subject to equation (3.1), $R(t) = -\dot{S}(t)$, and $K(0) = K_0$ and $\int_0^\infty R(t)dt \leq S_0$.

That is, the controls $R(t)$ and $C(t)$ satisfy

$$\frac{\partial H(t)}{\partial C(t)} = 0 \text{ or } U_C(C(t)) = \lambda(t) \tag{3.2}$$

and

$$\frac{\partial H(t)}{\partial R(t)} = 0 \ \text{ or } \ \lambda(t)F_R(t) = \phi(t) \tag{3.3}$$

where $H(t)$ is the current value Hamiltonian:

$$H(t) = U(C(t)) + \lambda(t)[F(K(t), R(t), N) - C(t)] - \phi(t)R(t) \tag{3.4}$$

$\lambda(t)$ and $\phi(t)$ are shadow asset prices for $K(t)$ and $S(t)$ respectively. Formally they are co-state variables. We identify $H(t)$ with current net national product, measured in utils. Using (3.2) and (3.3), (3.4) can be written as

$$\frac{H(t)}{U_C(t)} = \frac{U(C(t))}{U_C(C(t))} + \dot{K}(t) + \dot{S}(t)F_R(t) \tag{3.5}$$

which we identify as the green net national product, valued in numeraire units or dollars.[19] $\dot{S}(t)F_R(t)$ is the current economic depreciation of oil stock $S(t)$. Net investment at zero involves $\dot{K} = -\dot{S}(t)F_R(t)$, which is the expression for 'investing resource rents' (Hartwick, 1977). Note that traditional net national product ($C + I$) can be identified with the first two terms on the right-hand side of (3.5). Green national accounting involves incorporating the economic depreciation of natural resource stocks (disinvestment) in net national product. Expressions for the economic depreciation of other natural stocks for a variety of cases are in Hartwick (1990, 1992, 1993 and 1995b). See also Mäler (1991) and Hamilton and Atkinson (1995) for additional cases involving the depletion of environmental capital, or pollution.

The co-state variables $\lambda(t)$ and $\phi(t)$ satisfy necessary conditions for optimality

$$-\frac{\partial H}{\partial K} = \dot{\lambda} - \rho\lambda \ \text{ or } \ -\lambda(t)F_K = \dot{\lambda}(t) - \rho\lambda(t)$$

$$-\frac{\partial H}{\partial S} = \dot{\phi} - \rho\phi \ \text{ or } \ \dot{\phi}(t)/\phi(t) = \rho$$

which yield the asset equilibrium (dynamic efficiency) conditions

$$F_R(t) = F_K(t)F_R(t) \tag{3.6}$$

and

$$\lambda(t) = \int_0^\infty \exp\left(-(v-t)r\right)\lambda(v)F_K(v)dv. \tag{3.7}$$

Condition (3.6) is the Hotelling rule for this problem and was essential to our construction of constant consumption paths. Analogous dynamic efficiency conditions for problems involving other natural stocks appear in Hartwick (1978), Dixit, Hammond and Hoel (1980), Becker (1982), Hung (1993), Dockner and Hartwick (1994) and related papers dealing with constant consumption paths. The derivation of (3.6) above illustrates how the appropriate dynamic efficiency conditions are obtained.

We know from dynamic programming that the optimal solution satisfies

$$\rho\int_t^\infty U(C^*(v))\exp-(v-t)r\,dv = U(C^*(t)) + U_C(C^*(t))\dot{K}(t) + U_C(C^*(t))F_R(t)\dot{S}(t).$$

This can be written as

$$U_C(C^*(t))\{\dot{K}(t) + \dot{S}(t)F_R(t)\} = \rho\int_t^\infty [U(C^*(v)) - U(C^*(t))]\exp\left(-(v-t)r\right)dv.$$

This indicates that current net investment, in braces, measured in utils is proportional to the discounted gap between the actual optimal $[U(C^*(v))]$ and a hypothetical path involving $C^*(t)$ constant. Roughly speaking, current net investment measures the discounted 'gain' in the value of consumption, given factor of proportionality ρ. This result could be inferred from Weitzman (1976). (See also Aronsson, Johansson and Lofgren, 1995.) If $[C^*(v)]$ is the unique optimal path, and $[C^*(v)]$ is not constant, then $\dot{K}(t) + \dot{S}(t)F_R(t) = 0$ does not imply that $C^*(t)$ is sustainable. The reason is that $\int_t^\infty U(C^*(v))\exp\left(-(v-t)r\right)dv = \int_t^\infty U(C^*(t))\exp\left(-(v-t)r\right)dv$ is attainable only if $[C^*(v)]$ is followed, not $[C^*(t)]$. This is the basis of Asheim's (1994) remark that zero net investment *per se* is not a perfect indicator of sustainability.

TECHNICAL CHANGE AND VARYING INTEREST RATES

Exogenous technical change raises difficulties in interpreting conventional net national product or, roughly speaking, $C + I$, consumption plus net investment (Kemp and Long, 1982; Aronsson and Lofgren, 1993, 1995; Usher, 1994; and Weitzman, 1995). Endogenous technical change is easier to deal with since it can be viewed as a particular form of capital accumulation. The knowledge stock becomes an indicator of the level of technical advancement and R. & D. (research and development) activity is current investment in the knowledge stock.

See, for example, Hartwick (1994). With *exogenous* technical change the economy's production function becomes $Q = F(K,R,N,t)$ where Q is aggregate output, K is machine capital, R is natural resource flow, N is labour services, treated as constant, and t is time, representing exogenous technical change. Then dt becomes a shift to the production function caused by technical change. If we return to the Weitzman (1976) framework, we have

$$\frac{\rho V - \partial V / \partial t}{U_c} = \frac{U(C)}{U_c} + \dot{K}(t) - RF_R,$$

from dynamic programming. ρ is the social discount rate and V is discounted optimal consumption into the indefinite future, $\int_t^\infty U(C^*(\tau))\exp((t-\tau)\rho)d\tau$. The right-hand side is NNP, inclusive of natural stock depreciation. Weitzman associates $\rho V/U_c$ with a hypothetical constant consumption level, i.e., sustainable consumption. $(\partial V/\partial t)/U_c(t)$ is the new wedge between net national product and sustainable consumption and it reflects the exogenous technical progress.[20] (See Appendix II.) Weitzman (1995) estimates this wedge to be about 50 per cent of current net national product (assuming $\rho = 0.05$, NNP growth to be at rate 0.03 and total factor productivity growth to be at rate 0.01).[21] Moreover, he argues that natural stock depreciation will be less than 10 per cent of the wedge representing technical progress. Hence, he contends, net national product is a poor measure of sustainable consumption, primarily because it fails to capitalize future technical progress, not because it fails to include natural stock depreciation.

Asheim (1995) has explored the Weitzman (1976) interpretation of net national product when the discount rate moves exogenously over time. Then a weighted sum of all future discount rates plays the role of the familiar constant rate and the revised definition of net national product includes a current interest rate change adjustment. This adjustment includes the term, currect wealth, and so could be large. See also Hartwick and van Long (1995), where varying interest rates and other non-autonomous cases are treated.

OTHER APPROACHES TO THE CRITERION OF SUSTAINABILITY

Solow (1974) was motivated to investigate constant consumption programmes because they exhibit a reasonable notion of intergenerational equity. No generation is doing better than another, particularly those with larger stocks of exhaustible resources, relative to those with lesser stocks.[22] But a constant consumption programme seems excessively conservative in the sense that there is no period in the future with a generation being better off. A cynic would infer, 'once a caveman, always a caveman'. But with positive discount rates and no technical progress, consumption must eventually decline because of the finiteness of essential oil stocks. Asheim (1988, 1991) investigated the possibility of an initially rising phase of consumption with a subsequent non-declining phase. He set out preferences that would yield such a programme. Individuals are altruistic and care about the consumption of their children. The maximin criterion (maximize the welfare of the worst off generation) is applied to the utility of the consumption stream of all future generations. This is a natural approach, once the specification of altruism is made. Asheim (1991) links his preference structure to a concept of justice based on the Lorenz formalization of inequality. Pezzey (1989) and others have also focused on non-declining consumption as a criterion for sustainability. Anand and Sen (1994, Appendix) indicates how declining consumption is closely tied to a positive discount rate (see also Pezzey and Withagen, 1995).

Chichilnisky has been concerned that the utilitarian criterion is excessively present oriented. Discounting leads to over consumption by the present generation. She has amended the utilitarian criterion so that the welfare of generations in the distant future is not slighted by decision makers in the current generation. Her criterion values utility streams as a sum of two terms, one that is an integral of the stream of discounted utility and one that is the utility of the consumption of the generation in the limiting future. Heal (1993) applies the Chichilnisky criterion to two models with a steady state at some finite future date. In each case, there is more current 'investment' in anticipation of the steady state than there would be under the utilitarian criterion. Elsewhere, Chichilnisky, Heal and Beltratti (1995) have linked sustainability to a 'Green Golden Rule', the configuration of capital and resources which supports the maximum indefinitely sustainable level of utility.

SUMMARY

We derived constant consumption paths for an economy with an essential exhaustible resource in partial and general equilibrium settings. We related such paths to those 'maintaining capital intact' or constant wealth paths. The links between such constant consumption paths and measures of sustainability and 'green national accounting' were set out. Complications posed by discrete time in deriving constant consumption paths were analysed. Complications posed by parametric resource price paths facing small open economies enjoying constant consumption were reported on. Finally, we reported on the complications posed by implementing constant consumption paths in an overlapping generations framework. With no explicit altruism (positive bequests), a role for government in making necessary transfers from old to young was set out.

APPENDIX I: ECONOMIC DEPRECIATION

We are interested in economic depreciation of an extractive firm or oil exporting nation facing constant oil prices p and with a stationary extraction cost $C(q(t))$ for $q(t)$ tons extracted from current stock $S(t) - q(t) = S(t)$. $C(0) = 0$ and $C_q(q(t))$ and $C_{qq}(q(t))$ are assumed strictly positive. The necessary conditions for the maximization profits

$$\int_0^T [pq(t) - C(q(t))] \exp(-rt)dt$$

subject to

$$\int_0^T q(t)dt = S_0$$

are

$$\frac{d[p - C_q(q(t))]}{dt} = [p - C_q(q(t))]r \qquad 0 \le t \le T$$

and at exhaustion date T,

$$\frac{q(T)d[p - C_q(q(t))]}{dt} = pq(T) - C(q(T)).$$

When combined with our assumptions on costs $C(q(t))$, this latter condition implies that $q(T) = 0$. We have then an optimal extraction path $(q^*(t))$ satisfying the above conditions. Then optimal profits at any date are

$$V(S(t)) = \int_t^T [pq^*(v) - C(q^*(v))] \exp(-(v-t)r)dv$$

and

$$\frac{dV(S(t))}{dt} = rV(S(t)) - [pq^*(t) - C(q^*(t))].$$

Note that T depends on the 'starting date' t but we can ignore dT/dt because T satisfies its optimality condition above, i.e., $pq^*(T) - C(q^*(T)) = 0$. From dynamic programming we know that

$$rV(S(t)) = pq^*(t) - C(q^*(t) - q^*(t)\,[p - C_q(q^*(t))]$$

for the optimal extraction programme. Combine this with the equation above and we obtain

$$\frac{dV(S(t))}{dt} = -[p - C_q(q^*(t))]q^*(t)$$

our basic economic depreciation expression. Our results can be summarized as shown in Figure 3.1.

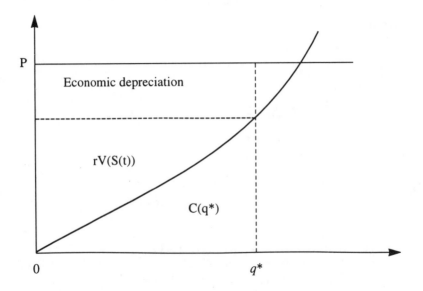

Figure 3.1   Economic depreciation, $-[p-C_q(q^*(t))]q^*(t)$, is the negative of exhaustible resource rent along the optimal extraction path

APPENDIX II: WEITZMAN (1995) ON SUSTAINABLE CONSUMPTION AND EXOGENOUS TECHNICAL PROGRESS

In Weitzman (1976) the point was made that current net national product y(t) could be viewed as interest on wealth as in rV(t) where wealth was interpreted as the discounted stream of optimal consumption $(C^*(\tau))$. Thus current net national product could be interpreted as a level of consumption, sustainable indefinitely. Consider that argument with exogenous technical change and a constant discount rate r. $\dot{K}(t) = F(K(t), N, t) - C(t)$ yields current 'output exhaustion'. $\dot{K}(t)$ is net investment in new person-made capital, N is the constant labour force and $F(K(t), N, t)$ is the aggregate production function. Optimal savings implies, via the Bellman equation of dynamic programming, that

$$rV(t) - \frac{\partial V(t)}{\partial t} = C(t) + \dot{K}(t) \equiv y(t)$$

where

$$V(t) = \int_t^\infty C^*(\tau) \exp(-(\tau-t)r)d\tau.$$

Weitzman (1995) shows that $\partial V(t)/\partial t$ takes the form

$$\int_t^\infty [\exp(-r(\tau-t))\partial y(\tau)/\partial \tau]d\tau$$

$$= \lambda y_t \int_t^\infty \exp(-(r-g)(\tau-t))/\partial \tau$$

for $[\partial y(\tau)/\partial \tau)/y(\tau)] = \lambda$, a constant, and y_t growing at a constant rate g. Hence $\partial V(t)/\partial t = y_t \lambda/(r-q)$, and $rV(t) = y(t) + y_t\lambda/(r-g)$. For $\lambda = .01$ (exogenous technical progress), $g = .03$ (growth in y(t)) and $r = .05$, $\lambda/(r-g) = .5$ and y_t is a poor estimate of sustainable consumption, $rV(t)$. Hence with exogenous technical progress, current net national product can be a large underestimate of sustainable consumption.

NOTES

1. I am grateful to Geir Asheim, Henk Folmer, Kirk Hamilton, John Livernois, Robert Solow and Tom Tietenberg who made helpful comments on an earlier draft.
2. This is not a hands-on manual for measurers of sustainability. Three papers (Hartwick and Hageman 1993; Hartwick 1993b; and Vincent, Panayotou and Hartwick 1995) constitute something of such a guide. There, among other things, are expositions of measures of El Sarafy, Repetto, and others.
3. Economic depreciation is defined as the loss in value of an asset over a specific period from optimal use. Keynes used the term 'user cost' in this context. People use the word depreciation for many kinds of decline in value of an asset and one must distinguish true economic depreciation from other sorts being referred to.
4. See also Lozada (1995) where non-autonomous cases are also taken up.
5. Pearce and Atkinson considered more capital goods than just K(t) and oil stocks S(t) in their measure of net investment. The constant consumption framework extends itself quite naturally

to a vector of capital goods, including knowledge stocks, durable exhaustible resource stocks, renewable resource stocks and environmental capital stocks. See, for example, Dixit, Hammond and Hoel (1980).

6.   Asheim (1994) notes that such a local-in-time measure is not an exact indicator of sustainability. We report on his critique in detail under 'National Accounting' (see p.72).

7.   In a reworking of the study by Repetto *et al.* (1989) for Indonesia, Vincent, Panayotou and Hartwick (1995) suggest that the cumulative terms of trade effect dominates the simple measure of economic depreciation of oil stocks. Price shift windfalls are large in this case. Weitzman (1995) makes a similar point for the case of exogenous technical improvement for a large closed economy.

8.   It would be exactly the triangle in question if the upward sloping marginal cost curve were a straight line, through the origin. We do assume $C(0) = 0$ but have not required the marginal cost curve to be a straight line.

9.   Investment in stock K can be generalized to a vector of stocks, including knowledge capital (Robson, 1980).

10. Dixit, Hammond, Hoel (1980) represented our problem quite generally. In particular, they allowed for C to be a vector of consumption goods and considered 'constant consumption' as the utility of the consumption vector constant. Hammond (1994) surveys this and other extensions in an interesting survey. He makes the point that an outstanding problem is the introduction of uncertainty into the model. Baranzini and Bourguignon (1994) view sustainability as forestalling declines in consumption at uncertain dates. However, their model has an extremely simple production sector. We could deal with extraction costs for our oil. Cairns (1986) has explored quite complicated extraction costs in the constant consumption model.

11. The Cobb–Douglas case is central because aggregate consumption can be held positive and constant indefinitely when the share of capital exceeds the share of oil in production (Solow, 1974). In this case the services of more $K(t)$ substitute precisely for the declining service flow $R(t)$ from the oil stock. Recall that the elasticity of substitution between inputs in the Cobb–Douglas case is unity. See generalizations of the result on the infinite sustainability of consumption in Cass and Mitra (1991).

12. Solow (1986) defined capital value by $K(t) + S(t)F_R(t) \equiv W(t)$. This, for efficient paths, has the property $\dot{W}(t) + C(t) = W(t)F_K(t)$, a generalized asset equilibrium relation (Hartwick, 1995a). However, $W(t)$ is not constant under investing resource rents.

13. This result extends to cases involving stocks in the production function as in recyclable durable exhaustible resources (Dockner and Hartwick, 1994), resource flows in the utility function as for fish harvested from stocks, and resource stocks in the utility function (Becker, 1982). See Hartwick (1994b).

14. Since Z is human capital, Z positive suggests technical progress with a constant population. With initial Z and K at very small values at the beginning of human civilization, we have an oil theory of development. The depletion of oil stock S_0 'allowed' $K(t)$ and $Z(t)$ to increase. In a precise sense, human civilization, in this view, is based on the depletion of natural capital. The asymmetry between labour and person made capital, and natural resources appears in Alfred Marshall (Book VI, Chapter II, p. 562, (1981)): 'The labour and capital of the country, acting on its natural resources, produce annually a net aggregate of commodities, material and immaterial, including services of all kinds.'

15. For the Cobb–Douglas case, $K^\alpha R^\beta N^{1-\alpha-\beta}$, $C_{t+1} - C_t$ reduces to

$$Q_{t+1} - Q_t - \frac{1}{\beta}\left(\frac{Q_t R_{t+1}}{R_t} - \frac{Q_{t-1} R_t}{R_{t-1}} \right).$$

16. One follows the steps we traversed at the beginning where $Y(t)$ became $\dot{Y}(t)$, $\dot{H}(t)$ became $\ddot{H}(t)$, etc.

17. Accounting principles, based on the Hicksian concept of 'income', require that replacement investment (that is the capital consumption allowance) include terms representing the decline in value of stocks of natural capital. This accumulation of one form of capital to balance off

the decline in value of another form of capital is, in a narrow sense, the same as investing resource rents (for constant consumption). However, accounting is a labelling of components of output and inputs for certain purposes; for accounting for things, if you will. The achievement of a constant consumption path is the realization of an investment strategy, the investing of resource rents. Hence, generalized Hicksian income and constant consumption paths are related but are not implied by one another. An economy can expand or contract given accounting based on Hicksian principles since NNP gets divided into actual current consumption and net capital augmentation. Hicksian income, by definition, equals actual current consumption plus actual net capital accumulation. The account for replacement investment gets expanded under green accounting to account for all current diminutions in capital stocks, including natural stocks such as oil deposits, fish stocks, watersheds, etc.

18. The maximization of

$$\int_0^\infty U(C)(t)) \exp(-\rho t) dt.$$

where ρ is the discount rate and $U(C(t))$ is the concave utility function.

19. Pemberton, Pezzey and Ulph (1995) indicate that current output minus economic depreciation of stocks, $F(.) - FR_R$, can be identified with 'Hicksian Income', a current output measure corresponding to the level of maximum current potential consumption that coincides with 'capital preserved intact'. It follows that, by identifying Hicksian income with net national product, one has net national product = $C(t) + \dot{K}(t) - R(t)F_R(t)$.

20. Aronsson and Lofgren (1995) emphasize this wedge but do not attempt to measure it. See also Nordhaus (1995).

21. For g at 1 per cent, the wedge is 25 per cent of NNP(t).

22. Though the social rate of discount does not appear in Solow's model, the interest rate (consumption discount rate) remains positive and declines toward zero over time. This set-up is compatible with the instantaneous social utility of consumption having infinite concavity in a limiting sense (Dasgupta and Heal, 1979, p. 307).

REFERENCES

Anand, S. and A. Sen (1994), 'Sustainable Development: Concepts and Priorities', Center for Population and Development, Harvard University, mimeo, forthcoming in *World Development*.

Aronsson, T. and K.–G. Lofgren (1993), 'Welfare Measurement of Technological and Environmental Externalities in the Ramsey Growth Model', *Natural Resource Modeling*, **7**, 1, 1–14.

Aronsson, T. and K.–G. Lofgren (1995), 'Natural Product Related Welfare Measures in the Presence of Technical Change, Externalities and Uncertainty', *Environmental and Resource Economics*, **5**, 321–32.

Aronsson, T., P.–O. Johansson and K.–G. Lofgren (1995), 'Investment Decisions, Future Consumption and Sustainability under Optimal Growth', Economic Studies No. 371, University of Umea, Sweden.

Asheim, G.B. (1986), 'Hartwick's Rule in Open Economies', *Canadian Journal of Economics*, **19**, 395–402.

Asheim, G.B. (1988), 'Rawlsian Intergenerational Justice as a Markov-Perfect Equilibrium in a Resource Technology', *Review of Economic Studies*, **55**, 469–84.

Asheim, G.B. (1991), 'Unjust Intergenerational Allocations', *Journal of Economic Theory*, **54**, 350–71.

Asheim, G.B. (1994), 'Net National Product as an Indicator of Sustainability', *Scandinavian Journal of Economics*, **96**(2), 257–65.

Asheim, G.B. (1995), 'The Weitzman Foundation of NNP with Non-Constant Interest Rates', typescript..

Baranzini, A. and F. Bourguignon (1994), 'Is Sustainable Growth Optimal?', mimeo.

Becker, R. (1982), 'International Equity: The Capital Environment Trade-Off', *Journal of Environmental Economics and Management*, **9**, 165–85.

Cairns, R. (1986), 'Intergenerational Equity and Heterogeneous Resources', *Scandinavian Journal of Economics*, **88**, 401–16.

Cass, D. and T. Mitra (1991), 'Infinitely Sustained Consumption Despite Exhaustible Resources', *Economic Theory*, **1**, 119–46.

Chichilnisky G., G.M. Heal and A. Beltratti, (1995), 'The Green Golden Rule', *Economic Letters*, **49**(2), August, 175–9.

Dasgupta, P. and G.M. Heal (1979), *Economic Theory and Exhaustible Resources*, Cambridge: Cambridge University Press.

Dasgupta, S. and T. Mitra (1983), 'Intergenerational Equity and Efficient Allocation of Exhaustible Resources', *International Economic Review*, **24**, 1, 133–53.

Dixit, A., P. Hammond and M. Hoel (1980), 'On Hartwick's Rule for Regular Maximum Paths of Capital Accumulation and Resource Depletion', *Review of Economic Studies*, **47**, 551–6.

Dockner, E. and J. Hartwick (1994), 'Recycling, NNP, and Constant Consumption Paths', mimeo.

Hamilton, K. and G. Atkinson (1995), 'Air Pollution and Green Accounts', *Energy Policy* (forthcoming).

Hammond, P. (1994), 'Is There Anything New in the Concept of Sustainable Development?', in L. Camriglio, L. Pineschi, D. Siniscalo and T. Treves (eds), *The Environment After Rio: International Law and Economics*, London: Graham and Trotman.

Hartwick, J.M. (1977), 'Intergenerational Equity and the Investing of Rents from Exhaustible Resources', *American Economic Review*, **66**, 972–4.

Hartwick, J.M. (1978), 'Investing Returns from Depleting Renewable Resource Stocks and Intergeneration Equity', *Economics Letters*, **1**, 85–8.

Hartwick, J.M. (1990), 'Natural Resources, National Accounting and Economic Depreciation', *Journal of Public Economics*, **43**, 291–304.

Hartwick, J.M. (1992), 'Deforestation and National Accounting', *Environmental and Resource Economics*, **2**, 513–21.

Hartwick, J.M. (1993a), 'Notes on Economic Depreciation of Natural Resource Stocks and National Accounting', in A. Franz and C. Stahmer (eds), *Approaches to Environmental Accounting*, Heidelberg: Physica-Verlag.

Hartwick, J.M. (1993b), 'Forestry Economics, Deforestation, and National Accounting', in E. Lutz (ed.), *Toward Improved Accounting for the Environment*, Washington, DC: World Bank.

Hartwick, J.M. (1994), 'National Wealth and Net National Product', *Scandinavian Journal of Economics*, **96**(2), 253–6.

Hartwick, J.M. (1995a), 'Constant Consumption Paths in Open Economies with Exhaustible Resources', *Review of International Economics*, **3**(3), October, 275–83.

Hartwick, J.M. (1995b), 'Decline in Biodiversity and Risk Adjusted NNP', in T.M. Swanson (ed.), *The Economics and Ecology of Biodiversity Decline: The Forces Driving Global Change*, Cambridge: Cambridge University Press.

Hartwick, J.M. and A. Hageman (1993), 'Economic Depreciation of Mineral Stocks and the Contribution of El Serafy', in E. Lutz (ed.), *Toward Improved Accounting for the Environment*, Washington, DC: World Bank.

Hartwick, J.M. and N. van Long (1995), 'Constant Consumption and the Economic Depreciation of Natural Capital: The Nonautonomous Case', typescript.

Heal, G.M. (1993), 'Valuing the Very Long Run: Discounting and the Environment', Columbia University Business School, working paper, PW-94–04.

Hung, N.M. (1993), 'Natural Resources, National Accounting, and Economic Depreciation: Stock Effects', *Journal of Public Economics*, **51**, 379–89.

Kemp, M.C. and N.V. Long (1982), 'On the Evaluation of Social Income in a Dynamic Economy', in G.R. Feiwel (ed.), *Samuelson and Neoclassical Economics*, Boston: Kluwer-Nijhoff, 185–9.

Long, N.V., T. Mitra and G. Sorger (1995), 'Equilibrium Growth and Sustained Consumption with Exhaustible Resources', Cornell University, discussion paper, CAE –95–02.

Lozada, G.A. (1995), 'Resource Depletion, National Income Accounting, and the Value of Optimal Dynamic Programs', *Resource and Energy Economics*, **17**(2), August, 137–55.

Mäler, K.G. (1991), 'National Accounts and Environmental Resources', *Environmental and Resource Economics*, **1**, 1–15.

Marshall, A. (1981), *Principles of Economics*, London: Macmillan.

Nordhaus, W.D. (1995), 'How Should We Measure Sustainable Income?', Cowles Discussion Paper No. 1101.

Pearce, D. and G. Atkinson (1993), 'Capital Theory and the Measurement of Sustainable Development: An Indicator of Weak Sustainability', *Ecological Economics*, **8**, 103–8.

Pemberton, M., J. Pezzey and D. Ulph (1995), 'Measuring National Income and Measuring Sustainability', typescript.

Pezzey, J. (1989), 'Economic Analysis of Sustainable Growth and Sustainable Development', Environment Department, working paper no. 15, World Bank.

Pezzey, J. and C. Withagen (1995), 'Single-Peakedness and Initial Sustainability in Capital-Resource Economies', typescript.

Repetto, R., W. McGrath, M. Wells, C. Beer and F. Rossini (1989), *Wasting Assets: Natural Resources in the National Income Accounts*, Washington, DC: World Resources Institute.

Robson, A. (1980), 'Costly Innovation and Natural Resources', *International Economic Review*, **21**(1), February, 17–30.

Solow, R.M. (1974), 'Intergenerational Equity and Exhaustible Resources', *Review of Economic Studies*, Symposium, 29–45.

Solow, R.M. (1986), 'On the Intergenerational Allocation of Resources', *Scandinavian Journal of Economics*, **88**, 1441–9.

Usher, D, (1994), 'Income and the Hamiltonian', *Review of Income and Wealth*, **40**, 123–41.

Vincent, J., T. Panayotou and J. Hartwick (1995), 'Resource Depletion and Sustainability in Small Open Economies', Harvard Institute for Economic Development, Environment discussion paper no. 8.

Weitzman, M. (1976), 'On the Welfare Significance of National Product in a Dynamic Economy', *Quarterly Journal of Economics*, **90**, 156–62.

Weitzman, M. (1995), 'The Welfare Significance of National Product in a Dynamic Economy Revisited', typescript.

4. The economics of biodiversity[1]

Dominic Moran and David Pearce

THE ISSUE

'Biodiversity' is short for biological diversity, the range of living things on Earth which in turn comprises the legacy of all living things. Since biodiversity relates to all life forms, the loss of any significant proportion of those life forms has potentially far-reaching consequences. According to some, loss rates are substantial, and hence the consequential damage to human well-being and ecological functions is enormous. Thus, Ehrlich and Ehrlich (1982, p. xiv), likening Earth to a spacecraft, declare that: 'extinction of other organisms must be stopped before the living structure of our spacecraft is so weakened that at a moment of stress it fails and civilization is destroyed'. For others, the focus is on marginal changes in the 'stock' of biodiversity, and the proper policy response is measured by a comparison of the costs and benefits of loss rates at the margin.

Diversity is measured by the numbers of different genes, different species and ecosystems, rather than by the population numbers for a given species, say. It is customary to distinguish genetic diversity, species diversity and ecosystem diversity. Genetic diversity refers to the variations in the genetic make-up of individuals within a population of a given species and between populations of species. Genetic diversity is important as the means whereby evolutionary processes occur and, increasingly, because it provides the basis for biotechnological manipulation of genetic material. Species diversity refers to the variety of living organisms. Only about one million species have been identified and described, but there are anything from 10 to 50 million species in existence (McNeely *et al.*, 1990; Pimm *et al.*, 1995). Eco-system diversity refers to the variety of habitats and ecological processes. In practice, biodiversity tends to refer both to the variety and number of living things. The rationale for this commonly observed generalization – encompassing biological resources and their variability – is that reductions in the stock of resources tend to be the precursors of extinction processes which reduce variability as well.

The problem is widely regarded as being one of unprecedented rates of biodiversity loss and the expected consequences. This raises several issues: at exactly what rate is biodiversity disappearing? And, whatever the rate, why does it matter?

Estimates of rates of biodiversity loss are very uncertain because knowledge about species is limited and because the remains of extinct species exist in only a limited number of cases. Thus inferences have to be made from past extinction rates based on fossil records, or on some assumption about the fate of existing threatened species, or about the relationship between species and land area. The last approach links species to land area and then uses records of historical land conversions to determine extinction rates. Pimm *et al.* (1995) suggest recent extinction rates of around 20 to 200 species per one million species years. For example, if a species lasts one million years, its extinction rate would be one per million species years. This rate is substantially above that in 'pre-human' times or some 100 to 1000 times background rates. Current extinction rates thus appear to be far higher than 'natural' or 'background' rates. Projections of species loss are fraught with difficulty, but Pimm *et al.* (1995) suggest that if all species listed today as being threatened become extinct in the next 100 years, then future extinction rates will exceed current rates by a factor of ten. While some authors doubt these orders of magnitude (some of them producing absurdly low figures – see Simon and Wildavsky (1995)) it is hard to doubt rapid rates of current human induced extinction, whilst the case for accelerating rates in the future seems persuasive. The issues remaining, then, are why it happens, why it matters and what can be done to slow the rate of loss.

FUNDAMENTAL CAUSES OF BIODIVERSITY LOSS

The economic theory of species extinction has its origins in the theory of the fishery (Gordon, 1954) and further developed by Clark (1973a, 1990). These models and subsequent elaborations emphasize the threat to economically significant biological resources arising from inappropriate property rights, and the relative (intertemporal) rates of return to conservation and exploitation. Failure to invest ownership in biodiversity is widely regarded as one of the basic causes of extinction: much biodiversity is either itself unowned, or resides in ecological resources, such as forests or open seas, which are unowned or owned but with poorly defined property rights. The result is a lack of incentive on the part of those using the biodiversity, or using the 'base resource' (e.g. land, sea) to conserve biodiversity. The property rights issue can be formulated in another way: it effectively amounts to saying that the perceived rate of return to conservation is less than the rate of return to the activity which displaces or destroys the biodiversity, whether it is land conversion, habitat modification, global and local pollution and the introduction of exotic species (Kerr and Currie, 1995; Vitousek, 1986). The issue of valuation of the biodiversity resource is then seen to be central to the biodiversity problem and a principal concern of this chapter. For if biodiversity has economic value this must first be shown to be the case – the 'demonstration' phase of any conservation action. Thereafter, that value must be appropriated by those who have power to destroy the resource, the 'capture' phase. Demonstration is insufficient without capture, and the captured rate of return must then exceed the opportunity cost of conservation. In this way, renewable resource harvesting models provide a cogent explanation for the observed depletion of many economically important resources and a useful introduction to the economic parameters of species loss.

The central features of the Gordon–Clark approach are twofold: the first is the property rights regime, the second concerns the intertemporal issue of the relationship between a resource owner's discount rate and the rate of growth of the resource. Even for species of whose existence we are aware, ownership and use rights over the vast majority of biological resources are ill-defined. This important factor reduces the conservation incentives relating to the use and

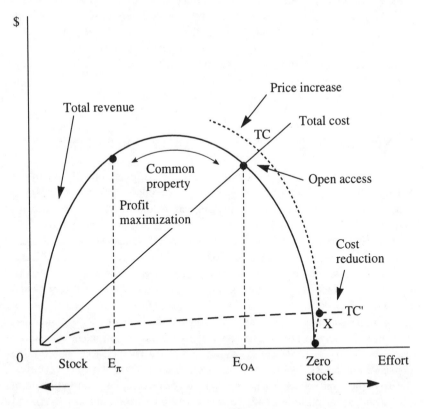

Figure 4.1   Gordon–Clark harvesting model and alternative equilibria

investment in species by any single interested party. In the context of harvesting models, specific regimes may be characterized as 'open access', common property, single private owner, or single state owner. Open access differs from common property in that the former regime has no owners and hence no rules for restricting or managing access to the fishery. Common property regimes involve sets of rules and regulations limiting access and catch rates, these rules being enforced by communal law or communal custom. Under single ownership, access is restricted to any outsider not part of the ownership regime, and the community in question is now a private organization or the nation state. Fairly self-evidently, the greater the restrictions on access, the less the harvesting effort applied to the resource and hence the more likely it is that biological stocks will be large. With open access, however, effort is unconstrained until the newest new entrant finds that stocks have depleted to the point where effort is only just rewarded by the extra revenues obtained from the sale of the harvest: the 'zero rent' point. Zero rents provide the condition for the equilibrium amount of open access effort – see Figure 4.1. In itself, then, open access does not generate extinction of the resource because further entry beyond the open-access equilibrium does not occur. As long as the costs of harvesting are positive, some of the resource is left intact, though with low sustainable yields. Nonetheless, population dynamics are ill understood and hence the risk of extiction is higher, the lower are the stocks. It is quite possible, therefore, for open access to create the conditions in which harvest levels give rise to stock levels that are below minimum viable sizes. For example, having a 'Noah's ark' solution in which just two members of a species survive is not sufficient for expansion of the population. Family bonds may be broken and reproduction cycles interfered with. Extinction may arise where price (relative to cost) incentives are sufficient in the neighbourhood of critical thresholds and in contexts where minimum viable size is influenced by family or group dynamics, as is the case for some land-based animals such as elephants. Removing critical family members may render the remaining population non-viable. Note also that, while common property regimes are far more likely to protect the resource against extinction, common property tends itself to be vulnerable to external influences, including human population growth which places pressure on the regime to continue managing the resource in the interests of the whole community.

Particular combinations of cost of effort and resource price will also make the open access situation more risky still. In terms of Figure 4.1, the initial open access equilibrium is at E_{OA}. Now suppose that technological change occurs such that the costs of harvesting, or 'effort' as it is usually described when the resource is a fishery, are reduced substantially from TC to TC'. Suppose too that the resource attracts a higher price, so that, for the same level of harvest, total revenue increases. The new open access equilibrium is at X, which is now much closer to the zero stock level. This 'high price, low cost' combination appears to fit certain land-based species well, e.g. elephants. Ivory prices can be very high and the use of vehicles and high velocity rifles makes costs low.

The first cause of extinction in this model, then, is the property rights regime, with open access having the highest risk of extinction for the species, and common property having a far lower but non-zero level of risk. Species attracting exotic demand, such as for elephant ivory, and being subject to advances in technological change which reduce effort costs are particularly at risk. As we shall see, specific policy actions to correct these situations automatically follow.

The second cause of extinction in the harvesting model arises in the single owner, profit-maximizing context. Whereas extinction under open access can be regarded partly as the outcome of ignorance about population dynamics and partly the outcome of a failure to comprehend the risks inherent in unrestricted access, extinction under single ownership can be the outcome of deliberate planning. In terms of Figure 4.1 the private owner equilibrium is seen to be E_π where profits are maximized. The high price, low cost combination no longer threatens the species, although it will lead to changes in the profit maximizing level of effort. It is when the picture is changed from the (essentially unrealistic) static one of Figure 4.1 to a more dynamic context that the risks arise. The essential condition for dynamic profit maximization is that the growth rate of the species stock should equal the single owner's discount rate.[2] The growth rate of the resource is effectively the rate of return on the resource. It then follows that if this rate of return is less than the rate of return the single owner can get by investing elsewhere (with discount rate equal to the opportunity cost of capital) the resource will be run down to zero with immediate effect. Under such conditions of 'optimal extinction' it will pay to 'mine' the resource to extinction. Open access then magnifies this effect since the resource harvester has no incentive to conserve the resource for the future. Looked at this way, the two causes of extinction become one: rates of return to conservation are less than rates of return to immediate exploitation. Nonetheless, there is value in keeping the first cause separate. Open access may be a stable equilibrium when knowledge is perfect, but ignorance of threshold population sizes is pervasive, particularly in the realistic case where species interact in predator-prey or synergistic relationships.

Again, the analysis is suggestive since slow growth species will almost automatically be at risk on this model: their 'own rate of return' will be low. And this is how it tends to be in practice. Elephants, rhinoceroses and whales are endangered whilst most (but not all) species of deer and seals are not. The former grow slowly, the latter more fast.

The Gordon–Clark harvesting model, developed very largely in the context of the fishery, can be applied to land-based species with some adaptation. Hence the analysis has tended to be in terms of property-rights regimes, the price/cost ratio, and the discount rate/own growth comparison. For an application of the Gordon–Clark model to the African elephant, see Barbier *et al.* (1990).

But Swanson (1990, 1994) stresses an additional pressure to those in the Clark model once the resource in question is land-based, an adjustment that augments the policy implications. This argument is rooted in the fact that land-based biological resources are typically subject to greater human management than marine resources, and are just one of many forms of land use. Considering all uses as part of a potential asset portfolio, the issue becomes one of relative returns to the scarce factor. Whereas fisheries occupy space that can be argued to have low opportunity costs – there are few competing uses of the seas – this is categorically untrue of land-based biodiversity. This is because land-based biodiversity depends on a base resource, the land itself, and this land does have alternative uses. The most obvious conflict is between land for conservation and land for 'development' uses such as agriculture. The critical point here is that whereas marine resources may be depleted because their growth fails to exceed the harvester's discount rate, in the land-based case they may be depleted because the returns from conservation fail to compete with the returns from land conversion to agriculture, roads, urban expansion, etc. The focus in the Swanson model shifts from the resource itself (fish, elephants, seals) to the 'base resource', the space occupied by the resource. The second feature relevant to this discussion is that whereas marine resources have a (generally) fixed carrying capacity, this is not true of land-based resources. Carrying capacity is no longer a 'given': it is something that is determined by choices about the level of base resources allocated to biodiversity.

There are two ways of viewing the elements of the sea and land-based depletion models. The first consists of a contrast between the profit maximizing equations in practice. In both the Clark and Swanson models, what is being maximized is the difference between revenues from the sale of the resource and the direct costs plus opportunity costs of harvesting them. In the case of the fishery the opportunity cost is not, however, the cost of changing the use of the base resource, the sea. It is simply an alternative use of the resources tied up in the fishing fleet. In the land-based version, what is being maximized is the difference between the proceeds of sale and the sum of the costs of 'harvest' and the foregone return to the alternative use of the land. Put another way, in both models the net benefits of land-based conservation have to be greater than the total opportunity costs of conservation, i.e. the foregone net returns from developing the land. But for the sea resource, the opportunity cost of the base resource (the sea) tends to be zero: fisheries tend not to compete with alternative land uses in the ocean. Where they do, as in near-shore coastal areas, the relevance of positive opportunity costs (drainage, marinas, shipping lanes) makes the analysis very close to the land-based model. Pearce and Moran (1994) review the rates of return to biodiversity conservation and note the relevance of the varying levels of opportunity cost.

The second way of viewing the difference between the two models is to look at the policy implications. Taking the elephant example again, the Gordon–Clark model blames high prices for ivory for the decline of elephant populations. High prices encourage poaching. The Swanson model suggests the very opposite, i.e. that ivory prices need to be kept high to encourage investment in sustainable management of elephant populations. By way of illustration, the range states that invested in elephant conservation in a significant way were the southern African states – South Africa, Botswana, Zimbabwe and Namibia. These were the states where ivory sales were (largely) controlled and authorized, and where elephant populations grew dramatically. States that 'underinvested' in elephants, including even a country like Kenya where the tourist value of the elephant was high, were the ones that lost elephants to poachers. Embedded in this explanation is a wider view of investment which includes the value of investing in property rights, but also the position of wildlife outside protected areas, the potential economic role of trophy hunting and the area-specific economic incentives which drive poaching. Thus, while high prices retain the incentive to poach, they also provide the incentive to protect and conserve, as the southern African range states have demonstrated. The insights from the land-based model are clear. It is not enough to take the property-rights regime as given, as in the harvesting models. For the property-rights regime is a matter of choice and management. Thus, it is incorrect to cite open access, say, as a 'cause' of environmental degradation, for the question should be why open access is allowed to prevail. Put another way, why has an open-access state not invested in changing the rights regime so as to allocate the base resource – land of suitable characteristics – to biodiversity?

Once it is understood that biodiversity is competing with alternative uses of the land, many things fall into place. First, human population growth becomes immediately relevant because population growth simply intensifies the conflict as humans demand 'niches' to occupy as residences or as locations for crops, roads, etc. Second, if markets in the 'products' of biodiversity are non-existent, the rate of return to conservation will almost certainly fail to compete with the rate of return to the alternative uses of land. Biodiversity is doomed. It is in the creation of markets for biodiversity and the equitable sharing of benefits that hope for conservation resides, although the extent to which even this solution will succeed may rest with the development of an environmental economics which captures the life-support functions of biodiversity. While this conclusion offends the instincts of many environmentalists, it is the perpetuation of myths about moral obligations to, and rights of, other species that reinforces the fate of biodiversity. The myth does not lie in the moral obligation – many would share that view – but in the belief that moral obligation alone will generate the right incentives to conserve the biodiversity resource. The moral view, for example, tends to result in bans on trade in species and restrictions on access to biologically rich areas. Yet both actions leave unsatisfied the wants and needs of those who still need access or who still find profit in extinguishing biodiversity. Unwittingly perhaps, the 'deep ecologist' is contributing to the demise of biodiversity. This is a strong conclusion, but one that follows from a closer understanding of the economic dynamics at work. Bans and moral outrage serve to 'disinvest' value in biodiversity: they take economic value away, when what is required is the investment of economic value in conservation through more and better markets for the sustainable output of conservation practices.

An alternative model would focus on government regulation as the major salvation of biodiversity, e.g. via land-use zoning. In practical terms, such regulations require institutional capacity which all too often is missing in areas of high biodiversity, i.e. tropical developing countries. As such, there may be a better chance to conserve biodiversity by demonstrating and capturing economic values through market creation than through regulation. Monitoring and enforcement of property rights are more likely under a decentralized than a regulatory regime. Moreover, governments have typically behaved schizophrenically with respect to conservation, enacting protected areas legislation whilst simultaneously pursuing policies, such as subsidized land conversion, which destroy biodiversity. But clearly, the regulatory model has a role to play in many contexts.

The fundamental causes of biodiversity loss can now be summarized. They lie in the following broad areas (Pearce, 1996):

(a) human population growth which leads to more and more of the base resource, land, being converted to non-conservation uses;
(b) market failures, i.e. the failure to create markets or modify existing markets for biodiversity such that biodiversity fails to secure economic value to compete with alternative uses of the base resource in which biodiversity resides; and
(c) intervention failures, i.e. government-provided incentives such as subsidies which simply exaggerate the rate of return to the developmental uses of land, thus further biasing the equation against biodiversity.

THE ECONOMIC VALUE OF BIODIVERSITY

'Value' is a pluralistic concept: it is possible to speak of biological resources possessing intrinsic value independent of humankind, ecological value, economic value, cultural and spiritual value, evolutionary value, and so on. In what follows we focus on economic value. In so doing we do not deny the relevance of other 'value dimensions', but we argue that economic value has a special role to play in policy towards biodiversity conservation. Furthermore, refinement of one particular economic value category – option value – reveals a common line of enquiry relating economic (preference-based) and biological (non-preference based) values. This interface emerges in the area of diversity theory which also provides the basis of subsequent discussion of conservation priorities.

Total Economic Value

Economic valuation approaches to biodiversity have been motivated by the context of biodiversity loss. Essentially, this is the process of land-use change. Historically, these changes have involved loss of 'natural' habitat, especially forests, in favour of agricultural exploitation, and, to a lesser extent, urban expansion, roads, etc. Biodiversity conservation therefore has to compete with the economic values of converted land, values which are expressed in market prices. This is the essential result of the extended theory of extinction discussed previously. Not surprisingly then, the focus has been on the search for economic values of conservation which bear a direct comparison with the economic values of development. This explains why the literature on biodiversity valuation is replete with information on the values of non-timber forest products, 'eco-tourism', pharmaceuticals and the indirect values of natural systems in terms of 'carbon storage' (the locking-up of carbon dioxide). In themselves, valuation studies are an attempt to rationalize the conservation decision from the perspective of the unregulated land user, say at the forest frontier. Simply put, if conservation is to stand a chance, it must compete in the market-place. As we show below, this past focus, whilst still very relevant, is gradually giving way to a wider systems-focused analysis of value. In this wider perspective, biodiversity is seen to have a systematic 'life support' function not easily captured by existing approaches to economic valuation and perhaps not easily amenable to market capture.

Typically, development benefits and costs can be fairly readily calculated because there are attendant cash flows. Timber production, for example, tends to be for commercial markets and market prices are observable. Conservation benefits, on the other hand, are a mix of associated cash flows and 'non-market' benefits. This fact imparts two biases. The first is that the components with associated cash flows are made to appear more 'real' than those without such cash flows. There is 'misplaced concreteness: decisions are likely to be biased in favour of the development option because conservation benefits are not readily calculable. The second bias follows from the first. Unless incentives are devised whereby the non-market benefits are 'internalized' into the land-use choice mechanism, conservation benefits will automatically be downgraded. Those who stand to gain from, say, timber extraction or agricultural clearance cannot consume the non-marketed benefits. This 'asymmetry of values' imparts a considerable bias in favour of the development option.

Conservation benefits are measured by the total economic value (TEV). In turn, TEV comprises use and non-use values, the latter sometimes being called passive use values. Direct use values are fairly straightforward in concept and offer the best chance of being measurable. Thus minor forest products output (nuts, rattan, latex, etc.) should be measurable from market and survey data. The value of medicinal plants for the world at large is more difficult to measure but several attempts have been made (see below).

Indirect use values correspond to one set of the ecologist's concept of 'ecological functions'. A tropical forest might help protect watersheds, for example, so that removing forest cover may result in water pollution and siltation, depending on the alternative use to which the forest land is put. Wetlands cleanse pollutants from the water – indeed, effluent problems may be controlled through the actual creation of wetlands. Similarly, tropical forests 'store' carbon dioxide. When they are burned for clearance much of the stored carbon dioxide is released into the atmosphere, contributing to the greenhouse gas effect. Tropical forests also store many species which in turn may have ecological functions – one of the values of biological diversity.

Option values relate to the amount that individuals would be willing to pay to conserve biodiversity for future use. That is, no use is made of it now but use may be made of it in the future. Option value is thus like an insurance premium to ensure the supply of something, the availability of which would otherwise be uncertain. While there can be no presumption that option value is positive, it is likely to be so in the context where the resource is in demand for its environmental qualities and its supply is threatened. Examples of option values include the chances that some species, described or otherwise, may generate a cure for some types of cancer, or provide the genetic base for a new breed of crops which can withstand pest attacks or drought conditions. In short, biodiversity is also information and information has economic value.

Existence, or non-use, or passive use value relates to valuations of the environmental asset unrelated either to current or potential future use. Its intuitive basis is easy to understand because a great many people reveal their willingness to pay for the existence of environmental assets through wildlife and other environmental charities but without taking part in the direct use of the wildlife through recreation. To some extent, this willingness to pay may represent 'vicarious' consumption, i.e. consumption of wildlife videos and TV programmes, but studies suggest that this is a weak explanation for existence value. Empirical measures of existence value, obtained through questionnaire approaches (the contingent valuation method), suggest that existence value can be a substantial component of total economic value. This finding is even more pronounced where the asset is unique. Total economic value can be expressed as:

TEV = Direct Use Value + Indirect Use Value + Option Value + Existence Value

(Note that use values can be measured as an 'option price' which is defined as the expected value of the benefits from the resource plus option value. In this case, option value would not appear as a separate component of TEV, but as a component of use values.)

While the components of TEV are additive, care has to be taken in practice not to add competing values. There may be trade-offs between different types of use value and between direct and indirect use values. The value of timber from clear-felling cannot be added to the value of minor forest products since clear-felling tends to destroy the minor products, but timber from selective cutting will generally be additive to forest products. It is important to note that the TEV formula above has no predetermined geographical boundaries. Technically, TEV may arise from local, national, international and global sources. This is important because a great deal of biodiversity may attract quite low local economic value (relative to the opportunity cost of use) but may attract a very high 'global' value. Conspicuous examples include some species of African wildlife which are a nuisance and a risk to local people, but which are highly 'prized' by foreign tourists. The issue here becomes one of measuring the TEV regardless of political boundaries, and then designing mechanisms for the 'capture' or appropriation of that value, especially for adversely affected communities.

It is tempting to think that economists have captured all there is to know about economic value in the concept of TEV. Conceptually this may be so, but the systems perspective suggests that the practice of economic valuation may not be comprehensive. First, economists are not claiming to have captured all values, merely economic values. It is legitimate at least to talk of the 'rights' of Nature or the obligations of humankind to natural systems and their occupants, and many have a philosophical or religious concern with 'stewardship' or a respect for the 'living' planet Earth – Gaia. But ecological scientists are also trying to say that TEV as estimated in practice is still not the whole economic story. There are some underlying functions of ecological systems which are prior to the ecological functions that we have been discussing (watershed protection etc.). Bateman and Turner (1993) calls them 'primary values'. They are essentially the system characteristics upon which all ecological functions are contingent. There cannot be a watershed protection function but for the underlying value of the system as a whole. There is, in some sense, a 'glue' that holds everything together and that glue has economic value. If this is true, and it is difficult to pinpoint what is at issue here, then there is a total value to an ecosystem or ecological process which exceeds the sum of the values of the individual functions. If this is something which cannot be counted as some form of use value, TEV may not, after all, be total. It seems more likely that 'primary' value is best seen as a form of indirect use value, a value of the state of the system rather than its component functions. The problem then is whether this value is captured in practice, and that appears to be an open question.[3]

A further caveat is that the TEV framework allows little to be inferred about the value of diversity *per se*. From a biological perspective it is often suggested that existing economic approaches fail to capture the essence of diversity value which seems to be located between existence and option value categories. Some refinement of the latter category seems appropriate, and methods to quantify diversity value are examined below. The first approach is a potential use-related view, and places a lower bound on future value based on current or expected uses. Second, more precise biological diversity measures are explored as a potential basis for ranking relative diversity 'value' of species and sets of species. While the resulting measures do not immediately imply monetary valuation, the unit of account or numeraire of difference they employ may be the most objective currency of diversity or flexibility value and possibly a best approximation to the aforementioned 'prior' eco-system value which appears to elude the restricted TEV approach.

The Characterization of Option Value

Option value is the category of economic value that sums up a general preoccupation with the biodiversity portfolio function. Although it is the most frequently cited rationale for conservation and the focus of common interest in economics and biology, convincing quantitative assessments of option value are limited in number. This may reflect the view that conservation decisions can often be justified on more familiar economic criteria, e.g. the value of biodiversity as a source of ecological tourism. But such direct-use values may be insufficient to conserve biodiversity. If so, it is important to investigate the full range of values.

Fisher and Hanemann (1985) offer a now fairly standard interpretation of option value as 'the present benefit of holding open the possibility that a future discovery will make useful a species that we currently think useless'. This definition captures the essence of flexibility which is important in all options. Thinking in terms of quantifying the economic significance of diversity, the pertinent questions relate to the appropriate biological numeraire of flexibility or perhaps resilience, and how this might translate into some market-related direct or indirect use, and ultimately a (monetary) value commensurate with cost-benefit decisions. In effect, the attempt to cardinalize the biodiversity issue goes to the heart of what exactly is the nature of diversity-related value in all areas where the concept is considered to be important. The lesson from the following discussion is that the choice to maximize any of a number of possible numeraires or surrogates of option value will dictate correspondingly 'optimal' portfolios of species or their habitats. In other words, conservation decisions can never be value-free.

The quantification of diversity value represents an area of common interest between biologists and economists. Since such value can in theory be calibrated by information on a specific biological numeraire of diversity (e.g. genetic distance) of a pair or group of species, the definition of a consensus numeraire of inter-species difference represents a step in the development of a cardinal indicator of diversity. Of course such an indicator cannot tell us how much diversity is needed. But irrespective of valuation, such an approach may nevertheless provide some baseline for biodiversity assessment and for informing conservation priorities, an issue to which we return.

Given the basic interpretation of option value as flexibility value, the distinction drawn in the following discussion is somewhat arbitrary. In the first instance, the discussion highlights the probabilistic (use) value basis for maintaining the widest portfolio of species in the wild. In the models reviewed, the characterization of the variance of this portfolio around some desirable characteristic, or 'hit', can in fact be related to the biological unit measures used to differentiate the individual elements in any group of species. Any such measure of diversity also provides the basis for ranking competing sets of species (or their habitats), which is the very real conservation choice facing many countries today. The importance of selecting a suitable diversity measure is clear and, prior to economic valuation, it seems reasonable to appraise the extent to which any ideal diversity measure is consistent with biological criteria.

Use-Oriented Option Value

There have been numerous attempts to quantify the use-related benefits of biodiversity. These studies have attempted to derive some bound on option value, with reference to the expected returns to improved agricultural yield variability (Brown and Goldstein, 1984), non-timber forest products (NTFPs) (Peters, Gentry and Mendelsohn, 1989), and biochemical prospecting for pharmaceutical development (Pearce and Puroshothamon, 1995; Mendelsohn and Balick, 1995; Simpson, Sedjo and Reid, 1996). Apart from the largely theoretical contribution of Brown and Goldstein and the exceptionally pessimistic conclusions drawn by Simpson, Sedjo and Reid, these studies have successfully caught the collective conservationist imagination by suggesting considerable returns to sustainable uses. Full surveys can be found in Pearce and Moran (1994). In retrospect however, some of the optimism about the returns to these activities is likely to have been premature. For example, in the case of NTFPs, re-evaluation of the harvest potential at other sites has shown that returns are highly sensitive to alternative assumptions regarding the full costs and frequency of harvesting plus the logistics of market access and location. In short, the prudent conclusion emerging from these studies is that the economic case for conservation may need to go beyond these values alone. Even if some NTFPs turn out to have significant economic value, the chances are that commercialization of those products will occur, just as it did with plantation rubber in Asia based on wild rubber trees from the Amazon. As Southgate (1996, p. 79) remarks:

> ... for non-timber extraction to save large tracts of rainforests, the problem of ill defined property rights will have to be resolved, just as it must be resolved if eco-tourism, logging or any other activity is to be conducted in an environmentally friendly way. Furthermore, attempts to raise the market value of non-timber products, and therefore rural incomes, could be self-defeating if agricultural production of commodities originally found in the wild is the result. The contribution of extractivism to rainforest conservation could turn out to be very limited indeed.

No less seductive are the frequently-cited figures on pharmaceutical value. These depend on a combination of *ex post* and speculative assessments related to quantities of undiscovered samples, possible screens, competing company activity and probabilities of the eventual development of a viable commercial product given the advances in synthetic chemistry.

Simpson, Sedjo and Reid (1996) have focused on the probabilistic basis of these studies, showing that while they make important contributions to an understanding of the industry, they fail on their (*ex post*) treatment of potential redundancy in sampled compounds. This argument is developed in the specific case of the value of a marginal species (and by extension the incentives for the conservation of the marginal hectare), and a process to describe the behaviour of prospecting agents. In essence, in the search for a particular characteristic, a species either has it (is a 'hit') or it does not. Once one species has been found to have this characteristic there is no value in finding it in other species (all hits are perfect substitutes). The search through many species will encounter redundant resources which are not scarce and therefore should not (as is the case of cruder studies) be part of the equation when grossing up the value of prime habitats. This redundancy simply increases the search cost and eats into the net revenue of any ultimate 'hit' which, as a result, has a low marginal value. Basically when there are many species, the marginal value of any one of them has to be low. By contrast, if the hit probability is high, then some other species will have the characteristic. Either way, according to the authors, the marginal value is low. This assessment is in stark contrast to 'back of the envelope' estimates, multiplying the probability with which a randomly sampled organism contains *some* commercially valuable chemical compound (whether unique to that organism or not), by the expected value of a commercial product. These types of exercise tend to produce very high values for genetic materials.

It is possible to modify the assumptions made in the Simpson, Sedjo and Reid (1996) study to correspond to alternative hypotheses about the nature of the prospecting process. In relating revenue to 'hit' potential, the model of Simpson *et al.* reflects redundancy by assuming that a binomial hit terminates the search process. In other words, species are considered to be independent rather than sharing any commercially valuable traits. As Polasky and Solow (1995) show, it is possible to think of hits as imperfect substitutes. They suppose instead that a hit allows a draw from a distribution that determines the value of that particular hit. Having multiple hits is valuable because there is some chance that a more valuable hit will be found. In this model the marginal value of a species need not decline to insignificance nearly as quickly as in the limiting case suggested by Simpson *et al.* Thus Polasky and Solow generalize for different substitutability and independence assumptions, using distinct probabilities for the hit and value parts of the expected value equation.[4] These assumptions are both a more accurate reflection of bioprospecting experience[5] and an attempt to consider how the expected value of a set of species may be determined from the extent of substitutability between individual species. The significance of this substitutability indicates an immediate economic reason to focus on the biological relatedness or 'distance' between species as a potential indicator of diversity value of species sets. In theory, it is possible to calibrate such expected value models with precise distance information relating the set of species of interest. This observation introduces an explicit link between the use-related view of option value models and the biological basis for interpreting diversity and assigning relative value, to which we now turn.

System Oriented Option Value

Biological interpretations of option value emphasize the features of difference and relatedness, and require some investigation of the fundamental biological characterization of diversity. Such an investigation establishes a common cause with other areas for which biodiversity serves as a useful, if somewhat complex, metaphor. Attempts to formalize a diversity measure in other fields include those for linguistic diversity (Lieberson, 1964), industrial concentration (Horowitz, 1970), and income inequality (Theil, 1967). The common preoccupation in most of these fields is about measuring diversity value for prioritizing based on unquantified option and existence motives. As previously mentioned, the characterization of biological diversity is also particularly important in terms of potential links to broader questions of resilience, system integrity and productivity (Tilman, Wedin and Knops, 1996), and, ultimately, human adaptation. This understanding is closest to that of taxonomists and ecologists (see Faith, 1994; Humphries, William and Vane-Wright, 1995), and the main objective of species taxonomic classification with a view to decisions on area conservation.

In terms of economic value, the quantification of diversity relates directly to informing the use-related option value models discussed above. Alternatively, one may wish to think of the whole enterprise in terms of maximizing existence value or as being somehow prior to the assignment of value. Yet even a prior 'glue' value must have some physical basis upon which one might derive a formalized treatment of diversity. If a consistent measure can be derived, the next step might be to speculate about assessing the welfare effects of increasing or decreasing such a diversity measure. Abstracting from the subjective nature of the science of phylogenetics, one can say that such a measure may be the most objective measure of option value.

Measuring Biological Diversity

The complexity of diversity is given some order by the discipline of systematics – a branch of taxonomy which is the study of the diversity of organisms and any and all relationships among them (Heywood, 1995, p. 28; Simpson and Cracraft, 1995). Systematic classification of species evolution is typically by means of family tree-like structures, with branches scaled according to the character differences between adjoining member species. The specific character chosen to quantify this difference may be a specific gene or a specific morphological structure or behavioural trait. For the information encoded in this character, the resulting structure, or *phylogeny*, therefore offers an explicit account of the unit differences separating a pair of species; denoted by a count of the units which two commonly-rooted species do not have in common. By extension, each species differs by, and is valued according to, the amount of evolutionary information that is unique to it, compared with parts shared with other species in the set joined by the tree. But construction of tree structures encoding such information is statistically complex (Felsenstein, 1985). Character data can be generated from raw material assayed at various levels of the biological individual, and in this sense any tree-related difference measure or resulting index is subjective. Furthermore, it is necessary to make use of specific evolutionary models to infer and extrapolate the unobserved series of changes relating the same bit of genetic material assayed from, say, two different species from the same family. The same models explain how the appropriate family tree evolved through time giving the existing biological character differences of species currently observed at the tree tips. Constructed using the most basic biological character unit (e.g. DNA sequence), such structures provide an abacus-like structure for the assessment of diversity-related option value for a particular family or group of species. It is important to note that the precision of exact scaled branch length cardinal measures of this nature represent the most information-intensive measures. It is also possible to formulate cruder summary measures of tree diversity on the basis of unscaled trees relying solely on the number of internal branching points and also measures relying only on pairwise distance measures (Solow and Polasky, 1994).

Phylogenetic structures offer several appealing properties as the basis of a diversity measure, and variants of the basic pattern model are central to contributions on the issue of measurement proposed by Weitzman (1992), and to measurement and area selection as proposed by Vane-Wright, Humphries and Williams (1991) respectively.

Weitzman (1992) proposed a biodiversity measure as a general approach to diversity problems. Inspired by the taxonomic tree form, his 'bead model' represents an evolutionary branching process giving rise to the set of species S, acquiring and discarding unique beads (representing unique alterations to a generic character trait), as they move away from a common ancestry in a tree-like process. Thinking of each branch tip as an individual species consisting of a constant number of uniquely coded beads, evolution *ideally* proceeds by a process of simultaneous accumulation and discard of beads per unit of time. Two new species occur at a nodal (branching point) bifurcation, the difference between them subsequently being defined as the distance back to a common ancestor, corresponding to the time elapsed over which beads have been independently accumulated.

An important contribution of this model is the formulation of a set of internally consistent diversity axioms to describe the matrix of distances which summarize the tree (Weitzman, 1992). These axioms permit the use of a novel recursion which reconstructs the most parsimonious representation of the relationships between the set of species, in a manner that accurately reflects the taxonomic evolutionary process for a given evolutionary model. By extension, the loss of value associated with the extinction of a species is the branch length of character differences 'snapped' from the tree which, in totality, might be viewed as an index of diversity value for a set of species.

The crucial assumption about this tree is the model of a constant rate of character accumulation, allowing branch length to be exactly scaled according to the number of mismatched beads (characters) between any two adjoining species. Weitzman recognizes this ultrametric assumption to be a simplification of biological reality since accumulation may be independent of branch length. Faith (1994) discusses the potential problems of using Weitzman's algorithm to summarize tree diversity when this is the case, demonstrating how potential double-counting may actually result in an erroneous measure of the diversity of a set. As Faith shows, it is possible to devise alternative measures of evolutionary pattern, which in theory provide more accurate diversity measures. However, even if the measure is technically limited, the axioms underlying the approach are sufficiently rigorous to be the basis of several subsequent diversity measures (e.g. Polasky, Solow and Broadus, 1993). Weitzman himself goes on to demonstrate the ultimate use of the ultrametric tree approach in a cost-benefit decision model, where the benefit (higher probability of prolonged survival of more diversity), is traded-off against the cost of conservation programmes to save all but the least desirable species in terms of its character complement. As previously mentioned, another use of this summary distance information is for the calibration of the expected value models according to assumptions on compound substitutability and the nature of the search process (Polasky, Solow and Broadus, 1993; Polasky and Solow, 1995). Such an approach could conceivably extend to the development of a biodiversity adjustment to conventional wealth indicators.

Away from these anthropocentric developments, but similar in spirit to Weitzman's objectives, Faith (1994) and Vane-Wright, Humphries and Williams (1991) show some of the assumptions necessary to translate phylogenetic pattern into area selection for conservation. This is Weitzman's ultimate objective, but both authors avoid making unwarranted assumptions about the evolutionary process giving rise to respective tree models. Given the inference of a relevant phylogenetic relationship between a set of species, the question arises as to how this information should be used in area selection to maximize option value. Inevitably the conservation decision raises the issue of the relative weights assigned to parts of the tree.

Phylogeny, Conservation and Area Selection: What are we Conserving?

Not all biodiversity can be saved, and hence it is necessary to select areas for priority conservation effort. Area selection can be conducted according to a specific definition of value inherent in a particular phylogenetic pattern, itself a construction based on a subjective decision about the biological unit of value. As discussed, value may derive from any number of criteria, ranging from basic diversity, reflected in phylogenetic tree pattern, to forms of diversity-related resilience. The latter may be maximized by specific combinations of characters in a set as opposed to their total number. The resulting choice for meeting such objectives may have little to do with the subset of species that happens to be physically appealing, traditionally protected or commercially valuable. Put another way, the choice of species and areas for conservation may be different to the choice that would result if the first approach to option value – based on identifiable use values – is used.

All objectives amount to a specific weighting decision for the tree structure. For example, if a species appears to have evolved along a path with relatively few nodes, then it seems reasonable to suspect that its weight should reflect the likelihood of it containing more unique characters than one evolved along a path with several nodes indicating potentially shared traits. Yet nodal information also has a role to play in explaining divergence, particularly when exact branch length information is unavailable. Figure 4.2, taken from Williams and Humphries (1994), illustrates the first element of the so-called 'agony of choice' by supposing that an appropriate weighting system would dictate which three of eight species described by a hypothetical phylogeny might be prioritized for conservation – perhaps within a subset of protected areas which can just be accommodated within an existing budget. Depending on which of the five distinct criteria is selected as most important, equally high scoring choices are bracketed by the dotted line. Groups that are essential to represent under the particular criteria, are shown in black. Groups that are alternatives and those of low priority are shaded and white respectively. Thus the selection of species giving weight to primitive characters nearer the root of the tree represents a diverse or dispersed set of evolved characters.

Williams and Humphries show that for this type of phylogenetic construct, higher taxon diversity and dispersion (regularity of representation across the tree), provide the best representation of character richness (total number), and character combinations respectively. Character richness simply means maximizing the total number of characters independent of one another. This can be achieved by selecting the subset of organisms from the metric tree which maximizes the subtree length of the branches in the path along the tree connecting all the species in the subset. In special circumstances,[6] this choice is akin to simply choosing higher taxon richness, and is most likely to be the favoured strategy if the aim is, say, prospecting for pharmaceuticals. Character combinations on the other hand, may be more important than mere numbers. Maximizing richness of *different suites* of characters may be more important for eco-system integrity, and can be attained by choosing organisms that are regularly spaced across trees, thereby evenly representing taxa at all levels of the hierarchy, and thus the different character combinations that diagnose these taxa.

Figure 4.2 is a simplified example, but such criteria have been combined into numerous measures developed to summarize the diversity of tree information. The search for an appropriate summary of the character representation is ongoing, but most measures use information on branch length and some variant of the relationship defining uniqueness as roughly inversely proportional to the number of internal nodes on an evolutionary path to the tip of a tree. Thus, Williams and Humphries (1994), present the advantages of nodal counts when exact branch length information is unavailable. Crozier (1992) combines both in his exact tree measure. Faith and Walker (1994), have drawn on a family of p-median measures originally designed for locating objects on networks which are similar to metric trees. Basically, the method is aimed at maximizing character richness and combinations by maximizing the intersection of a set of discs layed over the tree, the radii of which will define a unique set of character

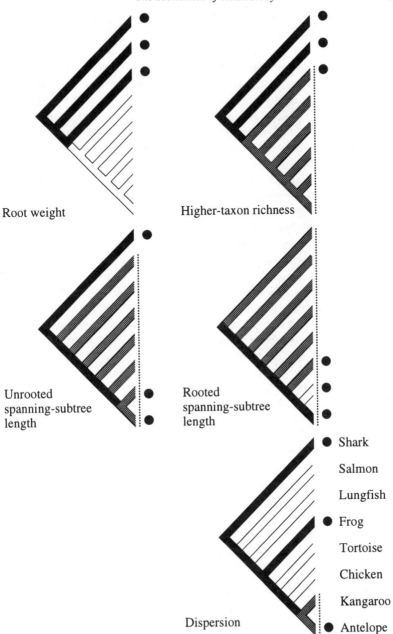

Root weight

Higher-taxon richness

Unrooted
spanning-subtree
length

Rooted
spanning-subtree
length

Shark

Salmon

Lungfish

Frog

Tortoise

Chicken

Kangaroo

Dispersion

Antelope

Source: Williams and Humphries (1994).

*Figure 4.2 Alternative conservation weighting criteria using phylogenetic
pattern*

combinations. The weighting pattern has been given a probabilistic angle (similar to that of Weitzman, 1995) by Witting and Loeschcke (1995), while, independently, Solow, Polasky and Broadus (1993) show a basic case where internal node counts are not sufficiently discerning to separate competing subsets. From the economic perspective, the obvious problem is that all these indicators are value-laden. Williams and Humphries (forthcoming) make much the same observation in indicating the contradiction inherent in alternative interpretations of basic phylogenetic information. Ideally, ignorance of how an organism may prove to be of value in the future means there can be no justification for attempting to weight differently the units of diversity value. Furthermore it turns out that there is no guarantee that weighting to maximize one desirable character set will be consistent with another. If the interest is in characters that are expressed in the phenotype of an organism, unexpressed difference, say in DNA, are of little interest. Yet, the lack of consensus over the level at which option value should be located, leads to valid arguments being made for weighting at any level of organization. As is evident from most conservation programmes the default choice appears to favour an attachment to the most charismatic species (Metrick and Weitzman, 1994).

A related point relevant to the discussion at species level has been made by Rojas (1992) in pointing out that disagreement among systematists and evolutionary biologists means that species are not circumscribed by any consistent definition. That is, the definition of a species in one taxonomic group (e.g. on the basis of morphological discontinuity or interbreeding capability) may mean little in the context of another group. This has been neatly summed up by the view that a species may be defined as whatever a competent taxonomist says it is, which may be decided with little regard for biological distance or evolutionary contribution. A worrying implication is that the number of existing species will immediately depend on how a species is defined (biological species, cladistic species or evolutionary species). Notwithstanding the analysis of Figure 4.2, a disproportionate focus on charismatic mega fauna and 'taxonomic flag ships' is difficult to reconcile with any specific concept of optimized biodiversity.

Abstracting from the weighting problem, further important aspects of the conservation dilemma have been highlighted by Vane-Wright, Humphries and Williams (1991). Figure 4.3 shows a tree structure corresponding to an hypothetical taxonomic tree for which 'importance' weights 'W' are assumed given for terminal taxa A through E. Three of the five taxa occur in three areas R1–R3, and, according to the weighting system, row T gives the total aggregate scores for the occurrence of the taxa. For each of the three regions row P1 gives the percentage diversity score, indicating that R3 is the top priority region. Row P2 gives the percentage diversity scores for the remaining two regions with respect to taxa complementarity – the concept which describes the use of cost-effectiveness to select the area adding the greatest *marginal* species difference to an existing set. In this case having chosen R3 it is possible to see that R1 is the second priority to achieve 100 per cent taxa coverage, rather than 89 per cent coverage had R2 been selected. This simplified example highlights several related to the important issue of priorities (see below). First, that *species richness* might be a less than perfect criterion for selecting priorities. By extension, the use of complementarity highlights the need to avoid double counting in character representation. Areas R1–R3 are equally species rich, but the sequential choice matters if a budget only covers the choice of two areas. Second, is the related question of cost. The simplifying assumption made here is that R1–R3 are three identical areas that may be acquired at equal cost. However, it is feasible that cost differentials might make the most biologically desirable sequence in this example too expensive to implement as an area selection programme. An issue that needs to be simultaneously addressed, therefore, is whether cost considerations can be integrated into this form of analysis.

The above form of analysis would seem to offer the beginnings of a calculus of option value-related diversity, and gives rise to practical developments on a number of fronts. Most immediately, the selection problem outlined is the basis of recent developments in algorithm-based methods for area selection using

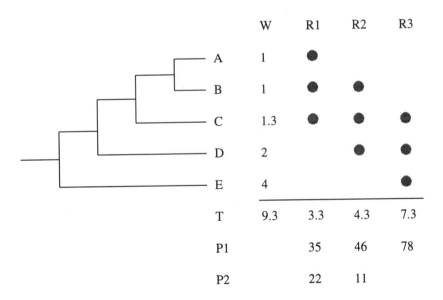

Figure 4.3   Theoretical priority area analysis (adapted from Vane-Wright, Humphries and Williams (1991))

surrogate information (see below). At this stage, however, it is difficult not to accord with Harper and Hawksworth (1994) who question how sufficient phylogenetic data could be generated in the near future to be able to compare the diversity of whole countries. They imply that traditional bottom-up classification obscures a bigger picture approach to conservation problems served by focusing on several geographical scales. The development and use of surrogate information is a recognized solution to this problem. Surrogacy can be applied at various scales, including the example of the predictive models used in phylogeny. As previously mentioned, the use of species-richness information may be sufficient for character richness or diversity and it is of some interest to address the economic criteria relevant to conservation decisions on this basis.

SURROGACY AND PRIORITY SETTING

Most of the current discussion is motivated by a belief that current *ad hoc* or opportunistic conservation efforts are inadequate, or in some sense suboptimal. The resulting financial and biological opportunity costs of making mistakes have given greater impetus to the assessment of the cost-effectiveness of conservation decisions, and the issue of biodiversity priorities (see Pressey and Tully, 1994; Prendergast *et al.*, 1993; Metrick and Weitzman, 1994).

There are many criteria complicating the issue of biodiversity priorities, but the basic economic objective can be stated as the maximization of diversity conserved for any given budgetary cost. This inescapable budgetary constraint applies at all geographical scales. As the analysis is typically conducted without the luxury of phylogenetic detail, some consideration of the role of surrogates is of considerable importance. Specifically, what methods are available to take the issue of priorities beyond a traditional focus on species hot spots, i.e. areas where species are under most threat?

Table 4.1   Taxonomic character differences within a well-defined hierarchy

Advantage: precision as a measure of character diversity	A scale of surrogacy for character diversity	Advantage: ease (/cost) of measurement
low	(ecosystems)	high
⇓	landscapes	⇑
⇓	land classes	⇑
⇓	species assemblages	⇑
⇓	higher taxa	⇑
⇓	species	⇑
high	(characters)	low

Source: Williams and Humphries (forthcoming).

Table 4.1 shows taxonomic character differences as lying within a well-defined hierarchy ranging from sub-species character traits (e.g. genetic), up to more indirect measures of overall diversity and corresponding cost of use. Thus, whereas eco-system characterization tends to be less data-demanding; analysis conducted at lower levels tends to be more painstaking and costly. Yet, if phylogenetic analysis implies that fundamental units of account (specifically genetic traits) are the real repository of biodiversity value, then some method to ensure correct representation is desirable. Indeed, the use of predictive tree models of diversity is already a recognition that all characters of all organisms cannot be counted directly. Table 4.1 suggests that there are several potential scales of surrogate information with the appropriate question relating to how well any surrogate predicts whichever character is thought to be the ultimate repository of option value.

Williams and Humphries (forthcoming) comment on an emerging consensus on the use of species richness (or its surrogate – higher taxon richness), as a reasonable surrogate for character richness. The conditions under which this is unlikely to be the case are where 'taxonomic clumping' occurs (i.e. species-rich areas that are character poor). Assuming data on a species exist in a geographic location, the problem is the maximization of species richness in a set of reserves subject to the existing budget. This area coverage objective can be set to address priorities both within and across countries and several heuristic and optimal programming algorithms for such coverage problems are available (Underhill, 1994; Csuti *et al.*, forthcoming).

Global Priorities

Increasing concern over the destruction of tropical habitats and concerted international efforts to implement the Biodiversity Convention, has focused considerable attention on the determination of global priorities. In this regard, much of the aforementioned analysis, particularly that of Vane-Wright *et al.*, indicates why traditional hotspot or endemic area assessment methods (Myers, 1988; Mittermeier, 1988) might be socially suboptimal at the national scale. In particular, area prioritization with limited regard to the taxonomic principles, inevitably trades-off distance or biological distinctiveness for more tangible benefits inherent in a species richness measure. As it happens, the analysis by Williams and Humphries suggests that the discerning use of richness surrogates may not always be completely misguided. This finding gives some scientific credibility to the issue of addressing priority-setting on a global scale.

Beyond strict species criteria, alternative suggested approaches have employed *ad-hoc* rankings based on threat indices such as deforestation rates, population growth, and the extent of existing protected areas (Dinerstein and Wikramanayake, 1993; Sisk *et al.*, 1994; Moran, Pearce and Wendelaar, 1996).

Only the last of these provides a unified ranking, which includes cost criteria relevant to the investment decision. A valid criticism of all global assessments is that their scale is necessarily too crude to account for the area-specific factors undermining biodiversity conservation. Nevertheless, there is a consensus that some areas will remain global priorities by any criterion, and that a global focus is not inconsistent with integrated conservation and development programmes at ground-level. Furthermore, the approach can be seen as complementary (rather than competing with) popular technologies such as Geographical Information Systems.

POLICY RESPONSE

It is clear that policy recommendations following from the preceding discussion will vary according to the precision with which conservation decisions should be informed. On the one hand, the taxonomic agenda of detailing the global family tree (see e.g. Savage, 1995) is consistent with a rigorous economic approach to the problem, as advanced in the Weitzman-type analysis. A formalized cardinal approach to the conservation problem appears to be the ultimate goal and most economists would be sympathetic to such a scientific agenda even if the interim losses are likely to be significant. On the other hand, such an undertaking is certainly long-term and as was the case in Figure 4.2, may not ultimately obviate the value judgements needed to differentiate species priorities even when phylogenetic information is available.

If policy tools are too characterized in terms of their proximity to the economist's tool-box then there is potentially much more to conservation policy than the specific essentially anthropocentric diversity measures that have been a central part of this chapter. Most immediately, historical patterns of land use, population pressure, and other aspects of global environmental change have all to be factored into conservation strategies. The pattern that emerges is inevitably an *ad-hoc* construction driven by opportunistic factors such as the availability of internal and external funding, and a range of competing policy objectives. To the extent that countries do have discernable biodiversity policies, these will typically be of low priority.

Looking beyond the hysteria which typically characterizes the extinction debate, a genuine policy hypothesis concerns the potential for the development process to be environmentally self-correcting. In other words, is the tendency towards habitat conversion attenuated at some sufficient level of economic development? This is simply another version of the 'environmental Kuznets curve' hypothesis, which has recently found favour for making development prognoses with regard to more common environmental pollutants (see Grossman and Krueger, 1995). For biodiversity, the contention derives support from similar arguments such as the diminishing marginal utility of money and a generally increased global awareness of the significance and uses of biological resources. Relative to other environmental problems, the importance of income distribution should be emphasized. Habitat conversion may have disproportionate impacts on low-income levels.

Given the many uncertainties and proximate and underlying causes of biodiversity decline there is a traditional tendency to shrink before the prospect of any general policy approaches to biodiversity. Growth may well be a long-term solution to extinction problems. However, in the proverbial long-run we are all dead and the tractable policy issue is how – given typical background rates of turnover – to contain accelerating extinctions.

Traditionally, individual cases of endangerment have motivated individual species recovery programmes, which have been controversial on both ecological and economic grounds (e.g. the Northern spotted owl and the IUCN 'Red Data Book'). The predictable economic concern relates to the opportunity costs of conservation, so much so that in most countries action plans for conservation and species recovery have some economic assessment as a standard requirement. Ecological criticism indicate a broader habitat approach, conserving biodiversity under a mosaic umbrella of representative biota. Such an approach also comes closer to dealing with the argument that a single species cost-benefit assessment abstracts excessively from the fundamental uncertainties surrounding the general erosion of biodiversity. The general thrust of this argument is that biodiversity is in some sense only maintained as an irreducible system which is more resilient to external shocks.

Whichever view is adopted, the ultimate conservation decision implies a cost, whereas efficient decisions ideally also require some assessment of conservation benefits. In the broadest sense this should include assessments of avoided uncertainty and potential irreversibilities. This however is much easier said than done. In the face of such unknowns the best default is to ascribe biodiversity some critical status implying limited substitutability in a strong sustainability sense. However, the result is that the relevant policy approaches involve ethical judgements and competing views about socially responsible or precautionary margins, or safe minimum standards (SMS) of exploitation. In theory, the SMS approach suggests a clear decision rule to avoid degradation beyond specified thresholds. This is a laudable objective, and one which should be the basis of more conservation decisions. However, it should noted that a SMS can be neither an undertaking on the indefinite survival of species, nor beyond the harsh realities cost-benefit analysis (Hohl and Tisdell, 1993). The difficulties of advocating such an approach are nowhere more evident than in developing countries, where the opportunity cost of resources tied up in conservation can make biodiversity seem like a superfluous luxury.

The Sectoral Approach to Biodiversity Policy

The diverse causes of biodiversity loss suggest a range of policy responses. Many sectoral policies in areas such as agriculture, transport and energy – all apparently unrelated to the issue – can be dressed up for the cause. Although advantageous in offering numerous potential instruments, a corresponding disadvantage arises where political expediency is served by a largely piecemeal approach to the issue. Nevertheless, as with other pollution problems, it is usually the case that the sectoral approach can offer considerable 'win-win' opportunities.

The effectiveness of any policy is of course determined by its particular objective. In this sense it is unclear how well current policies serve the objectives of biodiversity as defined here. Indicators of success are limited, since objectives are not always clearly articulated. No attempt here is made to review the menu of policies: these have been dealt with elsewhere (OECD 1996; Clark and Downs, 1995). Instead, noting the total absence of any empirical work on the issue of effectiveness, it is sufficient to sketch the basic objectives of instruments currently deployed for conservation purposes.

In response to *local market failure*, a range of policies has been suggested and employed. These include compensating farmers for the production of environmental goods in the form of miscellaneous management agreement, introducing user fees for the exploitation of biological resources and protected areas, and the use of corrective taxes, bonds and liability law to regulate damaging externalities. In several of these approaches, the instrument-fund dichotomy is apparent. In addition to financial incentives, many approaches rely solely on the stewardship motive, by which potential agents of destruction are themselves encouraged to foster and capture the production of positive externalities.

Modified *property rights* may also be classed as a response to local market failure, and are the basis of numerous schemes such as covenants and easements, habitat zoning and mitigation, and schemes such as tradeable emissions rights, development rights and miscellaneous quota schemes. With many competing social and economic objectives to be satisfied, there is nearly always some form of government *intervention failure* impacting on biodiversity. Subsidies to polluting industries, less than full-cost pricing, and sub-optimal taxation are all contrary to the polluter pays principle, and reflect the extent to which biodiversity concerns remain peripheral to policymaking.

Market failure is not confined to country borders, and concern for biodiversity in the developing world has focused attention on the nature of *global market failure*. As in the area of climate change, biodiversity loss has highlighted the absence of markets or conduit mechanism for international transfer payments. Such markets are emerging, however. The Framework Convention on Climate Change, for example, enables 'joint implementation' – the crediting to one country of reductions in *net* greenhouse gas emissions in another country, and with the credited country paying for the reductions. Since one of the mechanisms for reducing net emissions is to sequester carbon in biomass, joint implementation includes transactions in which rich country enterprises pay for afforestation and even avoid deforestation in developing countries. One additional benefit of such deals can be conserved biodiversity. Significant programmes of joint implementation exist, as with the United States Initiative on Joint Implementation, the 'FACE' deals between the Dutch public electricity utility and various countries, and emerging programmes in Japan, Scandinavia and elsewhere. In this way, global markets are beginning to emerge. While current contributions to conservation from these programmes are modest, the potential is thought by many to be very large (Jepma, 1995; Kuik, Peters and Schriver,1994). Other limited markets have also emerged. Such is the case in a few bioprospecting deals and debt-for-nature swaps. Bolder initiatives such as land purchase and cross-border attenuation of property rights, may have potential, but remain untested. Following a difficult inception period, the Global Environment Facility now attempts to fill the remaining significant global void by financing conservation costs incremental to some national baseline plan and which costs are judged to deliver a global benefit in the form of biodiversity conservation.

CONCLUSIONS

The economics of biodiversity conservation probably represent the most profound challenge to environmental economics. The necessity for seeking an economic valuation of biodiverse assets lies in the underlying causes of biodiversity loss. The main proximate cause is land-use change, but land conversion occurs because of human population change, misdirected economic policies which artificially inflate the rate of return to conversion, and 'missing markets' which effectively assign low, zero or even negative value to biodiversity. All the incentives are for 'homogenized' land-based production systems, i.e. for diversity reduction. But there is a real and growing debate about what it is that possesses this unrealized economic value. Is it diversity *per se* or is diversity being confused with the stock of biological resources rather than their genetic and species range? Use-values – for example, eco-tourism – attach to both stock and range of the resource, but may not be adequate to 'save' the resource when in competition with other land uses. This does not mean that the use-value approach should be neglected, only that 'something more' is also needed. Hence seeking values for, and setting priorities on, the basis of diversity *per se* becomes important. In this respect, developing a practical interface between economic values and biological non-preference value is the real challenge.

NOTES

1. We are deeply indebted to Tom Tietenberg, Steve Polasky and Per-Olov Johansson for extremely valuable comments on the earlier draft of this chapter. They are in no way responsible for the final outcome.
2. This is true only if harvesting costs are not functionally related to the size of the stock. We assume they are not for the sake of simplicity. For more detail see Clark (1990).
3. Steve Polasky has suggested to us a parallel with the value of the firm: total factor payments can be less than the value of the enterprise in the absence of constant returns to scale.
4. That is, whether a cure is unique to one member of the collection, or common to several but in varying degrees of quality and cost.
5. An example of this is the screening of close relatives of the pacific yew tree *taxus brevifolia* which was the original source of the anti-cancer agent taxol. The suggestion is not necessarily that the relatives will be as valuable as the original, but that they will have some economic value.
6. Again, providing these trees have branch lengths in proportion to character changes.

REFERENCES

Barbier, E., J. Burgess, T. Swanson and D.W. Pearce (1990), *Elephants, Economics and Ivory*, London: Earthscan.

Bateman, I. and R.K. Turner (1993), 'Valuation of the Environment, Methods and Techniques: the Contingent Valuation Method', in R.K. Turner (ed.), *Sustainable Environmental Economics and Management*, London: Belhaven Press, pp. 120–91.

Brown, G. and J. Goldstein (1984), 'A Model for Valuing Endangered Species', *Journal of Environmental Economics and Management*, **11**, 303–9

Clark, C. (1973a), 'The Economics of Overexploitation', *Science*, **181**, 630–4.

Clark, C. (1973b), 'Profit Maximisation and the Extinction of Animal Species', *Journal of Political Economy*, **81**(4), 950–61

Clark, C. (1990), *Mathematical Bioeconomics*, 2nd edn., New York: Wiley.

Clark, D. and D. Downes (1995), *What Price Biodiversity? Economic Incentives and Biodiversity Conservation in the U.S.*, Washington, DC: Centre for International Environmental Law.

Crozier, R.H. (1992), 'Genetic Diversity and the Agony of Choice', *Biological Conservation*, **61**, 11–15.

Csuti, B. *et al.* (forthcoming), 'A Comparison of Reserve Selection Algorithms Using Data on Terrestrial Vertebrates in Oregon', *Biological Conservation*.

Day, K. and G. Frisvold (1993), 'Medical Research and Genetic Resources Management', *Contemporary Policy Issues*, **11**, 1–11.

Dinerstein, E. and E. Wikramanayake (1993), 'Beyond Hotspots: How to Prioritise Investments to Conserve Biodiversity in the Indo-Pacific Region', *Conservation Biology*, **7**(1), 53–65.

Ehrlich, P. and A. Ehrlich (1982), *Extinction: the Causes and Consequences of the Disappearance of Species*, London: Gollancz.

Faith, D. (1994), 'Phylogenetic Pattern and the Quantification of Organismal Biodiversity', *Philosophical Transactions of the Royal Society of London*, B 345, 45–58.

Faith, D. and P. Walker (1995), 'Integrating Conservation and Development: Incorporating Vulnerability into Biodiversity Assessment of Areas', submitted to *Biodiversity and Conservation*.

Felsenstein, J. (1985), 'Confidence Limits on Phylogenies: An Approach Using the Bootstrap', *Evolution*, **39**, 783–91

Fisher, A. and M. Hanemann (1985), 'Option Value and the Extinction of Species', in *Advances in Applied Microeconomics*, vol. 4, pp. 169–90, JAI Press.

Gordon, H.S. (1954), 'The Economic Theory of a Common Property Resource: The Fishery', *Journal of Political Economy*, **62**, 124–42.

Grossman, G. and A. Krueger (1995), 'Economic Growth and the Environment', *Quarterly Journal of Economics*, **110**, 353–78.

Harper, J. and D. Hawksworth (1994), 'Biodiversity: Measurement and Estimation', *Philosophical Transactions of the Royal Society of London*, B 345, 5–12.

Heywood, V. (ed.) (1995), *Global Biodiversity Assessment*, Cambridge: Cambridge University Press.

Hohl, A. and C. Tisdell (1993), 'How Useful are Environmental Safety Standards in Economics? – The Example of Safe Minimum Standards for Protection of Species', *Biodiversity and Conservation*, **2**, 168–81.

Horowitz, I. (1970), 'Employment Concentration in the Common Market: an Entropy Approach', *Journal of the Royal Statistical Society*, Series A (133), 463–75.

Humphries, C., P. William and R. Vane-Wright (1995), 'Measuring Biodiversity Value for Conservation', *Annual Review of Ecology and Systematics*, 26, 93–111.

Jepma, C. (1995), *The Feasibility of Joint Implementation*, Dordrecht: Kluwer.

Kerr, J.T. and D.J. Currie (1995), 'Effects of Human Activity on Global Extinction Risk', *Conservation Biology*, **9**(5), 1528–38.

Kuik, O., Peters, P. and N. Schriver (1994), *Joint Implementation to Curb Climate Change*, Dordrecht: Kluwer.

Lieberson, S. (1964), 'An Extension of Greenberg's Linguistic Diversity Measures', *Language*, **40**, 4526–31.

McNeely, J., K. Miller, W. Reid, R. Mittermeier and T. Werner (1990), *Conserving the World's Biological Diversity*, Washington, DC: World Bank.

Mendelsohn, R. and M. Balick (1995), 'The Value of Undiscovered Pharmaceuticals in Tropical Forests', *Economic Botany*, **49**(2), 223–8.

Metrick, A. and M. Weitzman (1994), 'Patterns of Behaviour in Biodiversity Preservation', *Policy Research Working Paper*, No.1358, Washington, DC: World Bank.

Mittermeier, R.A. (1988), 'Primate Diversity and the Tropical Forest: Case Studies from Brazil and Madagascar and the Importance of the Megadiversity Countries', in E.O. Wilson and Francis M. Peter (eds), *Biodiversity*, Washington, DC: National Academy Press, pp.145–54.

Moran, D., D.W. Pearce and A. Wendelaar (1996), 'Global Biodiversity Priorities: A Cost Effectiveness Index for Investments', *Global Environmental Change*, **6**(2), 103–19.

Myers, N. (1988), 'Threatened Biotas: "Hot Spots" in Tropical Forests', *The Environmentalist*, **8**(3), 187–208.

OECD (1996), *Making Markets Work for Biological Diversity: The Role of Economic Incentive Measures*, Paris: Organization for Economic Cooperation and Development.

Pearce, D.W. (1996), 'Global Environmental Value and the Tropical Forests: Demonstration and Capture', in W. Adamowicz, P. Boxall, M. Luckert, W. Phillips and W. White (eds), *Forestry, Economics and the Environment*, Wallingford: CAB International, pp.11–48.

Pearce, D.W. and S. Puroshothamon (1995), 'The Economic Value of Plant-based Pharmaceuticals', in T. Swanson (ed.), *Intellectual Property Rights and Biodiversity Conservation*, Cambridge: Cambridge University Press, pp.127–38.

Pearce, D.W. and D. Moran (1994), *The Economic Value of Biodiversity*, London: Earthscan.

Peters, C., A. Gentry and R. Mendelsohn (1989), 'Valuing an Amazonian Rainforest', *Nature*, **339**, 655–6.

Pimm, S., G. Russell, J. Gittleman and T. Brooks (1995), 'The Future of Biodiversity', *Science*, **269**, 21 July, 347–50.

Polasky, S., A. Solow and J. Broadus (1993), 'Searching for Uncertain Benefits and the Conservation of Biological Diversity', *Environmental and Resource Economics*, **3**, 171–81.

Polasky, S. and A. Solow (1995), 'On the Value of a Collection of Species', *Journal of Environmental Economics and Management*, **29**, 298–303.

Prendergast, J., J. Quinn, J. Lawton, B. Eversham and D. Gibbons (1993), 'Rare Species, the Coincidence of Diversity Hotspots and Conservation Strategies', *Nature*, **365**, 335–7.

Pressey, R. and S. Tully (1994), 'The Cost of ad hoc Reservation: A Case Study in Western New South Wales', *Australian Journal of Ecology*, **19**, 375–84.

Rojas, M. (1992), 'The Species Problem and Conservation: What are We Protecting?', *Conservation Biology*, **6**(2), 170–8.

Savage, J.M. (1995), 'Systematics and the Biodiversity Crisis', *Bioscience*, **45**(10), 673–9.

Simon, H. and A. Wildavsky (1995), 'Species Loss Revisited', in J. Simon (ed.), *The State of Humanity*, Oxford: Blackwell, pp. 346–62.

Simpson, B. and J. Cracraft (1995), 'Systematics: The Science of Biodiversity', *Bioscience*, **45**(10), 670–3.

Simpson, D., R. Sedjo and J. Reid (1996), 'Valuing Biodiversity for Use in Pharmaceutical Prospecting', *Journal of Political Economy*, **104**(1), 163–85.

Sisk, T. D., A. Launer, K. Switky and P. Ehrlich (1994), 'Identifying Extinction Threats', *BioScience*, 44(9), 592–604.

Solow, A., S. Polasky and J. Broadus (1993), 'On the Measurement of Biological Diversity', *Journal of Environmental Economics and Management*, **24**, 60–8.

Solow, A. and S. Polasky (1994), 'Measuring Biological Diversity', *Environmental and Ecological Statistics*, **1**(2), 95–107.

Southgate, D. (1996), 'What Roles Can Ecotourism, Non-timber Extraction, Genetic Prospecting, and Sustainable Timber Play in an Integrated Strategy for Habitat Conservation and Local Development?', Report to Inter-American Development Bank, Department of Agricultural Economics, Ohio State University, mimeo.

Swanson, T. (1990), *The International Regulation of Extinction*, London: Macmillan.

Swanson, T. (1994), 'The Economics of Extinction Revisited and Revised: A Generalised Framework for the Analysis of the Problems of Endangered Species and Biodiversity Losses', *Oxford Economic Papers*, **46**, supplementary issue, 800–21.

Theil, H. (1967), *Economics and Information Theory*, Amsterdam: North Holland.

Tilman, D., D. Wedin, J. Knops (1996), 'Productivity and Sustainability Influenced by Biodiversity in Grassland Ecosystems', *Nature*, **379**, 718–20.

Underhill, L.G. (1994), 'Optimal and Suboptimal Reserve Selection Algorithms', *Biological Conservation*, **70**, 85–7.

Vane-Wright, R., C. Humphries and P. Williams (1991), 'What to Protect? – Systematics and the Agony of Choice', *Biological Conservation*, **55**, 235–54.

Vitousek, P. (1986), 'Diversity and Biological Invasions of Oceanic Islands', in E.O. Wilson (ed.), *Biodiversity*, Washington, DC: National Academy Press.

Weitzman, M. (1992), 'On Diversity', *Quarterly Journal of Economics*, May, 363–405.

Weitzman, M. (1995), 'Diversity Functions', in C. Perrings, K.-G. Maler, C. Folke, C. Holling and B.-O. Jansson (eds.), *Biodiversity Loss: Economic and Ecological Issues*, Cambridge: Cambridge University Press.

Williams, P. and C. Humphries (1994), 'Biodiversity, Taxonomic Relatedness and Endemism in Conservation', in P.L. Forey, C. Humphries and R. Vane-Wright (eds), *Systematics and Conservation Evaluation*, Oxford: Clarendon.

Williams, P. and C. Humphries (forthcoming), 'Comparing Character Diversity among Biotas', in K.J. Gaston (ed.), *Biodiversity: a Biology of Numbers and Difference*, Oxford: Blackwell.

Witting, L. and V. Loeschcke (1995), 'The Optimization of Biodiversity Conservation', in *Biological Conservation*, **71**, 205–7.

5. Nonpoint pollution[1]

James S. Shortle and David G. Abler

INTRODUCTION

Environmental regulation has become a prominent feature of the legal, political, and economic landscape of developed nations since the late 1960s. Yet, regulations are applied directly to only a small subset of polluters. Large point sources of pollution and manufacturers of environmentally harmful products, such as pesticides and automobiles, are the main targets of regulatory programmes. Nonpoint pollution sources, which are large in number but usually small in economic size, have largely escaped direct regulation. The comparative ease with which large point sources could be identified and controlled, and the political support for action against obvious polluters, made them a logical choice for first-generation environmental programmes. Similarly, regulation of chemical and automobile manufacturers has been easier politically and administratively, at least for governments at the helm of large economies, than direct regulation of the many households and small businesses that actually cause environmental harm through their activities and use of polluting products.

Much has been accomplished by first-generation environmental policies, but more aggressive measures for nonpoint sources are essential if environmental quality demands are to be met. Environmental assessments show nonpoint sources to be a major cause of environmental damages in developed and developing countries (Duda, 1993; OECD, 1991; World Resources Institute, 1988). Beyond limiting the extent of potential environmental quality improvements, the failure to extend pollution controls to nonpoint sources increases the costs of environmental protection by precluding efficient allocation of control between point and nonpoint sources (Freeman, 1990).

There is considerable support within environmental agencies and environmental groups for expanding nonpoint pollution efforts. However, there is little consensus about appropriate policies. There has been a heavy reliance on voluntary compliance approaches in the past, but these are generally acknowledged to have had limited impact. As with other types of pollution, significant reductions in nonpoint pollution will require the application of either enforceable regulatory approaches or economic instruments that have significant incentive effects. The appropriate choices among the range of options that fall within these boundaries is the subject of much debate.

Our goals in this chapter are to describe the nonpoint pollution control problem, the peculiar challenges it poses for policy design, and the policy-related contributions of the emerging theoretical and applied literature on the economics of nonpoint pollution. We begin with an overview of characteristics of nonpoint pollution problems that complicate the development of economically and politically appealing solutions. Next, we present a model of nonpoint pollution that helps to explain the nonpoint problem and establish benchmarks for the analysis of nonpoint policies. We then turn to nonpoint policy options. These are divided into two broad categories. The first encompasses more or less standard categories of pollution control instruments, such as moral suasion, regulations, and economic instruments. The second encompasses public investments in research and development and sectoral policy reforms that could reduce environmental pressures from nonpoint sources indirectly. Our treatment of these issues mirrors current applied research and policy debate in that we emphasize nonpoint water pollution. Analogous to the distinction between stationary and mobile sources in the context of air pollution, the distinction between point and nonpoint sources is especially meaningful and used most commonly in the context of water pollution (Callan and Thomas, 1996). This reflects the large contribution of nonpoint sources to water pollution and the difficulties governments have encountered in developing acceptable policies for major nonpoint sources of water pollution.

NONPOINT POLLUTION: SOURCES, CHARACTERISTICS, AND MANAGEMENT PROBLEMS

Nonpoint Pollution Sources

Pollution sources are generally distinguished as point or nonpoint according to the pathways the pollutants or their precursors follow from the place of origin to the receiving environmental media. Pollutants from point sources enter at discrete, identifiable locations. Industrial facilities that discharge residuals directly into air or water from the end of a smoke stack or pipe exemplify this class. Pollutants from nonpoint sources follow indirect and diffuse pathways to environmental receptors. Open areas such as farm fields, parking lots, and construction sites from which pollutants move overland in runoff into surface waters or leach through the permeable layer into groundwaters are examples.

The classification of pollution sources as point or nonpoint is not always clear-cut nor fixed. Urban storm runoff is generated by diffuse sources and is therefore generally considered a nonpoint source. However, it is a point-source pollution with respect to the receiving environmental medium when collected and discharged from the end of pipes at well-defined outfalls (Kneese and Bower, 1979). Similarly, storm runoff from livestock facilities, mines, and industrial facilities can be unmanaged and diffuse or collected and routed to treatment facilities. Conversion of nonpoint sources to point sources represents a policy option in the limited cases where it is technically and economically feasible (Boggess, Flaig and Fonyo, 1993; Duda, 1993; Malik, Larson and Ribaudo, 1994; US Environmental Protection Agency, 1994; Weinberg, Kling and Wilen, 1993b).

Conversely, with cross-media effects, point sources in one context may contribute to nonpoint pollution in another. In particular, air pollutants generated by point sources disperse and return to the Earth's surface where they may become nonpoint pollutants of soil or water (Chesters and Schierow, 1985; Puckett, 1995). In cases where atmospheric deposition is a large source of pollution, point-source controls represent an important nonpoint control option. An example is Chesapeake Bay. Elevated levels of nitrogen and phosphorous in Chesapeake Bay have led to a severe decline in highly valued fish and shellfish. For 1985, 23 per cent of the nitrogen and 34 per cent of the phosphorous were estimated to be from point sources with the remainder from nonpoint sources (Chesapeake Bay Program, 1995). Agricultural nonpoint sources were by far the most important, contributing 39 per cent of the nitrogen and 49 per cent of the phosphorous.[2] Twenty-seven per cent of the nitrogen was atmospheric nonpoint pollution, with 11 per cent falling directly on the water. Nitrogen oxides from fossil fuel combustion are the primary source of the atmospheric nitrogen.

Finally, some pollution sources that are point sources in a strict sense may have features that give their management more of a nonpoint character. Russell (1993) cites the example of discharges of storm runoff from older cities with many old and some possibly forgotten outfalls.

Dimensions of Nonpoint Pollution Management

Designing sensible pollution policies requires a substantial understanding of who is responsible for polluting discharges, their relative contributions, and the ecological and economic impacts of changes in polluter behaviour. A large degree of uncertainty about these matters is inherent in nonpoint pollution problems.[3]

Assigning responsibility

Uncertainty about how much any individual contributes to ambient pollution concentrations, or even whether a particular suspect has an adverse environmental impact is a key dimension of nonpoint pollution problems. Routine metering of pollutant flows from individual nonpoint sources is prohibitively expensive and often technically infeasible. For example, nitrogen fertilizer applied to cropland or suburban lawns can have a variety of fates depending on how and when it is applied, weather events during the growing season, and other factors. These fates include consumption by plants, leaching through the soil into groundwater, removal in surface runoff, or volatilization into the atmosphere. None of these fates, especially those that involve losses to the different environmental media, is easily measured or predicted. Nor can individuals' contributions be routinely inferred from ambient concentrations in environmental media because the latter are determined by the joint contributions of many unmeasured sources (both natural and anthropogenic).[4]

Uncertainty about who is responsible and the degree of responsibility creates significant problems for policy design. Regulation of households and businesses that cause little or no problem creates costs without offsetting benefits. Yet failure to cast the regulatory net broadly enough diminishes effectiveness and limits opportunities for cost-effective allocations. Fairness is clearly an issue when households and businesses are required to undertake costly activities in the public interest but there is uncertainty about whether the public interest is served at all. Similarly, political support for policies to regulate sources that may cause no actual or apparent environmental damage may be difficult to muster. The fairness and political considerations associated with uncertainty about individuals' responsibility may help to explain the frequent use of moral suasion and government-pays approaches to nonpoint pollution control rather than polluter-pays approaches.

Measuring and managing polluter performance

Unobservable pollution flows do more than cloud responsibility for environmental damages. They also complicate the choice of instruments. Economic research on environmental policy design has mirrored the legal and political focus on point sources. The bulk of the literature concerns emissions-based economic incentives (e.g., emissions charges, emissions reduction subsidies, transferable discharge permits) and emissions standards. This emphasis reflects economists' understanding that the preferred base for the application of incentives or regulations to manage pollution externalities is polluters' discharges of wastes into the environment (see, e.g., Oates, 1994). It also reflects a preoccupation with policy problems in which discharges can be metered with a reasonable degree of accuracy at low cost, obviously a necessary condition for the use of emissions-based instruments. However, with unobservable pollutant flows, other constructs must be used to monitor performance and as a basis for the application of policy instruments. The economics of designing policy instruments for nonpoint pollution externalities is therefore complicated by the fact that choices must be made between suboptimal bases as well as between types of regulations or incentives (Griffin and Bromley, 1983; Shortle and Dunn, 1986). Economically and ecologically desirable candidates will be more or less (1) correlated with environmental conditions, (2) enforceable, and (3) targetable in time and space

(Braden and Segerson, 1993). Options for bases proposed in the economic literature include inputs or techniques that are correlated with pollution flows (e.g., use of polluting inputs such as fertilizers), emissions proxies constructed from observations of inputs or techniques that influence the distribution of pollution flows (e.g., estimates of field losses of fertilizer residuals to surface or groundwaters), and ambient environmental conditions (nutrient concentrations in ground or surface waters). We look in detail at each of these bases below.

Site specific solutions

Solutions to nonpoint pollution problems are generally highly site-specific. Climate and characteristics of the physical environment (both built and natural) are key determinants of the volume of nonpoint pollution loads, the media receiving the loads (e.g., air vs. groundwater vs. surface water), and the timing of pollutant delivery.[5] These conditions also influence the feasibility, effectiveness, and costs of nonpoint pollution control technologies.

The critical role of site characteristics in determining technical feasibility and cost-effectiveness greatly limits the applicability of uniform technological prescriptions (e.g., technology-based emissions standards), long a favoured approach of environmental regulators, as a means for nonpoint pollution control. It also makes targeting pollution controls efforts to critical areas (e.g., groundwater recharge areas or the hydrologically active parts of watersheds in which most runoff originates) essential for cost-effective control.[6] Finally, the importance of site characteristics is an argument in favour of a degree of decentralization in the control of nonpoint sources (Shortle, 1996). Under the provisions of the Federal Water Pollution Control Act 1972 and subsequent legislation, the US Congress established federal primacy in the control of point sources of water pollution but assigned responsibility for nonpoint sources to the states. The site specific character of nonpoint pollution controls was a major reason for the division of responsibility (Greenfield, 1985).

Lags

Contemporary nonpoint pollution problems often reflect decisions and events that occurred many years in the past. For instance, time lags in the movement of agricultural chemicals from fields to wells of 30 to 60 years have been reported in southern California (Kim, Hostetler and Amacher, 1993). Similarly, the benefits of current control actions may not be fully realized for many years.

Many agents with limited information

Issues discussed above relate primarily to physical processes governing the formation and fate of nonpoint pollutants. Nonpoint pollution problems have two other important economic features: many agents, and agents with limited technical information.

The number of nonpoint sources in a region will often be multiples of the number of point sources. For example, there are approximately one hundred significant permitted point sources in the Susquehanna River Basin in Pennsylvania, but tens of thousands of farms, rural households, and other entities that are actual or potential sources of nonpoint pollutants.[7] With large numbers, the transactions costs associated with the design and administration of site-specific solutions could be enormous. Balancing the benefits of effective and informed differentiation against the transactions costs is a key aspect of the nonpoint policy problem. Similarly, large numbers in highly varied economic circumstances complicates differential policy treatment motivated by concern for fairness. In addition, large numbers along with the obscure and ambiguous character of nonpoint pollution are conducive to free-riding and a barrier to cooperative solutions (Tomasi, Segerson and Braden, 1994).

Traditional economic prescriptions for pollution control usually assume that polluters are more knowledgeable about the technical options for pollution control and corresponding costs than are government planners. This assumption is at the core of the economic critique of design standards. While reasonable for large industrial and municipal polluters with the resources to acquire engineering and other expertise, it is less applicable to typical nonpoint polluters such as homeowners and small farmers.

EFFICIENT NONPOINT MANAGEMENT

A Nonpoint Pollution Model

A model of the nonpoint pollution policy problem is useful for clarifying issues raised above and subsequent discussion of nonpoint instruments. We assume a particular resource (e.g., a lake) is damaged by a single residual (e.g., nitrogen). The ambient concentration of the residual depends on runoff from nonpoint sources, point-source discharges, and emissions from natural sources. Point- and nonpoint-source polluters are taken to be firms. The ambient concentration is given by

$$a = a(r_1, r_2, \ldots r_m, e, b, w, \lambda) \tag{5.1}$$

where a is the ambient concentration, r_i (i = 1, 2, ..., m) is runoff from nonpoint source i, e is discharge from the point source, b is the natural generation of the pollutant, w is a vector of weather variables that influence transport and fate, and λ is a vector of watershed characteristics and parameters.[8] The function a(.) can be thought of as representing an accepted theory of the relationship between the ambient concentration and the independent variables. Uncertainty about the relationship can be represented by taking λ to be uncertain.

Point-source emissions are observable and nonstochastic.[9] Runoff cannot be observed directly (at least not at an acceptable cost) and, via stochastic variations in weather, is stochastic. Accordingly, changes in resource use by nonpoint firms can only influence the distribution of runoff. Runoff from a firm's site depends on management decisions, weather, and site characteristics. Specifically, the runoff from firm i's decision is given by

$$r_i = r_i\,(x_i,\, w,\, \alpha_i) \tag{5.2}$$

where x_i is a vector of inputs chosen by the firm representing site management, and α_i is a vector of site characteristics such as soil type and topography and possibly other parameters that influence runoff. As above, the runoff functions can be thought of as representing an accepted theory about the relationship between pollution runoff, site management, and site characteristics. Uncertainty is introduced by taking α_i to uncertain. With this uncertainty, runoff cannot be inferred without error from observations of weather and resource use. Nor can runoff from any firm be inferred implicitly from observations of ambient conditions.[10]

Polluters are assumed to be risk neutral. The i-th nonpoint firm's expected profit for any choice of inputs is given by $\pi_i(x_i,\, \theta_i)$, where θ_i is a vector of site-specific parameters representing the firm's private knowledge.[11] Regulatory authorities may or may not have access to the information included in this vector. The expected profit of the point source is given by $\pi_e(e,\, \theta_e)$ where θ_e is analogous to θ_i.[12] The economic cost of damages caused by pollution are given by $D(a)$. The damage cost function is taken to be increasing in the ambient concentration of the pollutant.

There are empirical analogues to the model we have presented. The relationship between management variables and nonpoint pollution indicators is an active area of research and an array of models for simulating nonpoint pollution have been developed (e.g., Jackson and Flippo). Some models simulate the impacts of management practices and weather variables on the formation and movement of pollutants from particular sites. Our runoff functions (r_i) correspond to this category. Others simulate impacts of management and weather variables on ambient concentrations. Our linked runoff and ambient functions (a) correspond to this category.

Physical models have been linked with economic models to evaluate economic issues in nonpoint pollution control. Integrated modelling research on agricultural nonpoint pollution control is especially active. See Fox *et al.* (1991) for a survey of applications before the early 1990s. Discussions of approaches to integrated modelling for agriculture with implications for other nonpoint sectors are presented in Antle and Capalbo (1991, 1993) and Antle and Just (1993).

Ex-ante Efficient Management

The expected net benefit function of resource allocation decisions by point and nonpoint sources is given by

$$NB_0 = \pi_e(e, \theta_e) + \sum_{i=1}^{m} \pi_i(\cdot) - E_0[D(a(\cdot))] \tag{5.3}$$

where E_0 denotes the expectations operator over all the stochastic or inherently unknown variables (elements of w, α_i, λ).[13]With appropriate continuity and convexity assumptions, first-order necessary conditions for the efficient plan are:

$$\frac{\partial \pi_i}{\partial x_{ij}} = E_0 \left[D' \frac{\partial a}{\partial r_i} \frac{\partial r_i}{\partial x_{ij}} \right] \tag{5.4}$$

$$\frac{\partial \pi_e}{\partial e} = E_0 \left[D' \frac{\partial a}{\partial e} \right], \tag{5.5}$$

where x_{ij} is the jth element of x_i.

The first condition, (5.4), requires the expected increase in profit for firm j from its use of input j to equal the expected incremental environmental damage cost induced by the firm's use of the input. The expected marginal damage cost will be positive, negative, or zero depending on whether the activity increases, decreases, or has no effect on expected environmental damage costs. With market failure, the external costs of a firm's choices will not be considered in its resource allocation decisions. A nonpoint producer would therefore choose inputs such that the expected increase in its profit is zero for each input. Given that $\pi_i(x_i, \theta_i)$ is concave in x_i, condition (5.4) implies that nonpoint firms should stop short of fully exploiting the private gains from inputs that increase damage costs so as to avoid external costs in excess of the private gain. Conversely, (5.4) implies that nonpoint firms should make more use of inputs that reduce damage costs than they would otherwise in order to gain society damage costs reductions. The second condition is the more familiar requirement that the expected marginal benefit (in this case expected profit) of point-source emissions equal the expected marginal damage cost.

These conditions can be written in another way that brings out risk effects. Specifically, using fundamental results on mathematical expectations and a little manipulation, we can rewrite (5.4) as

$$\frac{\partial\pi_i / \partial x_{ij}}{E_0[(\partial a/\partial r_i)(\partial r_i/\partial x_{ij})]} = E_0[D'] + \frac{Cov\left(D', \frac{\partial a}{\partial r_i} \frac{\partial r_i}{\partial x_{ij}}\right)}{E_0[(\partial a/\partial r_i)(\partial r_i/\partial x_{ij})]} \qquad (5.6)$$

and (5.5) as

$$\frac{\partial\pi_e / \partial e}{E_0[(\partial a/\partial e)]} = E_0[D'] + \frac{Cov\left(D', \frac{\partial a}{\partial e}\right)}{E_0[(\partial a/\partial e)]}. \qquad (5.7)$$

The left-hand side of (5.6) is the opportunity cost of a reduction in the use of input j at site i normalized by the corresponding expected change in ambient quality. This term can be interpreted as the expected marginal cost of the improvement. The right-hand side is the expected marginal benefit of the environmental improvement, and is composed of the expected damage cost foregone at the margin plus a normalized covariance term that is analogous to a risk premium. An implication of (5.6) is that optimal use of an input affecting nonpoint pollution will differ from the level of use that would equate the expected cost of an environmental improvement with the expected marginal benefit. The sign and size of the difference will depend on the sign and magnitude of the risk effect. Similarly, the left-hand side of (5.7) can be interpreted as the opportunity cost of an improvement in ambient conditions by a reduction in point-source emissions. The right-hand side is the expected marginal benefit of the reduction plus a risk premium. The implication of (5.7) for point-source emissions is analogous to the implication of (5.6) for use of an input by a nonpoint source.

Cost-effective nonpoint pollution management

An alternative benchmark for economic analysis of resource allocation for pollution control is cost-effectiveness. Useful notions of cost-effectiveness for nonpoint pollution control must consider variations in the impacts of runoff from different sources on ambient concentrations and the natural variability of nonpoint loadings.[14] There are several possibilities. The simplest is a combination of point and nonpoint pollution control efforts that minimizes costs subject to an upper bound on the expected ambient concentration. For instance, if the ambient target is a_0, then the proposed allocation minimizes costs (or equivalently maximizes expected profits as in (5.3)) subject to $E[a(.)] \leq a_0$. However, this allocation may not have economically desirable properties. Suppose that allocations that produce lower mean concentrations, at least within the neighbourhood of the goal, also increase the variance of the concentration. In this case, the expected damage cost $E[D(a)]$ may be increased rather than decreased by the pollution control efforts unless the damage cost function is linear in the ambient concentration (e.g., Shortle, 1990). Generally, an allocation that minimizes the cost of satisfying an upper bound on the mean concentration need not be more efficient, in terms of expected net benefits, than an allocation that satisfies the constraint at a greater cost.

Another approach to defining least-cost allocations involves probabilistic constraints of the form Prob $(a \geq a_0) \leq \phi$ $(0 < \phi < 1)$. As above, allocations that satisfy this constraint at least cost need not be more efficient than allocations that satisfy the constraint at higher cost.

The most interesting cost-effectiveness concept when ambient concentrations are stochastic, but perhaps also the least practical, is an upper bound on expected damage costs, say D_0. Only in this case will allocations that achieve the target at least cost be unambiguously more efficient than allocations that achieve the target at higher cost (see Shortle, 1990). In the model above, the least cost solution would maximize expected profits subject to $E[D(a)] \leq D_0$. First-order necessary conditions for a least cost solution are

$$\frac{\partial \pi_i}{\partial x_{ij}} = \rho(D_0)E_0\left(D' \frac{\partial a}{\partial r_i} \frac{\partial r_i}{\partial x_{ij}} \right) \tag{5.8}$$

and

$$\frac{\partial \pi_e}{\partial xe} = \rho(D_0)E_0\left(\frac{\partial a}{\partial e} \right) \tag{5.9}$$

where $\rho(D_0)$ is the shadow price of the target as a function of the target. These conditions reduce to the conditions for the efficient solution if in equations (5.8) and (5.9), D_0 is set equal to the expected damage cost in the efficient solution. In this case, $\rho(D_0) = 1$.

Inferences about efficient allocation of inputs or activities across nonpoint sources or point/nonpoint trading can be derived from these results. Consider trades between nonpoint firm i and the point source. It would be tempting to define trades in terms of reductions in expected runoff and the point-source emissions. However, our analysis suggests that, in principle, trades should involve emissions and inputs or practices. In particular, for a given level of water quality protection defined in terms of expected damage costs, input j of firm i and point source emissions should trade such that

$$\frac{\partial \pi_i / \partial x_{ij}}{\partial \pi_e / \partial e} = \frac{E_0[D'] E_0[(\partial a/\partial r_i)(\partial r_i/\partial x_{ij})] + \mathrm{Cov}(D', (\partial a/\partial r_i)(\partial r_i/\partial x_{ij}))}{E_0[D'] E_0[(\partial a/\partial e)] + \mathrm{Cov}(D', \partial a/\partial e)}. \quad (5.10)$$

The left-hand side of (5.10) is the rate at which the input and emissions can be traded to hold expected profits constant. The right-hand side is the rate at which they can be traded to hold expected damage costs constant. Note that the optimal trades would hold the mean ambient concentration constant only if both covariance terms vanish. If this were the case, the right-hand side would simplify to the rate at which the input can be traded with point-source emissions to maintain a constant expected ambient concentration. Generally, however, optimal trading must consider the risk effects of changes in resource allocation. Similar considerations would apply when considering trades between nonpoint sources.

INSTRUMENTS FOR NONPOINT POLLUTION CONTROL

The absence of emissions-based instruments from the regulator's nonpoint tool-kit leaves it diminished but not empty. A variety of options are available to encourage decision makers with property rights in nonpoint sources to make socially desirable choices. The least intrusive are public persuasion combined with technical assistance to facilitate changes in behaviour. Conversely, choices can be constrained by regulations applied to suspected nonpoint polluters or by regulations applied to sectors that provide potentially polluting products (e.g., pesticides, leaded fuels, chlorofluorocarbons). Economic instruments for nonpoint pollution control can take a variety of forms. Major options that are used in practice or that have been proposed include taxes on polluting inputs, subsidies for purchases of pollution control equipment, liability for damages, environmental bonds, tax/subsidy schemes applied to ambient concentrations, and tradeable permits in polluting products.

Information and Education
Information and education programmes are an important part of nonpoint pollution programmes in many countries and will likely remain so. They supply

producers or consumers with information on practices for reducing nonpoint pollution, technical assistance to facilitate adoption, and encouragement to adopt, either out of self-interest or concern for broader societal well-being.

For example, there is evidence that much nonpoint pollution from consumer wastes is due to simple ignorance about the environmental consequences of improper disposal (see, e.g., Coburn, 1994). Consumers can make many changes to their behaviour at a low cost to themselves, such as disposing of used oil through approved means rather than in storm sewers or the garbage. If there is an adequate level of environmental concern or 'consciousness' among the general public, information programmes promoting activities to reduce nonpoint pollution can be very cost-effective.

Information and education programmes also may be effective in changing producer decisions, but their potential role here is more limited than in consumer decisions. They are most effective when encouraging 'environmentally friendly' actions that also happen to be profitable (Feather and Cooper, 1995; Musser *et al.*, 1995). Nonpoint problems often involve small producers who, because of their size and the fixed costs of acquiring information, may not invest much in information. Public agencies may have significantly better information than producers about pollution control or pollution prevention practices. Disseminating such knowledge could be particularly useful in reducing firms' costs of compliance with more direct regulatory or incentive-based approaches.

In agriculture, extension education to encourage and support the adoption of integrated pest management (IPM) is a key component of pesticide control programmes in Canada, Denmark, the Netherlands, the US, and Sweden. Basic IPM practices, such as pest scouting to detect whether it would be profitable to apply pesticides, are now used by a significant proportion of US farmers, although use of more sophisticated IPM techniques has been limited (Vandeman *et al.*, 1994). Pesticide use in Sweden has been greatly reduced since the early to mid-1980s through a mixed approach of regulations, incentives, and education, along with fortuitous developments in low-dose application and spraying pesticide technology (Bellinder, Gummesson and Karlsson, 1993; Pettersson, 1994; Weinberg, 1990). The independent contribution of education and other factors is unclear. Agricultural extension in most OECD countries now includes environmental components (OECD 1989, 1993).

Concerns have been raised about the effectiveness of traditional extension systems in disseminating environmental technology (Lichtenberg, Strand and Lessley, 1993; Thrupp, 1988). Similarly, there is ample evidence that public perceptions about environmental risks are often at odds with expert assessments and that people do not necessarily respond to risk information in ways that experts consider rational (e.g., Fisher, 1991; Smith, 1992; Lopes, 1992). To the extent that information programmes are used in an attempt to change producer and consumer behaviour, it is important that they be designed with a good understanding of the kinds of messages and delivery mechanisms that will have an impact on the target audiences.

While much can be said in favour of information and education, there are definite limits to what can be accomplished. The potential for information and education programmes to identify and disseminate techniques that are both environmentally friendly and profitable is clearly limited by the available technology. Moreover, continued survival as a producer in any industry requires a certain level of competence regarding the profitability of alternative production techniques. In agriculture, without good alternatives, significant changes in existing management practices would offer only small or negative economic gains to producers (Lee, 1992; Fox *et al.*, 1991). One might claim that farmers should reduce pesticide usage to protect themselves from exposure to harmful compounds or protect their own drinking water supplies from contamination. Here too, though, the perceived benefits to farmers of significant changes in existing practices are small (Beach and Carlson, 1993; Norton, Phipps and Fletcher, 1994).

Moral suasion is less likely to be an effective strategy for changing producer decisions than consumer decisions. Profitability and economic survival drive production decisions, and analyses of educational programmes to reduce nonpoint pollution suggest that concern for the environment is a poor substitute for more immediate economic imperatives (Cameron, 1990; Dubgaard, 1994; van Kooten and Schmitz, 1992; Feather and Amacher, 1993; Floyd and McLeod, 1993).

Input and Design Based Instruments

Nonpoint policies that involve more aggressive intervention in private decision-making than information and education, usually involve regulatory restrictions on choices or incentives to discourage the use of polluting inputs and encourage the use of pollution control practices. The emphasis on inputs and designs is not surprising given the general tendency in environmental policy to manage technology rather than emissions.

There are many examples of product and design standards. Pesticide registration is the principal method for protecting the environment, workers, and consumers from pesticide hazards in developed countries, and is used increasingly in developing countries (Dinham, 1993; OECD, 1986). Pesticide registration programmes have been very effective in many countries, but not at all in others (Dinham, 1993; Thrupp, 1988). Resources allocated to registration and enforcement activities, registration criteria, institutional capability and commitment are among key factors that differentiate results. Pesticide registration in the US has been effective and also relatively efficient, although at best it is only a crude instrument for pesticide management (Cropper *et al.*, 1992; Lichtenberg, 1992; Zilberman *et al.*, 1991).

Input regulations are also used to reduce other types of pollutants from agriculture and other sectors. For instance, standards governing the amount and timing of manure applications and restrictions on the numbers of farm animals are used to control ammonia, phosphorous, and nitrogen pollution from agriculture in the Netherlands (Broussard and Grossman, 1990; Dietz and Hoogervorst, 1991; Leuck, 1993). Architectural standards are a common way of regulating storm runoff from new urban developments.

Economic incentives applied to inputs are also a dimension of nonpoint pollution controls. Australia, Canada, Denmark, Sweden, and the United States provide subsidies for adoption of pollution control practices in agriculture and some other sectors. The Netherlands taxes manure production and feedstock oil. Sweden taxes fertilizers and pesticides at rates intended to have disincentive effects on use. A 150 per cent levy on nitrogen fertilizer has been proposed by the Danish government to reduce nitrate pollution. Dubgaard (1994) estimates the tax would reduce fertilizer purchases by 25 per cent. Iowa levies taxes above and beyond the usual sales taxes on fertilizers and pesticides. Sweden and the US offer subsidies for shifting land to activities with lower environmental hazards. The major programme in the US is the Conservation Reserve Program (CRP), which pays farmers to convert land from row crop production to grassed cover. The total water-quality benefits of the CRP when fully implemented have been estimated at nearly $4 billion (1988 dollars) (Ribaudo, 1989). However, the CRP has received low marks for cost-effectiveness (Miranowski, Hrubovcak and Sutton, 1989). In the US, Florida has offered a dairy herd buy-out programme as part of efforts to reduce nutrient pollution of Lake Okeechobee. Subsidies for conversion of farm land to forests in Sweden are justified in part as measures to reduce pesticide and fertilizer pollution. The Waste Water Management Division of the City of Denver charges property owners a modest annual runoff fee based on the percentage of impermeable surface area of a property.

Typically, input taxes are levied at such low rates that they offer little incentive to reduce input usage (OECD, 1994a). The purpose seems more often to be to generate revenue for environmental programmes than to reduce input use. Subsidies and regulations are the dominant mechanisms for reducing pollution. Subsidies are often used to reduce the costs of complying with mandated activities. In such cases, they serve primarily to spread costs and increase the political acceptability of direct regulations.

Designing input taxes and subsidies: theoretical issues
Input taxes and subsidies have long been recognized as substitutes for direct taxes on negative externalities. Plott (1966), Holtermann (1976), Griffin and Bromley (1983), Stevens (1988), and Dinar, Knapp and Letey (1989) show that taxing

inputs that increase a detrimental externality and subsidizing inputs that reduce it could replicate the results of taxing the externality directly. However, these studies have limited applicability to nonpoint pollution. In particular, each assumes that regulators have perfect information about the relationship between inputs and ambient conditions and that the pollution process is nonstochastic. Under these conditions, observing and controlling inputs is a perfect substitute for observing and controlling emissions, except for transactions costs differences.

Several recent studies provide theoretical support for input taxes for nonpoint pollution control using models that are more representative of the nonpoint pollution problem. Shortle and Dunn (1986) and Shortle and Abler (1994) analyse input taxes using a model analogous to the one we presented above. In this case, observations of inputs can reduce but not eliminate uncertainty about nonpoint emissions and their impact on ambient concentrations. Shortle and Dunn show that the efficient solution can be achieved by firm-specific taxes on all inputs entering the runoff functions. The optimal incentives essentially reproduce the marginal incentives on the right-hand side of (5.4). To construct these taxes would, however, require the taxing authority know firms' private information about their production functions. Shortle and Abler explore mechanisms that would induce firms to reveal their private information, and also second-best input taxes in which private information remains private. Dosi and Moretto (1993, 1994) present theoretical support for input taxes for nonpoint pollution control in a dynamic setting.

The real-world economic potential of input taxes is ambiguous. One limitation is the state of knowledge of the relationship between inputs and ambient concentrations. While perfect information about this relationship is not required to design input taxes with good economic properties, the information cannot be too imperfect (Braden and Segerson, 1993; Dosi and Moretto, 1993, 1994; Tomasi, *et al.* 1994). A second concern is set-up and administration costs. The development and regular application of complex models of pollutant transportation and fate would require the collection and processing of a considerable amount of data. The costs may well be so large as to negate the benefits.

Beyond these considerations, the input tax/subsidy structures that have been shown to have good economic properties are exceptionally complex. Tax/subsidy structures that can approximate the marginal incentives on the right-hand side of (5.4) must be applied to all inputs that directly affect emissions and firm-specific. Real-world tax/subsidy structures are much simpler. In practice, these incentives are applied to a few inputs or choices, and are uniformly applied across broad sets of agents.

While purchases of potentially harmful inputs or investments in pollution control structures can be easily tracked in some instances, many resource management decisions that can have a large impact on the actual consequences are too costly to monitor or verify. Information costs essentially require the tax/subsidy base to be truncated to a subset of choices that are both relatively easy to observe and correlated with ambient impacts. Truncation of the tax/subsidy base will reduce the cost-effectiveness of pollution control because it limits differential treatment of inputs according to their environmental impacts and control costs.

Truncation of the tax base has implications for the design of the incentives. Producers will substitute non-taxed inputs for those that are taxed. Adjustments in tax rates will be necessary to the extent that substitution effects are, on balance, environmentally adverse or beneficial (Laughland, Shortle and Musser, 1995). Similar considerations would apply to subsidies. The importance of policy-induced substitution effects has been recognized in the literature on agricultural nonpoint pollution (e.g., Bouzaher *et al.*, 1990; Braden and Segerson, 1993; Eiswerth, 1993; Hrubovcak, Le Blanc and Miranowski, 1989; Schnitkey and Miranda, 1993; Shogren, 1993). The literature suggests a variety of possible forms for substitution effects. These would include shifts that increase or decrease other hazards (e.g., policies for reducing sedimentation of surface water might increase or decrease pesticide or nitrate hazards in surface or groundwaters) and regional shifts (movement of activity from regions with regulation to regions without).

Uniformity of the tax/subsidy rates across polluters also reduces the cost-effectiveness of pollution control, in this case because it eliminates potential gains from differential treatment of polluters according to their relative impacts on ambient conditions. The inefficiencies that can occur from uniform taxation of inputs when differential taxes are optimal are analogous to the inefficiencies that can occur when uniform emissions charges are used in place of an optimally differentiated structure (Baumol and Oates, 1988). High control cost or low damage cost polluters will end up devoting too many resources to pollution control while low control cost or high damage costs polluters will devote too few resources to pollution control. Helfand and House (1995) find the costs of uniform taxation to be relatively small in the case of nitrate pollution from lettuce production in the Salinas Valley of California. The generality of this result is uncertain.

Taxes vs. subsidies
Pollution control subsidies can have the perverse effect of increasing the overall level of emissions by increasing profits and encouraging entry into the subsidized sectors (Baumol and Oates, 1988). Given the extensive use of subsidies in nonpoint pollution control, concern for the impact on the aggregate level of pollution is not unwarranted. For instance, Lichtenberg, Strand and Lessley (1993) suggest that subsidies for the adoption of pollution control practices in agriculture might increase agricultural pollution by encouraging conversion of pasture

and forest land to cropland even though pollution from existing land is reduced. The level and type of subsidy is clearly important to the outcome. Subsidies that remove land from relatively polluting uses, such as the US Conservation Reserve Program, clearly can have a beneficial impact, especially when targeted to critical areas.

Input standards

Efficient input standards can be defined in theory. They would simply be the efficient input choices, as determined by equations (5.4) and (5.5) in our model. As such, they would be firm-specific and selected using information on firm-specific costs and benefits. In practice, design standards are usually uniform across classes of polluters, applied to easily observed choices, and formulated with limited information on variations in costs. These simplifications are analogous to those discussed above with respect to input tax/subsidy schemes.

Studies of the cost-effectiveness of nonpoint policy approaches generally indicate that input standards applied in a uniform way are less cost-effective than performance-based standards or economic incentives. However, several cases can be identified in which standards make sense. One notable case is when the expected societal costs of the use of an input or process exceeds the expected benefits for essentially any level of use. Examples are extremely hazardous pesticides, especially when there are close substitutes with lesser risks and the use of certain types of pesticides in environmentally sensitive areas such as ground water recharge zones. A second case is when techniques exist that have the potential to yield significant environmental gains with little or no cost to the user. For example, several recent studies suggest that nitrogen soil testing in corn production in humid regions of North America can greatly reduce nitrate losses to ground and water resources with little negative economic impact on farmers (US Office of Technology Assessment, 1995). Similarly, no-till farming practices are very effective in reducing sediment pollution problems and can increase farm profits relative to conventional practices in some regions of North America (Eiswerth, 1993; Logan, 1993).[15] Finally, some least-cost techniques are essentially common knowledge. An example is the use of septic systems for domestic waste water treatment in rural areas.

Input trading

A plausible alternative to input taxes and standards would be tradable permits in rights to use potentially harmful inputs. Or, in the case of waste products such as manure, tradable permits in waste production rights. Optimally designed markets would satisfy the conditions for the efficient solution (ie., equations (5.4) and (5.5) in our model). However, like input taxes and subsidies, practical schemes can only be a pale reflection of what is optimal in principle. Markets could be developed for certain relatively easy to observe products but not for unobservables. Differentiation of regional zones could be used to a limited degree to account for differences in fate and transportation but optimal differentiation would be difficult and costly to define and enforce. Accordingly, significant reservations about the potential efficiency of input trading is warranted without careful empirical analysis.

Nevertheless, input trading does have appeal. Trading schemes could offer a mechanism for achieving aggregate input reduction goals in specified regions. Input reduction goals are relatively common in nonpoint pollution policy although the use of trading schemes to achieve them is exceptional.[16] The US used lead trading to improve the efficiency of the phased reductions of lead in gasoline (Hahn, 1989).

Input taxes (subsidies) vs. quantity controls, and mixed instruments

An important topic in the theory of environmental policy is the choice between quantity controls and emissions taxes under conditions of asymmetric information about pollution control costs and benefits. The seminal work is due to Weitzman (1974) based on a highly simplified model in which emissions are nonstochastic and the ambient concentration is linear in emissions. The standard result is that the choice depends on the relative slopes of the marginal benefit and cost functions. Temptation to generalize this result to choices between taxes and quantity controls on polluting inputs should be resisted.

Generalization of Weitzman's result to input taxation for nonpoint pollution control would be least problematic in the case where the taxes or quantity controls are linear, firm specific, and applied to all inputs that enter the runoff functions. Given these conditions, stable taxes and quantity controls can be set in principle such that firm-specific expected marginal benefits are equal to the firm specific expected marginal costs. We should note here that if there is more than one pollutant (e.g., nitrates and pesticides) or more than one receptor (e.g., ground and surface water), the firm specific marginal costs will be an aggregation across the hazards. Given that marginal cost is increasing, Jensen's inequality implies that uncertainty about the relationship between inputs and ambient conditions will increase the expected marginal cost of an input and act as a bias in favour of quantity controls.[17] Truncation of the base to a subset of inputs that enter the runoff functions introduces substitution effects into the tax rules like those discussed above. In this case, the information about the relative slopes of the expected marginal costs and benefits of the substitute inputs must enter into the analysis.

Mixed systems of input-based instruments can outperform single instruments. Shortle and Abler (1994) adapt Roberts and Spence's (1976) model to develop a mixed scheme of tradable input use permits, subsidies for reduced input use, and taxes on input use that would dominate any of the individual elements. Braden and Segerson (1993) discuss mixing an input tax with liability rules.

Some additional practical guidelines (see the above section on input standards) for the choice between quantity controls and economic incentives can be based on considerations of the acceptable degree of uncertainty about the level and geographic location of the use of inputs. Compared to fiscal incentives, standards and, to a lesser degree tradable permits, have a relatively certain impact on the use of polluting inputs and activities provided that they are adequately enforced. This suggests that quantity controls will be preferable to tax/subsidy schemes, at least as the main mechanism of control, when a high degree of certainty over the level and geographic distribution of polluting inputs and activities is desirable. Included would be pollutants for which the costs are highly uncertain but potentially high and/or irreversible, such as hazardous and toxic substances. Conversely, charges may be considered advantageous where some uncertainty about emissions is acceptable and where some growth in pollution is considered an acceptable cost of economic growth.

Ambient-Based Instruments

Rather than monitoring the choices of business or households that are suspected to contribute to environmental degradation, or firms that supply inputs to them, ambient-based instruments shift monitoring to the environmental media. Ambient instruments have received considerable attention in recent theoretical literature on nonpoint pollution control, but we know of no applications in practice.

Segerson (1988) first proposed an ambient tax/subsidy scheme that could achieve the efficient solution as a Nash equilibrium under very restrictive conditions. Firms would receive subsidies when ambient pollution concentration falls below a target and be charged taxes when the ambient concentration exceeded the target. Subsequent contributions include Cabe and Herriges (1992), Herriges, Govindasamy and Shogren (1994), and Xepapadeas (1991, 1992, 1994). This literature approaches the nonpoint problem as a moral hazard. Unobservable emissions mean that polluters' performance in the public interest cannot be observed directly. To the extent that input choices are costly to monitor and their relationship to ambient concentrations is uncertain, there will exist considerable uncertainty about the effort polluters are making in the public interest and thus a problem of moral hazard. The relative performance of nonpoint pollution controls in this context depends on their effectiveness in reducing 'environmental shirking'.[18] We should note that with uncertainty about the relationship between private activities and ambient concentrations, the meaning of environmental shirking may not be well defined in many nonpoint settings. However, the research to date on ambient-based instruments has avoided this issue by assuming that firms can observe their own emissions and control them deterministically, which is not typically the case in nonpoint problems.

An important aspect of Segerson's ambient taxes is that each polluter would pay the full expected marginal damage cost from a reduction in the ambient concentration rather than its share. This property is essential if the ambient tax is to provide optimal incentives, but implies that total payments will exceed the incremental cost. Building on the work of Holmström (1982) and Rasmusen (1987), Xepapadeas (1991) considers an alternative approach that is 'budget-balancing'. The regulator enters into contracts with polluters that subsidize each contracting polluter when the ambient concentration is at the target level. The target is taken to be the efficient level. If 'shirking' by one or more polluters results in an ambient concentration in excess of the target, then one of the contracting polluters is selected at random to pay a fine. The remaining contractors receive their normal subsidies plus a share of the subsidy that would have been paid to the firm that is fined, plus the fine it pays, less the marginal cost of the deviation from the optimum. Xepapadeas assumes firms to be risk averse and claims that if that all polluters participate, firm-specific subsidies and fines exist such that the efficient solution is a Nash equilibrium. Identifying the optimal contracts would, however, require that the regulator know abatement costs, damage costs, and transport and fate relationships. Herriges, Govindasamy and Shogren (1994) demonstrate that a degree of risk aversion is actually required for the instrument to be budget balancing.

An important feature of ambient approaches is that individuals are not rewarded or penalized according to their own performance. Rather, rewards and penalties depend on group performance. This makes polluters' expectations about other polluters behaviour, and the regulator's knowledge of these expectations, critical to the design and performance of ambient-based instruments. A second important feature is that a polluter's response to an ambient tax will depend on its own expectations about the impact of its choices, the choices of others, and natural events on ambient conditions. In other words, it will depend on the polluter's theory of fate and transportation. Cabe and Herriges (1992) explore the consequences of asymmetric prior information about transport and fate. If polluters' prior information about transport and fate differs from the regulator's, then incentives defined on the assumption that they are the same will not have the desired properties. For instance, a polluter may perceive no impact of its choices on pollution. In this case, an ambient tax may have either no impact, or it will result in a decision to escape the tax entirely by ending the suspect activity. The regulator has a choice between adjusting the incentives for the mismatch, educating the polluter, or a combination of both. The data collection and programme design issues involved in systematically measuring mismatches, developing educational programmes that would effectively close them, and adjusting incentives for their effects would undoubtedly be enormous. Similar concerns would apply to expectations about the behaviour of other polluters.

These considerations imply serious reservations about the potential effectiveness and efficiency of ambient instruments. Several other considerations also deserve mention. First, monitoring ambient conditions can be highly costly and subject to considerable error. This is illustrated by the uncertainty that exists about groundwater quality in many areas. Second, changes in observed conditions may have little relationship to contemporary actions. For instance, as noted earlier, nitrates and pesticides may take years to move from fields to wells. Similarly, eroded soils may take years before reaching receptor sites. Accordingly, incentives based on contemporary changes in ambient conditions may bear little relationship to current behaviour. In such cases, the incentives may do little to encourage improved performance. Finally, there is a capricious aspect to ambient-based taxes that would likely limit political and ethical acceptability. In particular, individuals who take costly actions to improve their environmental performance could find themselves subject to larger rather than smaller penalties due to environmental shirking on the part of others, natural variations in pollution contributions from natural sources, or stochastic variations in weather. Conversely, individuals who behave badly may end up being rewarded by the good actions of their neighbours or nature. Fining polluters at random, as Xepapadeas (1991) proposes, also raises troubling political and ethical questions.

Liability Rules
With this approach the regulator does not set the price for environmental damages as it does with a tax or subsidy. Instead, polluters are liable for damages they cause. The expectation of paying damages is the incentive the polluter has to modify behaviour. Liability can be established statutorily or by common law. An example of the former is the Comprehensive Environmental Response, Liability, and Compensation Act (CERCLA) under which the United States Congress established legal liability for damages to environmental resources. California and Connecticut have enacted statutes making farmers liable for groundwater contamination by agricultural chemicals. Nuisance and property law have been used under common law to secure compensation for damages (Dewees, 1992).

Theoretical research indicates that properly designed liability rules can result in efficient outcomes.[19] However, the characteristics of nonpoint pollution problems severely limit what can be expected from liability rules in practice (Menell, 1991; Segerson, 1990; Braden and Segerson, 1993; Segerson, 1995; Wetzstein and Centner, 1992). First, liability for damages may be viewed as an ambient-based instrument because it is triggered by the consequences of increased ambient concentrations of pollutants. As such, many of the issues raised above with regard to ambient-based instruments will apply in this case. Second, uncertainty about the relationship between individual behaviour and environmental conditions is a defining characteristic of nonpoint pollution, especially when large numbers are involved. Yet, assignment of liability to parties that are in fact responsible is an essential for efficient liability rules. Finally, courts are expensive and time-consuming, and should therefore be used sparingly if desired outcomes can be obtained by cheaper methods. These considerations suggest that other instruments should be used as the main mechanism for nonpoint pollution control, with liability as a complementary approach to address localized problems in which polluting events are infrequent, the number of parties involved is small, and cause and effect linkages are well understood.

Environmental Bonds

Environmental bonds take two general forms. One is the deposit-refund system, which involves a deposit at the time of purchase that is returned on evidence of proper disposal. Deposit-refund systems have considerable merit for management of waste materials that ought to be recycled or disposed of in particular ways after use. In particular, they are appropriate when the incentives for recycling or safe disposal are otherwise inadequate to induce users to choose the prescribed methods and where evasion of regulations or charges for improper disposal would be relatively easy. The method has a proven track record for beverage containers and some other products and could be an efficient method for a variety of products that can ultimately end up as nonpoint pollutants, such as unused pesticide containers, ingredients, and other wastes (Bohm, 1981; Bohm and Russell, 1985; OECD, 1994a). However, they have limited potential as a nonpoint pollution control method.

The second type is a performance or assurance bond. Like deposit-refund systems, performance bonds are an *ex ante* enforcement incentive. The method requires payment of a bond prior to initiating activities that may harm the environment. The bond is refundable if performance criteria are satisfied. This method is often used to mitigate adverse effects of land disturbances by construction, forestry, mining and other activities. For instance, strip mine operators in the United States are required to post bonds to assure proper reclamation of mine sites.

Shogren, Herriges and Govindasamy (1993) identify seven conditions that must be satisfied for performance bonds to work well for environmental protection:

1. producer performance criteria must be well defined and observable;
2. there must be a small number of agents that contribute to the problem;
3. damage costs must be well understood;
4. there must be well-defined states of the world;
5. the likelihood of their occurrence must be known;
6. there should be no irreversible effects; and
7. the horizon for remittance must be fixed.

These conditions are not generally satisfied by nonpoint problems. Malik, Larson and Ribaudo (1994) and Shogren (1995) discuss the limitations of performance bonds in the context of agricultural nonpoint pollution problems. These studies suggest that performance bonds, like liability rules, are best viewed as a complimentary approach applicable in specialized settings.

Emissions Proxies and Other Environmental Performance Proxies

With instruments based on metered discharges eliminated from the nonpoint choice set, perhaps the obvious next choice from an economic perspective is emissions proxies or other firm-specific environmental performance indicators (as opposed to aggregates like ambient conditions) that are constructed from firm-specific data. If close proxies can be easily constructed, then there would seem to be little lost. Indeed, many of the emissions taxes that are implemented in practice are in fact taxes on emission proxies (OECD, 1994a).

In the simplest cases, indicators are polluting inputs such as fertilizer or pesticide applications by a farmer, forester, or homeowner. Standards or charges applied to indicators of this form would be equivalent to product standards or product charges. More sophisticated indicators aggregate over inputs and other variables. One of the best known examples is the Universal Soil Loss Equation (USLE) developed by Wishmier and Smith (1978) for predicting gross soil loss from crop land. This indicator is used to assess compliance with 'cross compliance' programmes in the United States that require farmers with highly erodible soils who participate in farm income subsidy programmes to develop farm plans that meet specified erosion restrictions. Another widely used performance indicator is the balance between nutrient inflows and outflows in farm products (National Research Council, 1994). Farmers in the Netherlands are required to keep records of their nutrient balances.

The use of firm level performance indicators has been strongly advocated for nonpoint pollution control in a number of papers, most notably Dosi and Moretto (1993, 1994), Griffin and Bromley (1983), and Harrington, Krupnick and Peskin (1985). In general, efficient outcomes cannot be obtained by the management of firm-specific scalar measures of environmental performance. This point is illustrated by Shortle and Dunn (1986) who examine the efficiency of emission proxies constructed from observations of inputs and weather in the context of a single polluter. Assuming that the proxy is an unbiased estimator of emissions, which would seem to be a fairly desirable property, they demonstrate that the use of such proxies can be efficient only if the damage cost function is linear. With multiple sources of pollution the conditions would be even more restrictive.

Nevertheless, in the imperfect world of nonpoint pollution control, environmental performance indicators constructed from firm-specific observations have an intuitive appeal supported by empirical research. By emphasizing performance rather than means, proxies have several advantages compared to conventional input and design based instruments. First, well-constructed proxies can better correlate with environmental quality impacts than individual inputs when emissions are a function of more than one choice variable. For instance, in the case of nitrogen losses, the residual nitrogen available for leaching into groundwater is more highly correlated with the manageable nitrogen excess than with the fertilizer application (National Research Council, 1994). In addition, incentives applied to proxies tend to be more cost-effective in improving performance as measured by the proxy, than regulations or incentives applied to inputs or practices (see, e.g., Fontein *et al.*, 1994; Huang and Le Blanc, 1994; McSweeny and Shortle, 1990). As with the other schemes discussed above, incentives applied to performance indicators optimally applied would be firm-specific. However, as with those instruments, practical applications will more likely be relatively uniform across firms.[20]

Application of this approach requires the existence of proxies that are good indicators of measures of environmental pressures and not unduly burdensome to compute and enforce (Braden, Larson and Herricks, 1991; Braden and Segerson, 1993). The existence of such measures will vary.

Point/Nonpoint Trading

The concept of point/nonpoint-source trading has evolved within the particular institutional context of United States water pollution control laws. Under the provisions of the Federal Water Pollution Control Act 1972 and subsequent water quality legislation, the Federal government has primary responsibility for point-source pollution control while the states have primary responsibility for nonpoint sources. The Federal government has chosen stringent regulations for point sources while the states have generally taken voluntary approaches to nonpoint sources that have proven relatively ineffective (Cameron, 1990). Under these circumstances, it would seem likely that the incremental costs of water-quality improvements from unregulated nonpoint sources may be less than costs of squeezing further reductions from point sources. Point/nonpoint trading was offered in this context as a means for achieving water-quality improvements at lower costs by reallocating additional abatement from point to nonpoint sources (Elmore, Jaksch and Downing, 1985). Specifically, given the structure of property rights, point/nonpoint trading would allow point sources to avoid mandated emissions reductions by paying nonpoint sources to undertake measures.

Two trading programmes have been established. The first is a phosphorous trading programme that allows municipal sewage plants to trade for nonpoint reductions on Dillon Resevoir near Denver Colorado. A recent assessment reports one trade between a municipal sewage treatment plant and an urban nonpoint source (Malik, Larson and Ribaudo, 1994). The second is the recently established nutrient trading programme in the Tar-Pamlico basin in North Carolina. Feasibility studies suggest the potential for substantial cost saving in these and some other cases (Apogee, 1992; Letson, 1992).

Point/nonpoint trading is not strictly analogous to textbook transferable discharge permit markets (Crutchfield, Letson and Malik, 1994; Letson, 1992; Malik, Larson and Ribaudo, 1994). Because nonpoint emissions are unobservable, trades cannot involve the same commodity. Rather, the point source avoids a given reduction in emissions, say Δe, in return for actions by nonpoint sources that reduce estimated nonpoint emissions, by say Δr. The trading ratio is defined as $\Delta e/\Delta r$. As noted earlier, because of risk effects, efficient trades will not involve estimated nonpoint emissions and actual point-source emissions (see equation (5.10)). However, given the information requirements of optimal trades, trading in estimated reductions is more practical. The implications of risk effects, differential enforcement costs, and other considerations for trading ratios are discussed in Crutchfield, Letson and Malik (1994), Letson (1992), Malik, Letson and Crutchfield (1993), and Shortle (1990). In addition, the market is one-sided and essentially involves subsidizing nonpoint sources, with corresponding adverse incentive effects (Malik, Larson and Ribaudo, 1994). Government involvement in trading must also be extensive. Its function would include determination of acceptable trading ratios, certification of the types of management practice changes that will yield the required trades, monitoring and enforcement, and facilitating and coordinating trade (Malik, Larson and Ribaudo, 1994; Shabman and Norris, 1987). Assessments suggest that the transactions costs could be large.

A minimal condition for point/nonpoint trading is the presence of point and nonpoint sources of comparable pollutants in terms of type, timing, and quantity of pollutants in an air or watershed. Recent research on the feasibility of using trading programmes to protect coastal watersheds with agricultural sources in the United States found these conditions to be satisfied in limited cases (Letson, Crutchfield and Malik, 1993; Crutchfield, Letson and Malik, 1994).

INDIRECT POLICY APPROACHES

The potentially high costs of reducing nonpoint pollution problems using direct regulation or economic incentives suggest the potential desirability of indirect approaches to reducing environmental pressures. Prominent among these are 'environmentally friendly' technological developments and reform of economic policies that, as a side effect, contribute to nonpoint pollution.

'Environmentally Friendly' Research and Development

Research and development (R. & D.) on 'environmentally friendly' or 'green' technologies has attracted considerable interest as a potential means of reducing nonpoint pollution. This is particularly true with respect to consumer wastes, where, as noted above, there are few cost-effective ways to directly control methods of disposal. The past two decades have seen the introduction of a wide variety of consumer products in Western Europe and North America that do less environmental damage when disposed, including detergents, cleaning products, batteries, and products with biodegradable packaging.

There is also much interest in environmentally friendly production technologies. In agriculture, for example, a variety of innovations designed to substitute for fertilizers and pesticides are under development (OECD, 1993, 1994b; National Research Council, 1989, 1991). Biotechnology is beginning to yield crops with greater built-in resistance to pests and diseases. Biotechnology also brings the promise of cereal grains that can fix atmospheric nitrogen akin to the way that legumes do, although this innovation is years if not decades away.

Environmentally friendly products and production technologies could be classified in a number of ways. One common distinction is between pollution-prevention and pollution-abatement innovations. Pollution-prevention innovations provide alternatives to products or activities positively associated with pollution flows. The innovations in agriculture listed above fall within this category. Pollution-abatement innovations reduce pollution flows for any given set of polluting production or consumption activities. In agriculture, for example, a variety of cultivation practices or structural measures can be undertaken to reduce pollution, or at least redirect it from one environmental medium to another (Logan, 1993; Fawcett, Christensen and Tierney, 1994). Of course, it would be possible for a technology to have both pollution-prevention and pollution-abatement characteristics.

The environmental impacts of pollution-abatement technologies are reasonably obvious. However, since these technologies typically impose costs on users, adoption is unlikely in the absence of regulatory incentives, financial incentives, or some other perceived benefit to users.

The environmental impacts of pollution-prevention technologies are not as clear. Other things equal, the use of environmentally friendly products or production processes in place of environmentally unfriendly ones is environmentally beneficial. However, profit-maximizing producers will not voluntarily adopt new production processes unless they are less expensive than existing processes. If they are less expensive, they will be adopted and marginal cost will fall. At the market level, this will be passed on to consumers in the form of lower prices, which in turn will stimulate output demand to a greater or lesser degree depending on the price elasticity of output demand. As output demand increases, the derived demand for all inputs will increase, including inputs and activities that are correlated with point and/or nonpoint pollution flows. These inputs and activities may also change because of input substitution effects caused by the introduction of the new techniques. In any event, if the increase in derived input demand were large enough, total pollution could actually rise. Simulation analyses of grain production by Abler and Shortle (1991b, 1995) and econometric work on lumber production by Darwin (1992) indicate that such a scenario is not merely possible but plausible.

On the consumer side, the situation is also murky. The introduction of a new, environmentally friendly alternative to an existing product in effect reduces the 'price' of environmental consciousness, which one could view as a good purchased by consumers like any other good. This reduction in price will have income and substitution effects on the demands for all goods and services, including those correlated either positively or negatively with point and/or nonpoint pollution flows.

Regardless of whether or not R. & D. is likely to be a successful approach in and of itself, it could still have a role in reducing the costs of compliance with more direct regulatory or incentive-based approaches. One can find examples from many countries of how environmental policies have encouraged the development of new production processes, new products, and even entirely new industries (see, e.g., Porter and van der Linde, 1995; Kemp *et al.*, 1992; Caswell, Lichtenberg and Zilberman, 1990). However, the more extreme 'Porter hypothesis' that environmental regulations can systematically induce firms to develop and adopt innovations that would have been profitable even without regulation, but which for ignorance or some other reason were not developed or adopted, strikes us as highly implausible (Palmer, Oates and Portney, 1995; Jaffe *et al.*, 1995).

Economic and Environmental Policy Coordination

Production and consumption decisions associated with nonpoint pollution can be significantly affected by policy-induced distortions in output and input markets. Nonpoint policies should not be formulated in isolation but instead should bear in mind the distortions created by economic policies. Reform of distortionary economic policies would actually yield an efficiency gain from reduced deadweight losses, meaning that the costs of environmental protection would be negative.

In developed-country agriculture, the major policy-induced distortions are due to trade and commodity policies, which have a variety of different objectives and effects depending on the country and commodity (US Department of Agriculture, 1994). In developing country agriculture, subsidies for 'modern' inputs such as fertilizer and irrigation are common, while there are also a wide array of policies that elevate or depress output prices (US Department of Agriculture, 1994; Krueger, Schiff and Valdés, 1992). In forestry, many developing countries have policies that encourage deforestation, including open-access property-rights regimes for forest resources, aquisition of titles in land from the public domain through 'land improvement' (ie., clearing forest for other uses), subsidized credit for timber production or agricultural production on deforested land (particularly cattle ranching), road-expansion projects into forested areas, and preferential tax treatment for forest products (Munasinghe and Cruz, 1995; World Bank, 1992). Most developing countries also encourage rural-urban migration and, in turn, nonpoint pollution problems associated with urbanization through a variety of policies that discriminate against rural areas and favour urban areas (Tolley and Thomas, 1987).

Environmental Impacts of Economic Policies

Economic policies can affect nonpoint pollution in a variety of ways. Policies that affect output supply prices induce changes in output supply and, in turn, the derived demand for inputs, including inputs that are correlated either positively or negatively with nonpoint pollution flows. Policies that impose quotas on the usage of certain inputs, such as acreage controls in agriculture, have more ambiguous environmental effects. The answer depends on whether the inputs subject to quotas are correlated positively or negatively with nonpoint pollution flows. The answer also depends on the changes in demands for inputs not subject to quotas and the degree to which these inputs are correlated with nonpoint pollution flows. Like input quotas, policies that subsidize certain inputs can have environmental effects through their impacts on the demands for both subsidized and non-subsidized inputs. See Gardner (1990) for a general discussion of the impacts of various policies on input demands.

The economic policies of one country can affect the environment in other countries in a manner somewhat akin to environmental policies (see Chapter 7). However, whereas environmental policies are sometimes presumed to encourage the migration of 'dirty' industries from the north to the south, the reverse tends to be the case with respect to agricultural policies. A variety of applied partial-equilibrium models of world agricultural markets have shown that liberalization of agricultural trade and commodity policies in OECD countries would encourage a shift of grain, livestock, sugar, and horticultural production from OECD countries to developing countries (see, e.g., Goldin and Knudsen, 1990 ; Goldin, Knudsen and van der Mensbrugghe, 1993). The environmental impacts of these production shifts would depend on the relative usage of polluting inputs in developing countries vs. developed countries, pollution abatement strategies in the two regions, and the relative sensitivity of the environment to any given level of input usage under any given set of management practices.

Opportunities for Coordination

One clear opportunity for environmental and economic policy coordination involves the removal or liberalization of economic policies that both reduce social welfare and have undesirable environmental side effects (OECD 1989, 1993). Reform of these economic policies would reduce nonpoint pollution at a negative social cost.

For example, significant reductions in nonpoint problems associated with agriculture could be achieved through reform of agricultural trade and commodity policies (Abler and Shortle, 1992; Swinton and Clark, 1994) or input subsidies (Weinberg *et al.*, 1993; World Bank, 1992). Increases in nonpoint agricultural pollution resulting from international shifts in production patterns would, to a large degree, occur in areas in which less environmentally harmful techniques are used, areas which are less environmentally sensitive, or areas where people place a lower economic value on the environment. For instance, anticipated shifts in horticultural production from the US to Mexico under NAFTA (the North American Free Trade Agreement) are, on the whole, probably good from an environmental perspective because horticultural production techniques in Mexico are less fertilizer- and pesticide-intensive and because the willingness to pay for environmental quality is lower in Mexico (Abler and Pick, 1993).

However, one should not necessarily assume that economic policy reform can by itself eliminate all or even most nonpoint externalities, even in areas in which production or consumption activities associated with nonpoint pollution would contract significantly. For example, nitrogen surpluses (nitrogen applied to the soil through fertilizer, manure, and atmospheric deposition less uptake by crops) are so large in some parts of the EU that decreases in fertilizer usage and manure production of more than 50 per cent would be required to eliminate or significantly reduce them (Brouwer *et al.*, 1995). In developing countries, the fundamental economic forces driving urbanization are quite strong, and it is unclear whether elimination of policies with an urban 'bias' would significantly decrease urbanization (Tolley and Thomas, 1987; Williamson, 1988) and, in turn, urban nonpoint problems.

In the absence of economic policy reform, one could attempt policy coordination by using environmental policies to reduce the distortions caused by the economic policies. For example, quotas or taxes on estimated emissions or on production inputs/activities that are correlated with emissions could be structured taking into account the existence of distortionary economic policies. In general, social-welfare maximizing taxes or quotas on estimated emissions are probably stricter (from the producer's perspective) in the presence of policies that increase output prices than in the absence of these policies. However, if there were inputs that were negatively correlated with emissions, and if these inputs constituted a large share of total cost relative to inputs positively correlated with emissions, then the social-welfare maximizing taxes or quotas might actually be more lax (Laughland, Shortle and Musser, 1995). The reason is that stiffer taxes or quotas could encourage greater use of inputs negatively correlated with emissions, thereby increasing output and compounding the distortions created by trade and commodity policies.

Alternatively, and from a completely different perspective, one could view 'policy coordination' as the use of environmental policies to accomplish both environmental and economic policy objectives. This perspective is important if political considerations rule out penalizing producers along the lines of the polluter pays principle. To illustrate, producers unambiguously lose from taxes on estimated emissions or on polluting inputs/activities. Quotas have more ambiguous effects on producer welfare. By shifting the output supply curve inward and making it steeper, an emissions or input quota reduces producer surplus by reducing the quantity produced. However, the remaining quantity is sold at a higher price, increasing producer surplus. If output demand were sufficiently price-inelastic, the former effect would outweigh the latter. Simulations for the US indicate that modest quotas on fertilizer and pesticides could in fact work to increase producer welfare (Abler and Shortle, 1992; Just and Rausser, 1992). However, agricultural output demands facing the EU are significantly more price-elastic than those facing the US, so that fertilizer and pesticide quotas would probably harm EU producers (Abler and Shortle, 1992).

The effectiveness of environmental policies structured along the lines of the polluter pays principle could be diminished if economic policies were changed in response so as to protect producer welfare. Shortle and Laughland (1994) examine the impacts of a tax on fertilizer and pesticides in US maize production in the context of a model in which the output subsidy is endogenous. They find that the cut in fertilizer and pesticide use in response to the tax is only about half as much in the case where the output subsidy is endogenous as in the case where it is fixed.

CONCLUSIONS

Environmental decision-makers have many options for addressing growing demands for nonpoint pollution control. While some have appealing economic properties in theory, there are significant limits to what can be accomplished in practice. It is impossible to recommend aggressive application of any approach without a sound empirical foundation. Nevertheless, some generalizations are possible.

First, while there is ample evidence and reason to establish the inherent limitations of voluntary approaches, the limited information households and small businesses have about the impacts of their choices on the environment, the technical options for pollution control, and the costs of each option suggest that information and education programmes should be a part of nonpoint pollution control programmes. At the same time, these programmes should be developed with realistic goals. Limited research also suggests that innovations in the types and methods of information delivery techniques are needed in order to improve effectiveness.

Beyond this, the basic tools for nonpoint pollution control should be based on inputs or performance indicators that aggregate over inputs. There is a substantial body of knowledge about practices that lead to nonpoint pollution, and pollution control technologies. Regulation or incentives applied to technologies and inputs, or to well-defined firm-specific environmental indicators that aggregate over inputs and technologies, offer solutions to planners that can be relatively easy to observe and understand. They also offer methods of compliance to polluters that they can control and understand. When applied in conventional ways, these instruments can deliver environmental improvements in relatively predictable ways. The challenge is to structure instruments in ways that are reasonably efficient as well as fair. We consider ambient-based instruments to be of little practical interest. Liability rules and environmental bonds have some potential applications in practice but the circumstances to which they are best suited are atypical of nonpoint pollution problems.

Nonpoint pollution control programmes in practice are often portrayed as evolutionary in nature because environmental, agricultural and other agencies are still grappling with the complexity and uncertainty of nonpoint problems. There are significant concerns regarding effectiveness, direct and indirect economic impacts, fairness, and in many cases the conflicting objectives of responsible agencies (see, for example, Boggess *et al.*, 1993; Dubgaard, 1994; Weinberg, 1990). These experiences suggest that nonpoint problems are difficult but not intractable. Experience and theory suggest some common elements of successful policy development. First, given the site-specific character of the nonpoint problem, decentralized planning is essential for cost-effective results. Where there are jurisdictional spillovers, institutional mechanisms are needed for coordinating action. Much remains to be learned about how best to coordinate environmental protection programmes both within and between countries (e.g., see Braden, Folmer and Ulen, 1995). Second, except where environmental irreversibilities or unusual risks are involved, programmes should be flexible enough to accommodate learning and economic change. Third, strategies combining quantity controls and economic incentives should generally provide better results than individual instruments. Major challenges for environmental economists in nonpoint research are to learn more about the optimal design of inherently suboptimal instruments and to provide guidance based on empirical research.

Beyond direct measures, indirect approaches can play a significant role. In particular, it appears that economic policy reforms can offer a very cost-effective approach to reducing some nonpoint pollution problems.

NOTES

1. The authors greatly appreciate the research assistance of Andrew Fuentes and Richard Horan, and the helpful comments of Henk Folmer, Tom Tietenberg, Ann Fisher, and Olli Tahvonen.
2. The relative importance of different nonpoint sources varies from one problem to another. Agricultural and urban land uses are generally considered the most important nonpoint polluters of surface water. For instance, agricultural nonpoint sources are the leading cause of water-quality impairments in rivers and lakes and the third most important source of impairments in estuaries in the US (US Environmental Protection Agency, 1994). Urban runoff and storm sewers were identified as the second leading source of impairment of lakes and estuaries and the third most important source of river impairments. The situation in Western Europe is comparable (Duda, 1993). The importance of agriculture and urban activities is due to the quantity and quality of runoff from these land uses. Agricultural land-use is extensive, and by comparison to other extensive rural land-uses, contributes both a larger volume of runoff and a higher concentration of pollutants per unit of area. Urban land-use is much smaller in area than agricultural and other rural land-uses. However, paved streets, parking lots, roofs, and other impervious surfaces found in urban areas are hydrologically active, producing much more runoff and a higher concentration of pollutants per unit area than other land uses.
3. See Abler and Shortle (1991a), Braden and Segerson (1993), Dosi and Moretto (1993), Malik, Larson and Ribaudo (1994), Phipps (1991), Shogren (1993), and Tomasi, Segerson and Braden, (1994) for alternative discussions of information issues in nonpoint pollution control and their policy implications.
4. Nature can be a large source of some pollutants that are also contributed by anthropogenic nonpoint sources. Uncertainty about nonpoint contributions to acidification, nutrient enrichment, and other problems is due in part to limited information about the contributions from natural sources (Chesters and Schierow, 1985).
5. For instance, sediment pollution from cropland is largely associated with sheet and rill erosion of fields. Gross sheet erosion is a function of the intensity and frequency of rain storms, the inherent erosivity of the soil, the surface condition of the soil as determined by tillage practices, crop cover at the time that rainfall events occur and the length and slope of fields (National Research Council, 1994). Crop cover will depend on management choices (e.g., crop choice, tillage practices, fertilization and pesticide applications), but also on soil productivity and weather conditions influencing crop growth. Eroded particles may be redeposited in the field, at the edge of the field, in channels, and other sites. The amount of eroded soil that ultimately reaches water bodies and the time profile of sediment delivery will similarly be influenced by the interaction of management decisions, weather events, and geologic and geographic features.
6. Targeting has received considerable attention in the economic literature on agricultural nonpoint pollution control. The research shows that the cost-effectiveness of nonpoint pollution controls can be greatly improved by targeting, although the improvements depend critically on the targeting criteria (Bouzaher, Braden and Johnson, 1990; Braden *et al.*, 1989; Duda and Johnson, 1985; Lee, Lovejoy and Beasley, 1985; Park and Shabman, 1982; Ribaudo, 1986).
7. Personal communication with the Pennsylvania Department of Environmental Protection.
8. Dynamics, multiple pollutants, and multiple media in nonpoint pollution are explored in a number of studies, although few contain all of these elements and others that we introduce subsequently. Examples of theoretical models with multiple pollutants or multiple receptors include Cabe and Herriges (1992) and Eiswerth (1993). Nonpoint models with pollution accumulation, capital accumulation, or site dynamics include Shortle and Miranowski (1987),

Dosi and Moretto (1993, 1994), Kim, Hosteller and Amacher (1993), and Xepapadeas (1991, 1992, 1994).

9. Point-source emissions are in fact often measured with error and subject to stochastic influences. Nevertheless, this treatment is standard and helps to contrast the typical theoretical treatment of point sources with nonpoint sources.

10. In this specification pollution runoff at each site is independent of actions at others. In actuality, interdependencies can emerge in a number of ways. For instance, the runoff from a down-slope site may be affected by runoff from up-slope sites. In this case, we could have something like r_{i+1} entering the runoff function for r_i, r_{i+2} entering the runoff function for r_{i+1} and so on for subsets of nonpoint firms (Braden *et al.*, 1989). Essentially in this and other ways we are disregarding transferable (or shiftable) externalities (Bird, 1987) that can arise in the nonpoint pollution problem. See Shogren (1993) for further discussion of transferable externalities and the associated consequences of non-cooperative self-protection in nonpoint pollution.

11. For the case of a firm with one output and a well-defined production function, $\pi_i(.)$ can be viewed as the expected value of the profit equation. For multi-product firms, it can be viewed as a restricted expected profit function conditioned on x_i. In the latter case, x_i would be best interpreted as the subset of inputs that enter the runoff functions. In some cases, such as agricultural nonpoint-source pollution, the weather vector will be an argument of the production technology. If so, implicit in this specification is that the distribution of weather is common knowledge.

12. This function may be viewed as a restricted profit function conditioned on point-source emissions.

13. Implicit in this specification is the assumption that input and output prices are exogenous. Otherwise, welfare effects on consumers and resource owners would need to be considered.

14. Discussions of the implications of uncertain emissions for definitions of nonpoint pollution control and cost-effectiveness include Braden, Larson and Herricks (1991), Braden and Segerson (1993), Lichtenberg, Zilberman and Bogen (1989), McSweeny and Shortle (1990), Milon (1987), and Segerson (1988). Also see Beavis and Walker (1983), Forsund and Strom (1980), Mäler (1974), Nichols (1984), and Shortle (1990).

15. This case illustrates the need to consider substitution effects in the context of standards as well as taxes because no-till farming can also increase pesticide hazards.

16. In 1985 the Swedish Parliament established a goal for reducing pesticide use by 50 per cent by the year 2000. Similar goals exist for pesticides and fertilizers in Denmark. Phased reductions in manure production and application are key dimensions of Dutch policies to reduce associated air and water quality problems. In the mid-1980s, states surrounding the Chesapeake Bay in the United States set a goal of reducing nutrient loads from point and nonpoint sources by 40 per cent by 2000. In each case the goals have been pursued using a mixture of regulations and incentives. And, in each case, the cost effectiveness of the programmes is questionable (Dubgaard, 1994; Gren, 1994; Lichtenberg, Strand and Lessley, 1993).

17. See Varian (1992) for a definition of Jensen's Inequality and its use in the analysis of choice under uncertainty.

18. See Tomasi, Segerson and Braden (1994), Malik, Larson and Ribaudo (1994), Shogren (1995), and Xepapadeas (1991) for further discussion of moral hazard and environmental shirking in nonpoint pollution control.

19. See Segerson (1995) for a review of the relevant literature.

20. The choice between taxes and quantity controls applied to performance proxies in this setting is examined by Shortle (1984).

REFERENCES

Abler, D.G. and D. Pick (1993), 'NAFTA, Agriculture, and the Environment in Mexico', *American Journal of Agricultural Economies*, **75**, 794–8.

Abler, D.G. and J.S. Shortle (1991a), 'The Political Economy of Water Quality Protection from Agricultural Chemicals', *Northeast Journal of Agricultural and Resource Economics*, **20**, 54–60.

Abler, D.G. and J.S. Shortle (1991b), 'Innovation and Environmental Quality: The Case of EC and US Agriculture', in F.J. Dietz, F. van der Ploeg, and J. van der Straaten (eds), *Environmental Policy and the Economy*, Amsterdam: North-Holland.

Abler, D.G. and J.S. Shortle (1992), 'Environmental and Farm Commodity Policy Linkages in the US and EC', *European Review of Agricultural Economics*, **19**, 197–217.

Abler, D.G. and J.S. Shortle (1995), 'Technology as an Agricultural Pollution Control Policy', *American Journal of Agricultural Economics*, **77**, 20–32.

Antle, J.M. and S.M. Capalbo (1991), 'Physical and Economic Model Integration for Measurement of the Environmental Impacts of Agricultural Chemical Use', *Northeastern Journal of Agricultural and Resource Economics*, **20**, 68–82.

Antle, J.M. and S.M. Capalbo (1993), 'Integrating Economic and Physical Models for Analyzing Environmental Impacts of Agricultural Policy on Nonpoint Pollution', in C.S. Russell and J.F. Shogren (eds), *Theory, Modeling and Experience in the Management of Nonpoint-Source Pollution*, Dordrecht: Kluwer Academic Publishers.

Antle, J.M. and R.E. Just (1993), 'Conceptual and Empirical Foundations for Agricultural Environmental Policy Analysis', *Journal of Environmental Quality*, **21**, 307–16.

Apogee Research, Inc. (1992), 'Incentive Analysis for CWA Reauthorization: Point Source/Nonpoint Source Trading for Nutrient Discharge Reductions'. Report prepared for Office of Water, US EPA, April 1992.

Baumol, W. and W. Oates (1988), *The Theory of Environmental Policy*, Cambridge: Cambridge University Press.

Beach, E.D. and G.A. Carlson (1993), 'A Hedonic Analysis of Herbicides: Do User Safety and Water Quality Matter?', *American Journal of Agricultural Economics*, **75**, 612–23.

Beavis, M. and M. Walker (1983), 'Achieving Environmental Standards with Stochastic Discharges', *Journal of Environmental Economics and Management*, **10**, 103–11.

Bellinder, R.R., G. Gummesson, and C. Karlsson (1993), 'Percentage-Driven Government Mandates for Pesticide Reduction: The Swedish Model', *Weed Technology*, **8**, 350–9.

Bird, P.J.W.N. (1987), 'The Transferability and Depletability of Externalities', *Journal of Environmental Economics and Management*, **14**, 54–7.

Boggess, W.G., E.G. Flaig and C.M. Fonyo (1993), 'Florida's Experience With Managing Nonpoint Source Phosphorous Runoff into Lake Okeechobee', in C.S. Russell and J.F. Shogren (eds), *Theory, Modeling and Experience in the Management of Nonpoint-Source Pollution*, Dordrecht: Kluwer Academic Publishers.

Bohm, P. (1981), *Deposit-Refund Systems: Theory and Applications to Environmental, Conservation, and Consumer Policy*, Baltimore: John Hopkins University Press.

Bohm, P. and C. Russell (1985), 'Comparative Analysis of Alternative Policy Instruments', in A. Kneese and J. Sweeny (eds), *Handbook of Natural Resource and Energy Economics Vol. 1*, Amsterdam: Elsevier Science Publishers.

Bouzaher, A., J.B. Braden and G. Johnson (1990), 'A Dynamic Programming Approach to a Class of Nonpoint Pollution Problems', *Management Science*, **36**, 1–15.

Braden J.B. and K. Segerson (1993), 'Information Problems in the Design of Nonpoint Pollution', in C.S. Russell and J.F. Shogren (eds), *Theory, Modeling and Experience in the Management of Nonpoint-Source Pollution*, Dordrecht: Kluwer Academic Publishers.

Braden, J.B., A. Bozaher, G. Johnson and D. Miltz (1989), 'Optimal Spatial Management of Agricultural Pollution', *American Journal of Agricultural Economics*, **71**, 404–13.

Braden, J., H. Folmer and T. Ulen (eds) (1995), *Environmental Policy with Economic and Political Integration: The European Union and the United States*, Cheltenham: Edward Elgar.

Braden, J.B., R. Larson and E. Herricks (1991), 'Impact Targets vs Discharge Standards in Agricultural Pollution Management', *American Journal of Agricultural Economics*, **73**, 388–97.

Broussard, W. and M. Grossman (1990), 'Legislation to Abate Pollution From Manure: The Dutch Approach', *North Carolina Journal of International Law and Commercial Regulation*, **15**, 86–114.

Brouwer, F.M., F.E. Godeschalk, P.J.G.J. Hellegers and H.J. Kelholt (1995), *Mineral Balances at the Farm Level in the European Union*, The Hague: Agricultural Economics Research Institute (LEI-DLO).

Cabe, R. and J. Herriges (1992), 'The Regulation of Nonpoint-Source Pollution Under Imperfect and Asymmetric Information', *Journal of Environmental Economics and Management*, **22**, 34–146.

Callan, S.J. and J.M. Thomas (1996), *Environmental Economics and Management: Theory Policy and Applications*, Chicago: Irwin.

Cameron, D.M. (1990), 'Controlling Poison Runoff', *Environment*, **32**, 43–5.

Caswell, M., E. Lichtenberg and D. Zilberman (1990), 'The Effects of Pricing Policies on Water Conservation and Drainage', *American Journal of Agricultural Economics*, **72**, 883–90.

Chesapeake Bay Program (1995), *The State of the Chesapeake Bay 1995*, printed for the Chesapeake Bay Program by the US Environmental Protection Agency.

Chesters, G. and L. Schierow (1985), 'A Primer on Nonpoint Pollution', *Journal of Soil and Water Conservation*, **40**, 9–13.

Coburn, J. (1994), 'Cleaning Up Urban Stormwater: The Storm Drain Stenciling Approach (Or Getting to the Nonpoint Source)', *Journal of Soil and Water Conservation*, **49**, 312–16.

Cropper, M.L., W.N. Evans, J.J. Bernardi, M.M. Duclas Soares and P.R. Portney (1992), 'The Determinants of Pesticide Regulation: Statistical Analysis of EPA Decision Making', *Journal of Political Economy*, **100**, 175–97.

Crutchfield, S.R., D. Letson and A.S. Malik (1994), 'Feasibility of Point-Nonpoint Source Trading for Managing Agricultural Pollutant Loadings to Coastal Waters', *Water Resources Research*, **30**, 2825–36.

Darwin, R.F. (1992), 'Natural Resources and the Marshallian Effects of Input-Reducing Technological Changes', *Journal of Environmental Economics and Management*, **23**, 201–15.

Dewees, D. (1992), 'Tort Law and the Deterrence of Environmental Pollution', in T.H. Tietenberg (ed.), *Innovation in Environmental Policy: Economic and Legal Aspects of Recent Developments in Environmental Enforcement and Liability*, Cheltenham: Edward Elgar.

Dietz, F.J. and N.J.P. Hoogervorst (1991), 'Toward a Sustainable and Efficient Use of Manure in Agriculture: The Dutch Case', *Environmental and Resource Economics*, **1**, 313–32.

Dinham, B. (1993), *The Pesticide Hazard: A Global Health and Environmental Audit*, London: Zed Books.

Dinar, A., K.C. Knapp and J. Letey (1989), 'Irrigation Water Pricing to Reduce and Finance Subsurface Drainage Disposal', *Agricultural Water Management*, **16**, 155–71.

Dosi, C. and M. Moretto (1993), 'NPS Pollution, Information Asymmetry, and the Choice of Time Profile for Environmental Fees', in C.S. Russell and J.F. Shogren (eds),

Theory, Modeling and Experience in the Management of Nonpoint-Source Pollution, Dordrecht: Kluwer Academic Publishers.

Dosi, C. and M. Moretto (1994), 'Nonpoint Source Externalities and Polluter's Site Quality Standards Under Incomplete Information', in T. Tomasi and C. Dosi (eds), *Nonpoint Source Pollution Regulation: Issues and Policy Analysis*, Dortrecht: Kluwer Academic Publishers.

Dubgaard, A. (1994), 'The Danish Environmental Programs: An Assessment of Policy Instruments and Results', in T.L. Napier, S.M. Camboni and S.A. El-Swaify (eds), *Adopting Conservation on the Farm*, Ankeny, Iowa: Soil and Water Conservation Society.

Duda, A.M. (1993), 'Addressing Nonpoint Sources of Water Pollution Must Become an International Priority', *Water Science and Technology*, **28**, 3–5.

Duda, A.M. and R.J. Johnson (1985), 'Cost Effective Targeting of Agricultural Non-point Source Pollution Controls', *Journal of Soil and Water Conservation*, **40**, 108–11.

Eiswerth, M.E. (1993), 'Regulatory/Economic Instruments for Agricultural Pollution: Accounting for Input Substitution', in C.S. Russell and J.F. Shogren (eds), *Theory, Modeling and Experience in the Management of Nonpoint-Source Pollution*, Dordrecht: Kluwer Academic Publishers.

Elmore, T., J. Jaksch and D. Downing (1985), 'Point/Nonpoint Source Trading Programs for the Dillon Reservoir and Planned Extensions for Other Areas', in *Perspectives on Nonpoint Source Pollution*, Washington, DC: US Environmental Protection Agency.

Fawcett, R.S., B.R. Christensen and D.P. Tierney (1994), 'The Impact of Conservation Tillage on Pesticide Runoff Into Surface Water: A Review and Analysis', *Journal of Soil and Water Conservation*, **49**, 126–35.

Feather, P.M. and G. Amacher (1993), 'Role of Information in the Adoption of Best Management Practices for Water Quality Improvement', *Agricultural Economics* **11**, 159–70.

Feather, P.M. and J. Cooper (1995), *Voluntary Incentives for Reducing Agricultural Nonpoint Source Water Pollution*, US Department of Agriculture, Economic Research Service, Agriculture Information Bulletin No. 716, Washington, DC: Government Printing Office.

Fisher, A. (1991), 'Risk Communication Challenges', *Risk Analysis*, **11**, 173–9.

Floyd, D.W. and M.A. McLeod (1993), 'Regulation and Perceived Compliance: Nonpoint Pollution Control Programs in Four States', *Journal of Forestry*, **91**, 41–7.

Fontein, P.F., G.J. Thijssen, J.R. Magnus and J. Dijk (1994), 'On Levies to Reduce the Nitrogen Surplus: The Case of the Dutch Pig Farm', *Environmental and Resource Economics*, **4**, 445–78.

Forsund, F. and S. Strom (1980), *Miljo Og Ressurs Okonomi*, Oslo: Universitets Forlaget.

Fox, G., A. Weersink, G. Sarwar, S. Duff and B. Deen (1991), 'Comparative Economics of Alternative Agricultural Production Systems: A Review', *Northeastern Journal of Agricultural and Resource Economics*, **20**, 124–42.

Freeman, M. (1990), 'Water Pollution Policy', in P. Portney (ed.), *Policies for Environmental Protection*, Washington, DC: Resources for the Future.

Gardner, B.L. (1990), *The Economics of Agricultural Policies*, New York: McGraw-Hill.

Goldin, I. and O. Knudsen (eds) (1990), *Agricultural Trade Liberalization: Implications for Developing Countries*, Paris: Organization for Economic Cooperation and Development.

Goldin, I., O. Knudsen and D. van der Mensbrugghe (1993), *Trade Liberalisation: Global Economic Implications*, Paris: Organization for Economic Cooperation and Development.

Greenfield, R. (1985), 'Controlling Nonpoint Sources of Pollution – The Federal Legal Framework and the Alternative of Nonfederal Action', in *Perspectives of Nonpoint Source Pollution*, EPA 440/5–855–001, US EPA.

Gren, I.M. (1994), 'Cost Efficient Pesticide Reductions: The Case of Sweden', *Environmental and Resource Economics*, **4**, 279–93.

Griffin, R.C. and D.W. Bromley (1983), 'Agricultural Runoff as a Nonpoint Externality: A Theoretical Development', *American Journal of Agricultural Economics*, **70**, 37–49.

Hahn, R. (1989), 'Economic Prescriptions for Environmental Problems: How the Patient Followed the Doctors Orders', *Journal of Economic Perspectives*, **3**, 95–114.

Harrington, W., A.J. Krupnick and H.M. Peskin (1985), 'Policies for Nonpoint Water Pollution', *Journal of Soil and Water Conservation*, **40**, 27–32.

Helfand, G.E. and B.W. House (1995), 'Regulating Nonpoint Source Pollution Under Heterogeneous Conditions', *American Journal of Agricultural Economics*, **77**, 1024–32.

Herriges, J.R., R. Govindasamy and J. Shogren (1994), 'Budget-Balancing Incentive Mechanisms', *Journal of Environmental Economics and Management*, **27**, 275–85.

Holmström, B. (1982), 'Moral Hazard in Teams', *Bell Journal of Economics*, **13**, 324–40.

Holtermann, S. (1976), 'Alternative Tax Systems to Correct for Externalities and the Efficiency of Paying Compensation', *Economimca*, **46**, 1–16.

Hrubovcak, J., M. Le Blanc and J. Miranowski (1989), 'Limitations in Evaluating Environmental and Agricultural Policy Coordination Benefits', *American Economic Review*, **80**, 208–12.

Huang, W. and M. Le Blanc (1994), 'Market-based Incentives For Addressing Non-point Water Quality Problems: A Residual Nitrogen Tax Approach', *Review of Agricultural Economics*, **16**, 427–40.

Jackson, D.R. and H.N. Flippo (undated), *Development of Technical Procedures for Managing Nonpoint Source Pollution*, prepared for the Susquehanna River Basin Commission, SRB Publication No. 156.

Jaffe, A.B., S.R. Peterson, P.R. Portney and R.N. Stavins (1995), 'Environmental Regulation and the Competitiveness of U.S. Manufacturing: What Does the Evidence Tell Us?', *Journal of Economic Literature*, **23**, 132–63.

Just, R.E. and G.C. Rausser (1992), 'Environmental and Agricultural Policy Linkages and Reforms in the United States Under GATT', *American Journal of Agricultural Economics*, **74**, 766–74.

Kemp, R., X. Olsthoorn, F. Oosterhuis and H. Verbruggen (1992), 'Supply and Demand Factors of Cleaner Technologies: Some Empirical Evidence', *Environmental and Resource Economics*, **2**, 615–34.

Kim, C.S., J. Hostetler and G. Amacher (1993), 'The Regulation of Groundwater Quality with Delayed Responses', *Water Resources Research*, **29**, 1369–77.

Kneese, A.V. and B.T. Bower (1979), *Environmental Quality and Residuals Management*, Baltimore: Johns Hopkins University Press for Resources for the Future Inc.

Krueger, A.O., M. Schiff and A. Valdés (1992), *The Political Economy of Agricultural Pricing Policy, Vols. 1–5*, Baltimore: Johns Hopkins University Press.

Laughland, D., J. Shortle and W. Musser (1995), 'Nonpoint Pollution Control in a Second Best World', presented at the annual meeting of the American Agricultural Economics Association, Indianapolis, Indiana.

Lee, L.K. (1992), 'A Perspective on the Economic Impacts of Reducing Agricultural Chemical Use', *American Journal of Alternative Agriculture*, **7**, 82–8.

Lee, J.G., S.B. Lovejoy and D.B. Beasley (1985), 'Soil Loss Reduction in Finely Creek, Indiana: An Economic Analysis of Alternative Policies', *Journal of Soil Conservation*, **40**, 132–5.

Letson, D. (1992), 'Point/Nonpoint Source Trading: An Interpretive Survey', *Natural Resources Journal*, **32**, 219–32.

Letson, D., S. Crutchfield and A.S. Malik (1993), 'Point/Nonpoint Source Trading for Controlling Pollutant Loadings to Coastal Waters: A Feasibility Study', in C.S. Russell and J.F. Shogren (eds), *Theory, Modeling and Experience in the Management of Nonpoint-Source Pollution*, Dordrecht: Kluwer Academic Publishers.

Leuck, D.J. (1993), *Policies to Reduce Nitrate Pollution in the European Community and Possible Effects on Livestock Production*, Washington, DC: US Department of Agriculture, Economic Research Service Staff Report No. AGES 9318.

Lichtenberg, E. (1992), 'Alternative Approaches to Pesticide Regulation', *Northeastern Journal of Agricultural and Resource Economics*, **21**, 83–92.

Lichtenberg, E., I. Strand and B.V. Lessley (1993), 'Subsidizing Agricultural Nonpoint Pollution Control: Cost-Sharing and Technical Assistance', in C.S. Russell and J.F. Shogren (eds), *Theory, Modeling and Experience in the Management of Nonpoint-Source Pollution*, Dordrecht: Kluwer Academic Publishers.

Lichtenberg, E., D. Zilberman and K.T. Bogen (1989), 'Regulating Environmental Health Risks Under Uncertainty: Groundwater Contamination in Florida', *Journal of Environmental Economics and Management*, **17**, 22–34.

Logan, T.J. (1993), 'Agricultural Best Management Practices for Water Pollution Control: Current Issues', *Agriculture, Ecosystems and Environment*, **46**, 223–31.

Lopes, L.L. (1992), 'Risk Perception and the Perceived Public', in D. Bromley and S. Segerson (eds), *The Social Response to Environmental Risk: Policy Formation in an Age of Uncertainty*, Dordrecht: Kluwer Academic Publishers.

McSweeny, W.T. and J.S. Shortle (1990), 'Probabilistic Cost Effectiveness in Agricultural Nonpoint Pollution Control,' *Southern Journal of Agricultural Economics*, **22**, 95–104.

Mäler, K.G. (1974), *Environmental Economics: A Theoretical Inquiry*, Baltimore: Johns Hopkins University Press for Resource For the Future, Inc.

Malik, A.S., B.A. Larson and M.O. Ribaudo (1994), 'Economic Incentives for Agricultural Nonpoint Pollution Control', *Water Resources Bulletin*, **30**, 471–80.

Makik, A.S., D. Letson and S. Crutchfield (1993), 'Point/Nonpoint Source Trading of Pollution Abatement: Choosing the Right Trading Ratio', *American Journal of Agricultural Economics*, **75**, 959–67.

Menell, P. (1991), 'The Limitations of Legal Institutions for Addressing Environmental Risk', *The Journal of Economic Perspectives*, **5**, 93–114.

Milon, J.W. (1987), 'Optimizing Nonpoint Source Controls in Water Quality', *Water Resources Bulletin*, **23**, 387–96.

Miranowski, J.A., J. Hrubovcak and J. Sutton (1989), 'The Effects of Commodity Programs on Resource Use', in R.E. Just and N.E. Bockstael (eds), *Commodity and Resource Policies in Agricultural Systems*, Berlin: Springer Verlag.

Munasinghe, M. and W. Cruz (1995), *Economywide Policies and the Environment: Lessons from Experience*, World Bank Environment Paper No. 10, Washington, DC: World Bank.

Musser, W., J.S. Shortle, K. Kreahling, B. Roach, W. Huang, D. Beegle and R.H. Fox (1995), 'An Economic Analysis of Corn Nitrogen Test for Pennsylvania Corn', *Review of Agricultural Economics*, **17**, 25–35.

National Research Council (1989), *Alternative Agriculture*, Washington, DC: National Academy Press.

National Research Council (1991), *Sustainable Agriculture Research and Education in the Field*, Washington, DC: National Academy Press.

National Research Council (1994), *Soil and Water Quality: An Agenda for Agriculture*, Washington, DC: National Academy Press.

Nichols, A.L. (1984), *Targeting Economic Incentives for Environmental Protection*, Cambridge Mass.: MIT Press.

Norton, N.A., T.T. Phipps and J.J. Fletcher (1994), 'Role of Voluntary Programs in Agricultural Nonpoint Pollution Policy', *Contemporary Economic Policy*, **12**, 113–21.

Oates, W. (1994), 'Green Taxes: Can We Protect the Environment and Improve the Tax System at the Same Time?', *Southern Economic Journal*, 915–22.

OECD (1986), *Water Pollution by Fertilizers and Pesticides*, Paris: Organization for Economic Cooperation and Development.

OECD (1989), *Agricultural and Environmental Policies: Opportunities for Integration*, Paris: Organization for Economic Cooperation and Development.

OECD (1991), *The State of the Environment*, Paris: Organization for Economic Cooperation and Development.

OECD (1993), *Agricultural and Environmental Policy Integration: Recent Progress and New Directions*, Paris: Organization for Economic Cooperation and Development.

OECD (1994a), *Environmental Taxes in OECD Countries*, Paris: Organization for Economic Cooperation and Development.

OECD (1994b), *Towards Sustainable Agricultural Production: Cleaner Technologies*, Paris: Organization for Economic Cooperation and Development.

Palmer, K., W.E. Oates and P.R. Portney (1995), 'Tightening Environmental Standards: The Benefit-Cost or No-Cost Paradigm', *Journal of Economic Literature*, **9**, 119–32.

Park, W.M. and L.A. Shabman (1982), 'Distributional Constraints on Acceptance of Nonpoint Pollution Controls', *American Journal of Agricultural Economics*, **64**, 455–62.

Pettersson, O. (1994), 'Reduced Pesticide Use in Scandinavia Agriculture', *Critical Reviews in Plant Sciences*, **13**, 43–55.

Phipps, T.T. (1991), 'Commercial Agriculture and The Environment: An Evolutionary Perspective', *Northeastern Journal of Agricultural and Natural Resource Economics*, **20**, 143–50.

Plott, C.R. (1966) 'Externalities and Corrective Taxes,' *Economica*, **33**, 84–7.

Porter, M.E. and C. van der Linde (1995), 'Toward a New Conception of the Environment-Competitiveness Relationship', *Journal of Economic Literature*, **9**, 97–118.

Puckett, L.J. (1995), 'Identifying Major Sources of Nutrient Water Pollution', *Environmental Science and Technology*, **29**, 408A–414A.

Rasmusen, E. (1987), 'Moral Hazard in Risk Averse Teams', *Rand Journal of Economics*, **18**, 428–35.

Ribaudo, M.O. (1986), 'Considerations of Offsite Impacts in Targeting Soil Conservation Programs', *Land Economics*, **62**, 402–11.

Ribaudo, M.O. (1989), *Water Quality Benefits from the Conservation Reserve Program*, US Department of Agriculture, Agricultural Economic Report No. 606.

Roberts, M. and S. Spence (1976), 'Effluent Charges and Licenses Under Uncertainty', *Journal of Public Economics*, **5**, 193–208.

Russell, C.S. (1993). 'Foreword', in C.S. Russell and J.F. Shogren (eds), *Theory, Modeling and Experience in the Management of Nonpoint-Source Pollution*, Dordrecht: Kluwer Academic Publishers.

Schnitkey, G.D. and M. Miranda (1993), 'The Impacts of Pollution Controls on Livestock–Crop Producers', *Journal of Agricultural and Resource Economics*, **18**, 25–36.

Segerson, K. (1988), 'Uncertainty and Incentives for Nonpoint Pollution Control', *Journal of Environmental Economics and Management* **15**, 88–98.

Segerson, K. (1990), 'Liability for Groundwater Contamination from Pesticides', *Journal of Environmental Economics and Management*, **19**, 227–43.

Segerson, K. (1995), 'Liability and Penalty Structures in Policy Design', in D.W. Bromley (ed.), *The Handbook of Environmental Economics*, Cambridge, Mass.: Basil Blackwell.

Shabman, L. and P. Norris (1987), 'Coordinating Point and Nonpoint Control of Nutrient Pollution: Prospects for a Virginia Case Application', working paper SP-87-10, Department of Agricultural Economics, Virginia Polytechnic Institute and State University.

Shogren, J.F. (1993), 'Reforming Nonpoint Pollution Policy', in C.S. Russell and J.F. Shogren (eds), *Theory, Modeling and Experience in the Management of Nonpoint-Source Pollution*, Dordrecht: Kluwer Academic Publishers.

Shogren, J.F. (1995), 'Economic Incentives for Reduced Pesticide Use', in A. Weersink and J. Livernois (eds), *Potential Applications of Economic Instruments to Address Selected Environmental Problems in Canadian Agriculture*, Environmental Bureau, Agriculture and Agri-Food Canada.

Shogren, J.F., J.A. Herriges and R. Govindasamy (1993), 'Limits to Environmental Bonds', *Ecological Economics*, 109–33.

Shortle, J.S. (1984), 'The Use of Estimated Pollution Flows in Agricultural Pollution Control Policy: Implications for Abatement and Policy Instruments', *Northeastern Journal of Agricultural and Resource Economics*, **13**, 277–84.

Shortle, J.S. (1987), 'The Allocative Implications of Comparisons Between the Marginal Costs of Point and Nonpoint Source Pollution Abatement', *Northeastern Journal of Agricultural and Resource Economics*, **17**, 17–23.

Shortle, J.S. (1990), 'The Allocative Efficiency Implications of Abatement Cost Comparisons', *Water Resources Research*, **26**, 793–7.

Shortle, J.S. (1996), 'Environmental Federalism and the Control of Water Pollution from US Agriculture: Is the Current Allocation of Responsibilities Between National and Local Authorities About Right?', in J.B. Braden, H. Folmer and T.S. Ulen (eds), *Environmental Policy with Political and Economic Integration*, Cheltenham: Edward Elgar.

Shortle, J.S. and J.W. Dunn. (1986), 'The Relative Efficiency of Agricultural Source Water Pollution Control Policies', *American Journal of Agricultural Economics*, **68**, 668–77.

Shortle, J. and J. Miranowski. (1987), 'Soil Erosion: Is It Socially Excessive?', *Journal of Environmental Economics and Management*, **14**, 99–111.

Shortle, J.S. and D.G. Abler (1994), 'Incentives for Nonpoint Pollution Control', in T. Tomasi and C. Dosi (eds), *Nonpoint Source Pollution Regulations: Issues and Analysis*, Dordrecht: Kluwer Academic Publishers.

Shortle, J.S. and A. Laughland (1994), 'Impacts of Taxes to Reduce Agrichemical Use When Farm Policy is Endogenous', *Journal of Agricultural Economics*, **45**, 2–14.

Skea J. (1995), 'Environmental Technology', chapter 17, in H. Folmer, H.L. Gabel and H. Opschoor (eds), *Principles of Environmental and Resource Economics: A Guide for Students and Decision Makers*, Cheltenham: Edward Elgar.

Smith, V.K. (1992), 'Environmental Risk and Valuation: Conventional versus Prospective Reference Theory', in D. Bromley and S. Segerson (eds), *The Social Response to*

Environmental Risk: Policy Formation in an Age of Uncertainty, Dordrecht: Kluwer Academic Publishers.

Stevens, B. (1988), 'Fiscal Implications of Effluent Charges and Input Taxes', *Journal of Environmental Economics and Management*, **15**, 285–96.

Swinton, S.M. and D.S. Clark (1994), 'Farm-Level Evaluation of Alternative Policy Approaches to Reduce Nitrate Leaching from Midwest Agriculture', *Agricultural and Resource Economics Review*, **23**, 66–74.

Thrupp, L. (1988), 'Pesticides and Policies: Approaches to Pest-Control Dilemmas in Nicaragua and Costa Rica', *Latin American Perspectives*, **15**, 37–70.

Tolley, G.S. and V. Thomas (eds) (1987), *The Economics of Urbanization and Urban Policies in Developing Countries*, Washington, DC: World Bank.

Tomasi, T., K. Segerson and J.B. Braden (1994), 'Issues in the Design of Incentive Schemes for Nonpoint Source Pollution Control', in T. Tomasi and C. Dorsi (eds), *Nonpoint Source Pollution Regulation: Issues and Policy Analysis*, Dortrecht: Kluwer Academic Publishers.

US Department of Agriculture, Economic Research Service (1994), *Estimates of Producer and Consumer Subsidy Equivalents: Government Intervention in Agriculture, 1982–92*, Statistical Bulletin No. 913, Washington, DC: Government Printing Office.

US Environmental Protection Agency (1994), *National Water Quality Inventory: 1992 Report to Congress*, EPA841-R-94-001.

US Office of Technology Assessment (1995), *Targeting Environmental Priorities in Agriculture: Performing Program Strategies*, Washington, DC: US Government Printing Office, OTA-ENV-640.

Vandeman, A., J. Fernandez-Cornejo, S. Jan and B.H. Lin (1994), *Adoption of Integrated Pest Management in US Agriculture*, US Department of Agriculture, Economic Research Service, Information Bulletin No. 707, Washington, DC: Government Printing Office.

Van Kooten, G.C. and A. Schmitz (1992), 'Preserving Waterfowl Habitat on the Canadian Prairies: Economic Incentives Versus Moral Suasion', *American Journal of Agricultural Economics*, **74**, 79–89.

Varian, H.R. (1992), *Microeconomic Analysis*, New York: W.W. Norton.

Weinberg, A.C. (1990), 'Reducing Agricultural Pesticide Use in Sweden', *Journal of Soil and Water Conservation*, **45**, 610–13.

Weinberg, M., C.L. King and J.E. Wilen (1993a), 'Water Markets and Water Quality', *American Journal of Agricultural Economics*, **75**, 278–91.

Weinberg, M., C.L. Kling and J.E. Wilen (1993b), 'Analysis of Policy Options for the Control of Agricultural Pollution in California's San Joaquin Basin', in C.S. Russell and J.F. Shogren (eds), *Theory, Modeling and Experience in the Management of Nonpoint-Source Pollution*, Dordrecht: Kluwer Academic Publishers.

Weitzman, M. (1974), 'Prices versus Quantities', *Review of Economics and Statistics*, **41**, 477–91.

Wetzstein, M.E. and T.J. Centner (1992), 'Regulating Agricultural Contamination of Groundwater Through Strict Liability and Negligence Legislation', *Journal of Environmental Economics and Management*, **22**, 1–11.

Williamson, J.G. (1988), 'Migration and Urbanization', in H. Chenery and T.N. Srinivasan (eds), *Handbook of Development Economics, vol. 1*, Amsterdam: North-Holland.

Wischmeier, Walter H. and Dwight D. Smith (1978), *Predicting Rainfall Erosion Losses: A Guide to Conservation Planning*, Agriculture Handbook 537, Washington, DC: US Department of Agriculture.

World Bank (1992), *World Development Report 1992: Development and the Environment*, New York: Oxford University Press.

World Resources Institute (1988), *World Resources 1988–89: An Assessment of the Resource Base that Supports the Global Economy*, Washington, DC: World Resources Institute.

Xepapadeas, A. (1991), 'Environmental Policy Under Imperfect Information: Incentives and Moral Hazard', *Journal of Environmental Economics Management*, **20**, 113–26.

Xepapadeas, A. (1992), 'Environmental Policy Design and Dynamic Nonpoint Source Pollution', *Journal of Environmental Economics Management*, **23**, 22–39.

Xepapadeas, A. (1994), 'Controlling Environmental Externalities: Observability and Optimal Policy Rules', in T. Tomasi and C. Dosi (eds), *Nonpoint Source Pollution Regulation: Issues and Policy Analysis*, Dortrecht: Kluwer Academic Publishers.

Zilberman, D., A. Schmitz, G. Casterline, E. Lichtenberg and J.B. Siebert (1991), 'The Economics of Pesticide Use and Regulation', *Science*, **253**, 518–22.

6. Pricing what is priceless: a status report on non-market valuation of environmental resources

V. Kerry Smith[1]

INTRODUCTION

The theory and performance of the methods used for non-market valuation have been major preoccupations of environmental economists over the past decade.[2] This attention has been explained by a composite of public policy needs and the litigation-based interest arising from natural resource damage assessments (in the United States).[3] While there is little doubt that these two areas have provided important demands for valuation information, it may also be useful to consider non-market valuation in the context of what might be described as the 'larger landscape' of resource allocation decisions. Environmental resources, especially those providing amenities, seem to have become more scarce over the last half of this century. Most of this change has been due to the forces of economic growth raising incomes of households in more areas around the globe and, as a result, increasing their demands for the environmental resources embodied in local living environments and in resources supporting outdoor recreation. Both types of demands acknowledge that there are marketed goods and services demanded primarily when they can be combined with environmental amenities. Often, the quality of the environmental resources involved influences the economic value people place on these combinations of marketed and non-marketed resources. For example, estimates of the full expenditures on outdoor recreation activities that use environmental resources (including time and travel costs, but excluding lodging and food), would dwarf the gross domestic product (GDP) of a number of the developing nations. In the US alone, 270 million visitors are expected to use national parks and forests during the 1996 summer season.[4] As this sector continues to grow in significance, it should not be surprising that there is ever-increasing attention given to measures of the economic value of environmental resources.[5] These resources serve as the equivalent of essential inputs to each household's production of the outdoor recreational activities that would comprise an important part of the tourism sector.

To meet these needs, both the historically developed and newly developed countries have increased the restrictions on emissions leading to pollution and on land conversions that threaten natural environments. Pollution control requirements have created an economic sector whose product demands derive from these requirements. In developed economies, it is a growing component of the manufacturing sector and therefore also has a 'stake' in the indirect values assigned to environmental resources. Annual expenditures to control pollution in the developed world exceed the GDP of many developing countries.[6] These expenditures go to firms that develop, manufacture, and maintain environmental control equipment.

At a general level then one might interpret this interest as a reflection that the market-oriented systems around the world are being forced (by growing demands) to find ways of reflecting the economic values of environmental resources available outside markets in the decisions that are made about how they are used and protected.

This chapter provides a selective overview of what has been learned from efforts to develop monetary measures of the economic values for non-market environmental resources. It assumes a working knowledge of the theoretical principles underlying benefit measurement and highlights recent empirical developments in using indirect and direct methods for constructing these monetary measures. The first section outlines the typical objective – to measure willingness to pay for a specified change in some environmental resource – and then summarizes the approaches used by each method to accomplish this task. It provides a largely personal evaluation of what has been learned about the practice of using each method and concludes each subsection with a few suggestions for further research.

The next section considers two relatively new areas: calibration and conjoint analysis. Each has been proposed as offering insights (or approaches) that would improve upon existing methods for non-market valuation. The last section discusses how the uses of valuation estimates condition the way research is defined. It calls for different, less project oriented, approaches to research on benefit measurement.

MONETIZING ECONOMIC VALUES

Background

Beginning with the first edition of Freeman's *The Benefits of Environmental Improvement: Theory and Practice* in 1979, a variety of volumes have appeared in the intervening 17 years to enhance our overall understanding of the relationship between Hicksian and Marshallian measures of consumer surplus.[7]

The analytical definitions of monetary measures for the economic value of environmental resources usually treat these resources as rationed or quasi-fixed commodities. To define these measures more formally, assume q designates the amount of one such resource (or a vector of resources) that is (are) available to an individual. It is assumed to be outside an individual's direct choice in the conventional definitions of economic value. In later sections of this chapter this assumption is partially relaxed. Measures of economic value require that we observe people's choices, so our models will in fact assume some ability to select levels for q. As developed below, the interpretation and measurement of q has been often taken for granted.

In the literature as well as in the discussion of the concepts developed in the next few paragraphs, q will at times be referred to as an 'amount' of the environmental resource or as a quality dimension of an environmental resource. These practices can be confusing until we consider the same types of issues associated with marketed goods. Quantities of any commodity consumed by people should not be 'added up' unless they are exactly the same good. We encounter this issue when different types of the same commodity must be aggregated and these types vary in quality. Quantity and quality issues are interrelated. To adequately measure one it is essential to resolve how the other is measured and accounted for in any proposed quantity metric. At this stage in the development, having identified the issue, I will abstract from it, recall its relevance periodically and for now point out what is important about the role of q in the description of consumer behaviour. The definitions assume q (whether quantity or quality) is *outside* an individual's choice, and like each price will be treated as a parameter that affects choices.

The Hicksian willingness to pay (WTP) for an increase in one or more of these resources from q_0 to q_1 (with $q_1 > q_0$) is given in equation (6.1). $e(.)$ designates the function that describes the minimum expenditures necessary to obtain utility level, u_0, given the quasi-fixed commodities, q, and the vector of prices, p, for the marketed goods consumed by an individual. It describes how expenditures change with changes in any of these three determinants (including u).

$$\text{WTP} = e\,(p, q_0, u_0) - e\,(p, q_1, u_0) \tag{6.1}$$

The expenditure function cannot be estimated directly (Hausman, 1981), because the utility level realized in the baseline condition is not observed. Therefore it is convenient to recognize that this level of well-being is itself a function of the initial prices, initial level of environmental resource, q_0, and initial income (m_0).[8] Using this link (and the fact that $m_0 = e(p, q_0, u_0)$), we can rewrite (6.1) as equation (6.2) in terms of observable variables.

$$\text{WTP} = m_0 - e\ [p, q_1, v\ (p, q_0, m_0)] \tag{6.2}$$

where $v(p, q_0, m_0)$ is the indirect utility function evaluated for the baseline condition (i.e., p, q_0, m_0). Written in this form we see the arguments of equation (6.2) are, in principle, observable. WTP is not because q_1 is generally a proposed level, not one that has been realized. To measure WTP requires estimating what the expenditures with the environmental resource at the improved level would be. This is the point of any analysis of how people 'use' environmental resources.

In most policy applications we do not observe how specific individuals will react to an improvement in environmental quality. Thus, there may be no convenient way to observe the expenditures corresponding to $e(p, q_1, u_0)$ for the people whose WTP we wish to estimate. However, we may observe how *different* households have reacted to situations where the improved level of environmental quality was represented by q_1. For example, we might observe differences in households expenditures on health care associated with short-term morbidity episodes in areas with differing levels of air pollution. We could also consider the differences in distance travelled and other expenditures for specific types of recreation, for example sport fishing, for individuals in areas where the fishing opportunities (and quality) are different. Of course, as my examples suggest, they may also have different prices. In these circumstances, the restrictions we impose from economic theory become instrumental in using the choices across households to construct an estimate of the WTP. These types of assumptions are especially important for applications involving environmental resources because we rarely observe consumers confronting monetary trade-offs directly associated with these resources.

The second and equally important issue with this definition of WTP relates to the measurement of q. Writing it as either a scalar quantity or a vector in equations (6.1) and (6.2) gives the impression it can be readily measured in a well-defined metric that is understood by people in the terms to define q. In practice, we do not know how people perceive environmental resources or how different amounts should be represented to capture the way each person experiences them.

This issue does not arise for most market goods because the quantity measures can be defined from their prices. Developing a demand model for a particular brand of apples (e.g., Macintosh or Golden Delicious), for example, does not require understanding how people perceive the various types of apples. Rather we can observe how consumers respond to changes in their prices, using quantity measures as they have been defined in the pricing arrangements for these products.[9] If the needs of analysis are confined to understanding how a change in the price or income influences the quantity demanded (measured in these units), then incomplete information about how people perceive the 'amount of apples' becomes unimportant. To understand why one type of apple serves as a better substitute for another, or how demand would respond to a change in the attributes of a variety of apples, requires knowledge of these perceptions.[10] The existence of pricing rules allows for 'shortcuts' in the measures we accept as characterizing a consumer's preferences and is fundamental to the construction of quantity indexes.[11] As a rule, this advantage is not available for environmental resources. Indeed, it is fair to say that in many situations we don't have either quantity or price measures.

Finally, the last issue illustrated in equation (6.2) concerns the prospects for using assumptions about how q relates to private goods to estimate WTP. Substitution relationships are fundamental for measuring economic values. Trade-offs describe what each individual will give up to obtain something else and isolate a bound for an economic value.[12] As a result the linkages based on some form of substitution or complementarity between one or more private goods and the non-marketed environmental resource are the basis for non-market valuation.

Indirect Approaches for Non-Market Valuation – Theory

All monetary measures of economic value require a choice. Suppose, for example, we assume an individual could purchase an improvement in the environmental resource q from q_0 to q_1. If this $(q_1 - q_0)$ increment were offered for S dollars, then an individual's decision would isolate either a lower bound or an upper bound for the Hicksian WTP. We can see this by recognizing that a decision to make the purchase implies WTP must be greater than (or equal to) S, and one rejecting it implies that WTP must be less than S. For first choice, S isolates the lower bound, and the second (i.e., a rejection of the offer) an upper bound.

As a rule, we only observe choices involving private goods or services. Using them to estimate an individual's value for changes in a non-market environmental resource, that can be a public good, requires assumptions about how these choices were motivated by the resource. Bockstael and McConnell (1993) have noted the process of developing monetary measures of economic value requires the indirect methods to define two linked exchanges that compose each choice – one in an observable private good and one in the linked non-market environmental resource. We use the former (the private good) to reconstruct the implicit terms for the latter. The assumptions required for the Hicksian measures of the value can be described as establishing a correspondence between the Marshallian representation of the circumstances of the choice and measure of consumer surplus for the private good and the corresponding terms and surplus measure for the environmental resource.[13]

Table 6.1 Choice circumstances, models, and indirect methods for non-market valuation[a]

Method	Information observed	Information inputed	Behavioural model estimated	Link to WTP functions
Travel cost recreation demand	The quantity 'demanded' of a recreation sets measured as: a visit rate with aggregate data; a count of visits, or a single site selection for a specific trip with individual data	The price as the 'full' cost of using the recreation site; including the vehicle-related travel costs, access charges; on-site time costs; incremental costs of equipment and supplies directly related to activity	Demand or random utility model	[b] $x_i = \dfrac{-v_{p_i}}{v_m} = \left(\dfrac{-\dfrac{\partial WTP}{\partial p_i}}{1 + \dfrac{\partial WTP}{\partial m}} \right)$
Hedonic property (or wage) model	The housing price (or rent) for housing applications and the wage rate (hourly or annual) for wage models. Houses and jobs treated as differentiated goods so many different prices exist	People recognize attributes of houses; so equilibrium presumes no incentive to change; equilibrium assures that prices will be a function of attributes. Environmental resources enter as site specific amenities	Hedonic price (p_j) (or wage) function	[c] $-\dfrac{\partial p_j}{\partial q} = \dfrac{v_q}{v_m} = \left(\dfrac{\dfrac{\partial WTP}{\partial q}}{\dfrac{\partial WTP}{\partial m} - 1} \right)$
Averting behaviour (household production model)	An activity or actions that reflects implicit trade-off of costs to meet a specific objective such as improved air or water quality *experienced by the individual*	Quantity and incremental costs that were assumed to comprise the complete trade-off considered in deciding about the level of the averting or mitigating activity	Expenditure function or demand function for commodities (x_r) hypothesized to be involved in averting behaviour; direct link to marginal WTP when x_r is a perfect substitute for q	[c] $p_r \dfrac{\partial x_r}{\partial q} = \dfrac{v_q}{v_m} = \left(\dfrac{\dfrac{\partial WTP}{\partial q}}{\dfrac{\partial WTP}{\partial m} - 1} \right)$

Notes

[a] Subscripts to the indirect utility function refer to the partial derivative with respect to the identified argument, $v_q = \partial v/\partial q$.

[b] WTP refers to a different WTP function, one relevant to a change in access conditions: $\overline{WTP} = e(p^*, q_0, v(p_0, m_0)) - m_0$, with p^* = the choke price.

[c] WTP function relates to the one defined in equation (6.2).

Table 6.1 summarizes the information usually available, the information the analyst adds, and the link to the WTP model for each of the three indirect methods – travel cost, hedonic property value (and wage), and averting behaviour (household production) models. The last two columns in the table define the form of the function usually estimated, its relationship to conventional Marshallian measures for behaviour (through indirect utility function), and the connection to one type of willingness to pay function such as the one defined in equation (6.2). To use these choices to reconstruct measures of the monetary values requires enough information to isolate the WTP function. The first term in each of the expressions in the last column of Table 6.1 is usually observed. Assumptions about the other intermediate connections must be introduced to complete the connections. In the case of the travel cost model, for example, it is the demand function for trips to a recreation site. In this case, the objective is often to estimate the economic value of one of the site's characteristics such as water quality.

The restrictions to the WTP function implied by an assumption of weak complementarity between x_i and q provide one such example. In this case when $\partial WTP/\partial q$ is evaluated, at a price where $x_i = 0$ (the choke price), weak complementarity implies that the marginal WTP is zero. To interpret the specific implications of this result for Table 6.1, recall that equations (6.1) and (6.2) relate to the WTP for an improvement in q. If we considered the WTP for another type of change, say in the access conditions to a recreation site, the links would be different.[14] Moreover, if we impose a different relationship between the private good and q, the nature of what can be learned about the WTP function from observed behaviour changes. Prior restrictions are thus important, but they do not escape the fundamental dependency of these approaches on information about some type of choice.

Indirect Methods – Implementation and Performance

Travel cost

Two types of data have been instrumental in travel cost recreation demand studies. The early literature generally used aggregate origin zone data, where trips to a specific site from a given location (usually a county, but sometimes a distance or 'origin' zone, as envisioned in the original Hotelling (1947) letter) are related to round-trip distance (or distance scaled by a constant per mile cost factor). The trip is assumed to measure the quantity of the resource 'used' and was often measured relative to the population of the zone. Economic and demographic characteristics of the populations in each origin zone, as well as some substitution indexes for other recreation sites were 'attached' to each observation (as if they were relevant for the representative user in each zone). These data provided the basis for estimating site demand functions, both as individual demand equations and in systems of demand functions. While these early applications were 'successful' in developing plausible estimates for the price and income elasticities, they were also subject to concerns about using aggregate data under the mantel of a 'representative agent' argument.[15]

Individual records of recreational behaviour provide the second type of data. A record of problems with these data due to poor sampling procedures, infrequent consumption (of recreation trips), as well as the inherent complexity of the economic decisions involved, have made these applications a 'fertile' ground for advancing microeconometric methods. Initially borrowing from insights already developed in the models used in labour economics and modal choice decisions (for transportation applications), recreation applications are now leading other applications in their recognition of the important interaction between micro-theory and econometrics.[16] It is impossible to describe completely the full range of economic and econometric issues currently being discussed in this active literature. Instead, I have selected a few areas where research seems especially active.

Substitution and non-participation have been dominant concerns of the literature to date. Records of individual behaviour have usually been collected from on-site (which implies the surveys don't observe non-users and may over represent active users) or from surveys of user groups identified through licences, boat ownership, or some other eligibility criterion. Both surveys generally ask about recreation trips in a recent time period. For the former, that period usually includes the current trip so the quantity measure is a truncated random variable (at one). For the later, we do not learn how the state of environmental resources or the conditions of access influence people's decisions to become part of the sampled population (i.e., purchase a license, a boat, etc.).

Both types of surveys have had difficulty in either collecting information about substitutes or, when it has been collected, they have experienced empirical problems in incorporating substitutes' price and quality information into the analysis (see Smith, 1989).

In my opinion, most recreation economists, if polled, would likely identify some type of random utility model (RUM) as the preferred modelling strategy because it allows the effects of multiple sites (with different attributes) to be incorporated in a way that permits benefit measurement. Because of this judgement, this subsection considers some active research with the RUM approach.

The initial RUM applications focused on a single trip occasion and the selection of a recreation site for that trip. Each such decision was viewed as independent of other decisions. Preferences were described by a random, indirect utility function that hypothesized each individual would select the best site and then, conditional on that choice, make other allocation decisions (i.e., $v(p, q, m) = \text{Max}\,[V_i(p_i, q_i, m)\ i = 1,2, \ldots n]$, where p and q are assumed to be vectors that include the arguments p_i and q_i, $i = 1$ to n, with i indexing the recreation sites). Each conditional indirect utility function, V_i, is assumed to include an independent random error. This specification recognizes that we cannot describe people's recreation site choices perfectly. As a rule, the noise in the process is assumed to arise from the analyst's perspective. Usually (but not always), recreationists are assumed to know what they will do. This distinction is important because it affects the interpretation given to benefit measures from this model.

Selecting a Gumbel distribution allows a closed-form solution for the expression describing the probability any particular site(s) would be selected as in equation (6.3):[17]

$$\text{Prob}\,(\text{Max}\,(V_1, \ldots, V_n) = V_s) = \frac{\exp(\tilde{V}_s)}{\sum_j \exp(\tilde{V}_j)} \tag{6.3}$$

where $\tilde{V}_j$ is the nonstochastic component of v_j (i.e., $V_j = \tilde{V}_j + \varepsilon_j$) and this specification assumes ε_j follows an independent Gumbel error distribution.

From this basic form, the literature has considered a number of implementation and modelling questions, including the following issues:

- Because the simple RUM implies independence of irrelevant alternatives (IIA), nested models have been proposed as alternatives. In these specifications the Gumbel is replaced with a generalized extreme value distribution (McFadden, 1974). Models derived from this general structure consider an individual's choices in a sequence. For example, in Kaoru's (1995) model for sport fishing an individual is assumed to select a number of days for his (or her) fishing trip, then a region of the North Carolina coast, and then within the selected region a specific site. By sequencing the choices, the model restricts the nature of the substitution relationships among alternatives. A similar type of logic has been used in modelling substitution in the specification of preference or production functions with nested subfunctions. By separating commodities into specific subfunctions, these approaches control gross and net substitution elasticities and therefore the interrelationships among the commodities. The generalized extreme value function resembles a nested set of CES (constant elasticity of substitution) functions and constrains the substitution relationship among alternatives in an individual's choice set. Of course, they require some basis for developing the nesting structure and have been found to be sensitive to that structure as well as to the conditions required for the model to be consistent with constrained utility maximization (see Kaoru, 1995; Kling and Thompson,1996; and Kling and Herriges, 1995).

• The simple model's single trip orientation has led to efforts to expand the structure to repeated choice and sequential choice models, as well as to allow for the possibility of no trip being taken (see Morey, Shaw, and Rowe, 1991; Morey, Shaw, and Watson, 1993; and Parsons, 1991). Comparisons of the models using actual data sets imply highly variable benefit measures relative to conventional RUM formulations (see Liu, 1995; Kling and Thompson, 1996).

• The definition of the choice set and the specification of what is a site (especially when there is the possibility to aggregate across alternatives) have been found to be important influences on the benefit measures derived from RUM analyses (see Kaoru, Smith, and Liu, 1995; Parsons and Kealy, 1992; Parsons and Needelman, 1992; Feathers, 1994; and Parsons and Hauber, 1996).

• Developing seasonal measures of use and willingness to pay requires that either the RUM framework be specified in a way that links choices over time or that applications of the model for trip occasions be consistently related to the more conventional travel cost demand models that describe all trips taken in a season. Current discussion of this logic by Parsons and Kealy (1995), Feather, Hellerstein, and Tomasi (1995); Hausman, Leonard, and McFadden (1995) and Shonkwiler and Shaw (1996) have proposed, with varying levels of completeness, analytical descriptions of price and quantity index numbers derived from the models of site choice probabilities. The full implications of alternative definitions for the role of the time constraints in the definition of travel cost measures for these approaches have not been developed.[18]

Despite the fact that estimates of benefits from all versions of the RUM framework appear quite sensitive to strategic modelling decisions, enthusiasm remains high for continuing to base policy analyses on some type of RUM. The framework is attractive to practitioners because it *consistently* incorporates diverse sources of heterogeneous site characteristics. These characteristics provide the primary means to describe the status of the environmental resources supporting recreation uses. For example, in the case of recreational fishing, historic catch rates, emission loadings, contamination notices, as well as other proxy variables have served as the indicators of the quality of specific lakes, rivers, or areas along the coast that support this recreation. These would be difficult to include within standard travel cost demand models. Unlike cases where market prices are available, we cannot use some form of equilibrium condition linking prices of heterogeneous goods, such as the one underlying the hedonic price function, to estimate the marginal values of these features.[19]

One explanation for the sensitivity of the available results from these models to their assumptions is that considering the data generally available and the requirements for the valuation measures, it is clear that substantial prior information must be added to the models. These judgements are about: the functional forms assumed to characterize individual preferences, time horizons for choices, the assumed choice sequence (i.e., nesting), etc. Indeed, even in situations where extensive diaries can be assembled, there are limits to the details that can be reliably assembled. The only way to compensate for these informational limitations is to seek alternative sources of valuation information for the same resources.

This suggestion is not simply advocating 'more and better data'. Rather, my suggestion has a more practical goal. Travel cost demand models are developed to estimate use values for recreation sites or for characteristics of these sites. Given this goal, it seems reasonable to examine the potential for using other trade-offs involving the same sites or quality characteristics. It may be possible to use these related decisions jointly with models applied to trip-taking decisions in estimating the required values. By considering the other ways people adjust to the constraints it may be possible to isolate other substitutions that reveal the marginal value. The travel cost model relies on one type of trade-off involving the travel expenses and time required to acquire the services of recreational resources. People make others that have not been pursued in as much detail. For example, both fresh and sport fishing recreationists use boats. To the extent they purchase the boats (and subsequently maintain or upgrade them), these decisions can be expected to be influenced by the available recreational resources.[20] By maintaining a structural link (such as weak complementarity or perfect substitution) between the observable private good decisions and the environmental resource, it should be possible to recover from these decisions a measure of the economic value (due to use) of changes in the environmental resource even if they are made infrequently.[21]

My proposal is not simply for joint estimation, but calibrated assessments.[22] That is, consider using the valuation estimates from different trade-offs involving the same non-market resources with separate private goods to evaluate the benefit estimates implied by the RUM framework. To date, these strategies have been confined to linking travel cost and contingent valuation data (Cameron, 1992), or to the early efforts to evaluate contingent valuation estimates (see Brookshire *et al.*, 1982). In Cameron's application, both measures must be available for each individual. What is proposed here does not require this type of data because the objectives are more modest. Simple comparisons may help discriminate among the modelling assumptions.

A second type of composite strategy would exploit micro and aggregate data for the same recreational sites. Anderson, de Palma and Thisse (1988, 1992) have developed links between the simple RUM framework (expressed in terms of linear indirect utility functions) and demand functions for a representative individual. They have also shown the relationship for a constant elasticity of substitution specification for the representative consumer. This case directly links to a linear in the logarithms (of price and income) indirect utility specification for a simple RUM. More recently, Verboven (1996) has established this type of relationship for the cases involving the nested logit with linear indirect utility and the group constant elasticity of substitution utility specification for the representative agent's preferences.

These results permit consistent estimates of travel cost demand models based on aggregate, origin zone data (that relies on a representative agent model) to be connected to the results from RUM models developed with micro data. With this conceptual link, it is possible to calibrate findings from aggregate models to estimates based on surveys of users at the same sites.[23]

Hedonic price models
Hedonic price functions seem to provide one of the oldest and most durable of economists' methods for measuring consumers' responses to quality differentials. Waugh (1929) first used them to adjust prices for differences in the attributes of fresh vegetables. Tinbergen (1956) and Roy (1950) demonstrated that the framework described the conditions for equilibrium in the labour market with heterogeneous people and jobs. Applications for valuing air quality trace their origins to Ridker and Henning (1967). Using Table 6.1, the hedonic price function offers the most direct approach (largely free of specific assumptions about preferences) for measuring the marginal value of amenities (see Rosen, 1974). The equilibrium condition implies that the marginal price will measure the marginal rate of substitution between q and a numeraire good.

For the case of air pollution, the experience of numerous studies since Ridker and Henning confirms a significant negative relationship between air pollution and property values that holds over a wide range of conditions (Smith and Huang, 1993, 1995). Unfortunately, the recent research record ends largely with this finding of support. To my knowledge, no study has successfully estimated the WTP function as a second-stage model derived from the hedonic price functions. Zabel and Kiel's study (1994) provides the most recent attempt to implement a hedonic framework in a consistent way with measures of air pollution for multiple cities. They use a panel data framework to control for house and neighbourhood effects and focus on changes in air quality and their effects on changes in housing prices. The results yield both positive and negative estimates of air pollution's influence on property values. They do not support work on a second-stage model for the panel data base. Given the current understanding of the complexity of recovering estimates of the marginal WTP function from hedonic estimates (see Bartik, 1987; Epple, 1987; McConnell and Phipps, 1987; Palmquist, 1991), all of the original attempts to estimate the second-stage models would not meet conditions for identification. Moreover, they do not have the micro detail required to link the estimated marginal WTP to the economic and demographic characteristics of the households who purchased (or rented) the houses involved.

The primary focus of new research in this area has been on two issues. The first might be described as 'speciality' site-specific disamenities such as hazardous waste sites (Michaels and Smith, 1990; Kolhase, 1991; Kiel, 1995), incinerators (Kiel and McClain, 1995), odour due to private residences' proximity to hog farms (Palmquist, Roka and Vakim, forthcoming), shoreline erosion (Kriesel, Randall and Lichtkoppler, 1993; van de Verg and Lent, 1994), and others. The second uses the Rosen (1979) – Roback (1982) arguments for links between property value and wage markets to propose joint estimation of the marginal willingness to pay. A key application of the resulting estimates (suggested by Rosen, 1979) has been to use them to develop quality of life measures for locations.

Equation (6.4) reports an expression comparable to what is used to describe the proper 'joint market' analysis required to estimate the marginal value for a site-specific amenity (q_k):

$$\frac{\partial \mathrm{WTP}}{\partial q_k} = \frac{\partial r}{\partial q_k} - \theta_k \frac{\partial w}{\partial q_k} \qquad (6.4)$$

where r is the land rent, w is the wage rate under same time horizon as the land rent, and θ_k is a measure of exposure to amenity q_k at the job (i.e., wage related measure, q_k^w, is linked to q_k as $q_k^w = \theta_k \cdot q_k$). Quality of life (QOL) indexes are derived from the marginal WTP as a simple composite of the site specific amenities as in equation (6.5):

$$\mathrm{QOL}_i = \sum_j \frac{\partial \mathrm{WTP}}{\partial q_j} \cdot q_{ji} \qquad (6.5)$$

This formulation holds the function computing marginal WTP for each site-specific attribute constant across locations assuming a cross-city equilibrium as in Blomquist, Berger and Hoehn (1988). Land rents are positively affected by desirable amenities (i.e. $\partial r/\partial q_k > 0$ if q_k is desirable) and wages are negatively impacted (i.e. $\partial w\partial/q_k < 0$) so their contributions in equation (6.4) are both positive (after adjusting for the sign in the wage equation).

There are any number of difficulties that one could raise with the Rosen–Roback structure. The specific equilibrium result follows from the assumption that residential location and job are changed simultaneously when an individual adjusts location to improve site-specific amenities. This ignores the basic idea that households also move within larger communities to improve housing and site-related amenities. This was the original formulation and test of the Tiebout (1956) model (see Oates, 1969). Such changes do not require job changes. How does the marginal household evaluate its choices to obtain site-related amenities (and to avoid the disamenities)? It is not clear that the 'site/job story' is necessary.

To implement their framework we must have comparable data for both housing (i.e., land rents) and wages across cities. There is considerable evidence suggesting the existence of sub-markets for housing within a single large city, so the assumption that a national housing market determines site amenities seems untenable.[24] The same comment, though with less clear-cut evidence, applies to labour markets and the wage hedonic equation.[25]

If we accept the prospects for different adjustment processes, this does not invalidate the concept of a quality of life index. It does lead to questions about a single set of weights across sites and the substitution of estimates for $\partial w/\partial q_j$ from a framework like the one used in labour economics to investigate the structure of wages into equation (6.4).

More generally, several research issues do follow from this line of research. First, we might consider QOL as a welfare index (Diewert, 1993). This would require considering a more traditional approach for defining index numbers for QOL measures based on the *level* of the Hicksian expenditure function rather than a simple first-order approximation. The resulting $\tilde{QOL}_i$ would then be consistent with the welfare theoretic interpretation of price indexes as in (6.6):

$$\tilde{QOL}_i = \frac{e(p_i, q_{1i}, ..., q_{Ki}, \bar{u})}{e(p_N, q_{1N}, ..., q_{KN}, \bar{u})} \tag{6.6}$$

where the subscript N identifies a reference site N. It is worth noting that $e(.)$ could be interpreted as a partial expenditure function (i.e., in terms of exogenous income required to realize a given utility level, recognizing people make commodity as well as labour/leisure choices with given prices and wage rates as in Just, Hueth and Schmitz (1982) – in this case, local wage rates would be included as one of the determinants of $e(.)$ if the joint supply site/job model is not used). The importance of this distinction is that we don't escape the task of distinguishing the marginal willingness to pay function from the composite of marginal price relationships describing equilibria in housing and labour markets. To isolate the marginal WTP requires that there be sufficient information to separate preference from supply influences in the joint determination of the equilibrium. That is, consistency in *both* QOL indexes and benefit measures requires that we go beyond the estimates of marginal WTP at a single equilibrium.

A second issue follows from considering other approaches households might select to adjust to disamenities associated with their residences. Following the basic logic I used to begin this discussion (i.e., that indirect methods hunt for substitution and complementarity relationships with other private goods to construct monetary measures of the economic value of non-market goods), we might consider how these other types of adjustments influence the interpretation of the hedonic price equation. The opportunities for substituting related resources should influence the trade-offs we observe in markets. This offers an explanation for Clark and Kahn's (1989) decision to include a wide range of recreational resources at some distance from a household's residential location as sources of compensating differentials in their wage models. It does not tell how to determine the geographic extent or character of the resources that serve as substitutes for the ones available as the site-specific amenities.

There are two aspects of the Rosen–Roback analysis that should be distinguished. The first concerns the ways households adjust to site-specific amenities. It is central to most indirect methods for non-market valuation. The criticism raised with this dimension of the Rosen–Roback framework is that households are assumed to make simultaneous housing and job decisions. While we can acknowledge that there may be multiple opportunities for adjustment, this does not mean they are relevant to *all* individuals. Requiring that all would meet Rosen and Roback's proposed link would seem implausible. Indeed, existing literature suggests that it is possible to use the heterogeneity in individual circumstances to test aspects of the model. For example, retired households should not be influenced by the wage effects, and have the opportunity to realize site-specific amenities without experiencing the wage reductions. Graves and Waldman (1991) developed such an analysis and found direct support for a focus exclusively on housing market conditions for these types of households.

Equally important are those whose jobs require frequent travel to locations with considerable access to amenities (e.g. airline pilots, travelling sales personnel, telecommuters, etc.) and may select residences to economize on site rents. Other individuals with travel routes that do not provide the amenities or the time to enjoy them will consider the residential amenities where they live and can do so free from the lower wages paid by 'local' employers. Of course, these hypotheses rely on these types of individuals' wages being set independent of site-specific amenities. More generally, migration behaviour should be linked to the same factors affecting equilibria in the housing and labour markets and may offer opportunities for the types of calibrating evaluations discussed in the subsection on travel cost demand models.

The second aspect of the Rosen–Roback model concerns the determination of equilibrium prices in housing and wage markets. If their description offers a reasonable approximation, then we would expect the equilibrium prices and wages to be jointly determined. This can be expected to compound the complexity of identifying marginal willingness to pay functions from the information available in the marginal price and wage functions.

Averting behaviour models

Models to describe averting or mitigating behaviour can be developed using a household production framework that postulates a set of activities households can adopt to improve the amenities they experience. At one level, the hedonic model could be considered as one such adjustment – moving to change amenities. For the most part, the averting approaches envisioned in these models are not as 'drastic' and usually involve smaller resource or time reallocations. Ridker's (1967) original proposal suggested that the soiling effects of air pollution would require increased household cleaning activities to maintain the same level of cleanliness. We could also think of air-conditioning homes and cars to avoid air pollution, water filters or public water supplies as responses to avoid contamination of private sources of water, and other types of adjustments as examples (see Harrington and Portney, 1987).

To link the observed changes in expenditures or activities to Hicksian welfare measures requires further assumptions. Perfect substitution was recognized by Freeman (1979) as the assumption underlying Ridker's proposal. Subsequent work by Mäler (1985) and Smith (1991) formalized the link to household production and the assumptions required to assure expenditure changes will in fact measure willingness to pay for the desired amenity.

As a rule, empirical applications have demonstrated the plausibility of the hypothesized links (Smith and Desvousges, 1986b; Jakus, 1994; Abdalla, Roach and Epp, 1992), but not the fully defined valuation measures. Some recent developments may increase interest in the method. The first of these involves empirical models proposed by McConnell, Strand and Blake-Hedges, (1991) to explain the catch on sport fishing trips. In a subsequent application we (Smith, Liu and Palmquist, 1993) interpreted these models as providing direct estimates of the household production technology for sport fishing, given total catch can be assumed to provide a plausible output measure. Similar interpretations could be proposed to describe the yields of other consumptive recreational activities. To the extent that the resulting output is related to externalities (nutrient and pesticides loadings into the coastal areas used for fishing), it is possible to meet the theoretical requirements for consistent benefit measurement.

Building on an early proposal by Shapiro and Smith (1981), Robert Horst of Math-Tech (1982) developed measures of the effects of air pollution on household expenditures. This analysis could be interpreted as an attempt to use household budget information to estimate the 'input demands' for a household production technology. By adapting Pollak and Wales's (1981) proposal for translating parameters for pollution in linear expenditure models (their suggestion was for demographic effects), he linked household expenditures, as mitigating responses, to the local concentrations of air pollutants. Subsequent work by Gilbert (1985) extended the approach to consider how these adjustments in expenditures could be related to estimates from hedonic property value models.

In a more recent application of this logic, Liu and I (1996) have proposed using expenditures on a sport fishing trip with this framework as an alternative to a RUM for valuing site quality. The analysis interprets the expenditure categories as reflecting inputs to a household production function. By using the translating parameters we adopt a model consistent with the Horst–Gilbert proposals. It is also one that implicitly maintains an assumption of 'generalized' perfect substitution for the goods linked to the characteristics of site quality.

Finally, it is important to recognize two other ways that the averting behaviour framework has affected the current practice of non-market valuation. The first of these arises in the development of models to estimate an individual's valuation for risk reductions. The consumer response approaches to estimating the statistical value of a life[26] or the values implied by decisions to wear seat-belts, purchase smoke alarms, or adjust in other ways to reduce risk implicitly impose a perfect substitution assumption between the behaviour and the perceived reduction in risk. This follows from a simple description of the expected utility, EU, (without altruism toward one's heirs) to describe this behaviour. Let π designate the probability of survival and $v(m)$ the indirect utility associated with 'life' (recall m is income, and for this example p and q are treated as constants and dropped from the expression). π is assumed to be a linear function of the averting response ($\pi = a + b \cdot x$). This implies equation (6.7) describes the individual's behaviour:

$$EU = (a + bx) \cdot v(m) \tag{6.7}$$

The Hicksian marginal willingness to pay for risk reductions is measured by the incremental expenditures on the private good (x), offering a means to reduce the risk of dying. Thus, the arguments used in this setting to value risk can be directly related to the theory underlying valuation of environmental amenities.

The second line of influence is the framing of contingent valuation (CV) questions. Increasingly, the CV literature has described the proposed changes in environmental resource offered to survey respondents using a specific plan that could lead to the proposed changes. The Carson *et al.* (1992) effort to estimate the monetary loss people experienced due to the Exxon Valdez oil spill used a plan to prevent future injuries from oil spills in this area instead of the specific injuries. The proposed plan can be considered as a type of public averting (or mitigating) behaviour. This analogy highlights the implicit role of perfect substitution in framing CV surveys.

Direct Methods

Context
Contingent valuation (CV) seems deceptively simple – just ask people what a specific hypothetical resource change is worth to them and assume they will answer the question in exactly the terms it was asked. The standard response of CV skeptics is that 'hypothetical questions yield hypothetical answers'. The key word in this description and critique is *hypothetical* and the success CV has experienced in a large number of applications relates directly to the effort expended at the design stage of the CV survey to present choices that people feel are *real*. Unfortunately, there are no simple steps that will guarantee a survey question will be perceived by respondents as real. The present state-of-the-art recommends a mix of focus groups, cognitive interviews, and pre-tests to evaluate whether the set of information, visual aids, and circumstances framing the CV questions are being interpreted by most respondents the way the investigator intended.

Recently, contingent valuation questions and descriptions have been described as the *object of choice* and the proposed *circumstances of choice* (see Carson *et al.*, 1992, 1996). This terminology avoids using a commodity orientation and instead recognizes that what is presented in most CV applications is a proposed plan to alter some environmental resource (or set of resources).

I believe this distinction is important. Use of stated preference methods for private goods or services (as in applications in marketing and transportation, see Louviere (1996b)) can rely on respondents believing the plausibility of having a new type of orange juice, a new train route (or schedule), or some variation in the characteristics of currently available goods and services. People do not have similar direct choices available for environmental resources.[27] When people are unable to select an 'amount' for the environmental resource consumed, a CV question that allows some change is constructing a new choice. Respondents' decisions permit measures of economic value to be constructed. It is possible to use the analogy between 'CV-plans' and averting behaviour to suggest a direct relationship between stated choices and Hicksian WTP.

A simple framework for describing CV questions
To simplify the algebra, assume preferences can be described with a CES (constant elasticity of substitution) preference function with one composite private good, with price p_1, a private rationed commodity, x, that serves as perfect substitute for the non-market environmental resource, and the resource, q,

(retaining the earlier notation). Contingent valuation offers a plan to alter q. Here I treat this plan as a change in the amount of an existing private rationed good, x. In the framework I assume that x is fixed and each respondent has paid $c(x)$ for it. The framework is not affected by assuming there is a fixed price per unit. It is important to require that the plan is the only way x can change. Thus, people may recognize that they are paying for the initial amount of x (e.g., people do recognize that taxes pay for public services, but may well have little conception of the unit cost of these services). Alternatively, they may not. What is important is that they have no means available to alter either x or q. Assume the objective is to measure the WTP for a change from q_0 to q_1. This is given in equation (6.8).

$$\text{WTP} = m - c(\bar{x}) - p_1 \left(\left(\frac{p_1}{m - c(\bar{x})} \right)^\alpha + (\bar{x} + bq_0)^\alpha - (\bar{x} + bq_1)^\alpha \right)^{-\frac{1}{\alpha}} \qquad (6.8)$$

where $c(\bar{x})$ is the perceived cost for a specific amount of the rationed good, $\bar{x}$, and the indirect utility function is given by

$$v = \left[\left(\frac{p_1}{m - c(\bar{x})} \right)^\alpha + (\bar{x} + bq)^\alpha \right]^{\frac{1}{\alpha}}$$

The challenge with framing a CV question is to identify a plan that offers some change in x which is perceived to be a perfect substitute for q *and* to be assured respondents interpret the proposed financial consequence of the choice is *as an addition* to the existing costs of their initial holdings of x, designated here as $\bar{x}$ and $c(\bar{x})$ (for the costs). To illustrate how this comparison helps explain responses to CV questions, consider an offer of an addition of Δx to $\bar{x}$ at a total cost of t in comparison with direct changes in q. The threshold value of t, t^*, defining the willingness to pay for Δx is:

$$t^* = m - c(\bar{x}) - p_1 \left[\left(\frac{p_1}{m - c(\bar{x})} \right)^\alpha + (\bar{x} + bq_0)^\alpha - (\bar{x} + \Delta x + bq_0)^\alpha \right]^{-\frac{1}{\alpha}} \qquad (6.9)$$

To have $t^* = $ WTP for $(q_1 - q_0)$, Δx must be perceived as equal to $b(q_1 - q_0)$. The specification $x + bq$ implies perfect substitution. Mäler has demonstrated q need not enter in a linear form. It could be replaced by a function of q, $h(q)$.

This change means that the link between x and q can change as the 'amount' of q comprising each individual's baseline condition changes. Actually, Mäler's generalization implies that perfect substitution can be imposed for measures of q that might be different from observable technical measures. $h(q)$ can represent how an individual perceives the amount of the environmental resource. Thus, we are not required to use the number of acres of a wilderness area or the size of a population of wildlife as the 'correct' measure of individual perceptions of the amount of environmental resource contributing to well-being. Moreover, descriptions of plans to realize changes in q may need to be changed with the size of the baseline or the plan. They may differ across individuals. Thus, the development stage of a CV questionnaire can be viewed as a process attempting to find a framing that communicates in comparable terms to most respondents.

We can also use this framework to consider the consequences of imperfect perceived substitution between the changes described by the plan and the intended change in the environmental resource. This can be considered by replacing $\bar{x} + h(q)$ in the specified indirect utility function with a CES subfunction, say $(\bar{x}^\beta + (h(q))^\beta)^{1/\beta}$. As we change the assumed degree of substitution it is straightforward to demonstrate that the WTP for changes in x provide a *lower bound* estimate for the WTP associated with $(q_1 - q_0)$.[28]

Current evidence on the reliability of CV
Most questions about the reliability of CV arise either because the choices stated in response to these survey questions have not realized financial consequences or because they may be distorted by the strategic incentives (i.e., respondents who believe they will in fact pay understate their WTP, while those who do not and want what is offered will overstate their values).

There is no unambiguous way to resolve either question – any more than there is a means to fully validate the maintained assumptions underlying the indirect approaches to non-market valuation. Several methods have been used to gauge their importance. I will summarize what I believe has been learned from two of the approaches used for evaluation – simulated markets studies and reliability 'tests' for CV results based on conditions implied by the economic theory underlying WTP functions.

Following the pioneering work of Bishop and Heberlein (1979), a variety of studies have compared the outcomes in simulated markets for private goods with the results derived from CV surveys. These studies can never directly address applications where CV will provide the only means to estimate monetary benefits.[29] This conclusion follows because a financial consequence can be enforced (in the simulated market) only when it is possible to exclude those who do not pay.

Based on applications to date, it appears that the specific details defining each simulated market's rules for transactions can be important to comparisons made with CV choices. Adjusting for these details, it would appear the conclusions derived from the research to date depend on the 'eyes of the beholder'. To understand what I mean, consider five examples – three with private and two with public goods. Dickie, Fisher and Gerking (1987) sold strawberries as actual transactions and as stated purchases. After accounting for one enthusiastic team of 'sellers', they concluded that there was agreement in the two data sets' descriptions of individual preferences. By contrast, Hausman and Leonard (1992), analysing the same data, argue that there is a strong case for disparities and significant differences in the consumer surplus estimates implied by the simulated and actual sales.[30] My own analysis of these data (see Smith, 1994) suggested that both samples are small (72 observations) and the estimates are sensitive to the specification used for the demand functions. As a result, I concluded (given the inherent variability in demand models for any private product) there was not a basis for suggesting the two samples were derived from different behavioural processes.[31]

Cummings, Harrison and Rutström (1995) report three comparisons for juices, solar calculators, and chocolate candies. In all three cases they report significant and fairly striking differences in the proportion purchasing each product for the samples involved in actual sales in comparison to the stated purchases (juicer – 41 vs. 11 per cent; calculator – 21 vs. 8 per cent; chocolates – 42 vs. 8 per cent). Only one of these comparisons varied the price proposed for take-it or leave-it sales (i.e., the one involving solar calculators). When I analysed the sample, including cases with different prices for the calculator experiment, I found none of the choices (actual or stated) was influenced by the stated price (Smith, 1994). If one considers the comparison using the same sample as Cummings, Harrison and Rutström, and exclude those who currently own calculators, there was *no* significant difference in the proportions purchasing or stating an intention to purchase the calculator.[32]

The third application involves an experiment Carol Mansfield and I recently conducted within a willingness to accept (WTA) framework (see Smith and Mansfield, 1996). Using a sample of over 500 respondents who had completed a telephone-mail-telephone (TMT) survey we split the sample into two groups and attempt to recruit them into a follow-up survey for a new undefined issue involving the same type of TMT framework. Half of the sample were given real offers ranging from $5 to $50 for their participation in a new survey. The other half were told there was a plan to develop such a group and asked if it was possible to make this offer what would they decide. Our findings suggest that there are no differences in the two groups choices. This finding was quite robust, being confirmed using Chi-Square tests for the two groups choices (with 83.1 per cent accepting in the real offer and 81.7 per cent in the hypothetical) as well as in likelihood ratio tests for choice functions estimated based on the decisions. Using the pooled sample the amount offered, household income and a number of other variables were statistically significant and plausible determinants of respondents' decisions. While it is important to acknowledge that a WTA framework implies quite different financial consequences than a WTP format, the record prior to our study would argue that a close correspondence between stated and actual choices would be equally difficult to realize in this case.

The last two examples involve objects of choice that have some public-good characteristics (i.e., people cannot be excluded from enjoying the resource if it is provided, even though they did not pay). An important implication of this characteristic arises with a change in how the payment mechanism is described. For both the actual and stated responses, it is described as a donation, *not a price!* This may well change the perceived incentives. Nonetheless, for the case of increasing water flows to promote the habitat for a significant trout fishing area, Duffield and Patterson (1992) find consistency that is sensitive to how the differential rate of non-response is treated for the actual solicitation vs. the CV surveys.[33] When all non-respondents are treated as having zero values there are significant differences between the estimated means for actual and stated valuations.

Brown *et al.* (1996) considers a similar situation – contributions to return a hard soil road to natural conditions on the North Rim of the Grand Canyon. Respondents were told that volunteers would convert the road but that there were additional costs of about $640 per mile to restore it from dirt road to natural conditions. Discrete take-it or leave-it questions for stated amounts and open-ended questions were asked of independent sets of respondents requesting actual contributions and stated contributions. In the CV cases (both the discrete and the open-ended) the study informed respondents that they 'will not actually be asked to pay for the project'.

The results suggest significant differences in choices for all but one stated contribution level between actual and CV responses to the discrete (take-it or leave-it) choice format and significant differences in the estimated WTP for both the open-ended and discrete choice questions. The latter displayed larger differences with the ratio of stated to actual of 6.45 vs. 4.11 with the open-ended. While this evidence would seem decisive, it is also consistent with my initial comments about CV – the questions must strive to convince the respondent what is being asked is comparable to a real choice. That is, we do not know how much of the difference between actual and stated choices (and payments) is due to the assurances given to the CV respondents that no payments would be made.

The second set of research on the reliability of CV estimates has proposed 'tests'. This approach recommends that reliability be judged based on the practices used in conducting the survey and the properties displayed by the CV estimates of WTP. An important stimulus to this research was the recommendations of the National Oceanic and Atmospheric Administration's

(NOAA) Panel on contingent valuation (see Arrow *et al.*, 1993). Co-chaired by two Nobel laureates, Kenneth Arrow and Robert Solow, the Panel's report provides a set of guidelines for CV surveys that include recommendations for survey development activities, administration, and analysis. A subset of the items identified in their guidelines were given special emphasis and described as *burden of proof* requirements. They are described as follows:

> if a CV survey suffered from any of the following maladies, we would judge its findings 'unreliable':
>
> • a high nonresponse rate to the entire survey or to the valuation question
> • inadequate responsiveness to the scope of the environmental insult
> • lack of understanding of the task by the respondents
> • lack of belief in the full restoration scenario
> • 'yes' or 'no' votes on the hypothetical referendums that are not followed up or explained by making reference to the cost and/or the value of the program. (Arrow *et al.*, 1993 p. 4609)

Provided their guidelines were used and the burden of proof requirements met, the Arrow–Solow Panel concluded by noting:

> ... under those conditions (and others specified above), CV studies convey useful information. We think it is fair to describe such information as reliable by the standards that seem to be implicit in similar contexts like market analysis for new and innovative products and the assessment of other damages normally allowed in court proceedings.
> ... CV (contingent valuation) produces estimates reliable enough to be the starting point of a judicial process of damage assessment, including passive-use values (i.e., non-use values). (Arrow *et al.*, 1993, p. 4610)

Following the logic of this report, four characteristics have been identified by different authors as important to any judgement about whether CV estimates provide reliable measures of economic values. (I have attempted to identify the primary source(s) of the proposal in parentheses after each item).

1. CV choices should be responsive to the scope (or amount) of the object of choice offered to respondents. (NOAA Panel).[34]
2. CV choices should pass construct validity tests, indicating that they are related to a set of economic variables hypothesized to be important in actual choices. These variables include: the cost or financial consequence proposed to respondents; other measures of the terms of availability if they are relevant to access what is offered; the individual (or household) income, depending on how the choice is offered); factors related to the quality of the object offered; measures of the availability of substitutes; and, to a somewhat lesser degree, taste-related demographic variables and measures of individual

attitudes that are consistent with preferences for the object of choice. (Mitchell and Carson, 1989; NOAA Panel).

3. WTP estimates derived from CV surveys should be consistent with the 'adding-up' condition. That is, a proposed change in q, divided into components and presented as a sequence should yield separate WTP estimates that as a sum are approximately equal to the WTP for the full change in q, except for what are usually small income effects. (Diamond and Hausman, 1994; Diamond, 1996).

4. CV choices and their implied WTP estimates for objects, that can generally be argued to have different 'importance' to the 'typical' individuals, should be significantly different. (Kahneman and Ritov, 1994).

Not all economists would agree with these as reliability 'tests'. Moreover, recently Diamond (1996), using the Desvousges *et al.* (1993) bird loss example, has suggested that the scope test can be made more specific – with a bound on the WTP estimates for two different sized objects of choice (designated here by Δq_1 and Δq_2, with $\Delta q_1 > \Delta q_2$). For example, we could treat Δq_1 as 100,000 birds lost and Δq_2 as 1000 birds lost from a given overall population of birds. The WTPs would refer to avoiding these losses. Diamond's bound for such a case is given in equation (6.10):

$$\text{WTP}\,(\Delta q_1) \geq (\Delta q_1 \,/\, \Delta q_2)\,.\,\text{WTP}\,(\Delta q_2) \qquad (6.10)$$

This result follows from three assumptions: (a) Δq_1 and Δq_2 represent losses in a base level of q to be avoided; (b) the utility function is quasi-linear, so the marginal utility of income is constant; and (c) the plan described as providing the means to avoid the losses is perceived to provide outcomes that are perfect substitutes for the environmental resource q. The first two assumptions influence the specific form of the WTP function and, as Diamond has argued, seem plausible as descriptions of a number of CV applications. The last is not as plausible and plays a central role in Diamond's specific bound for responsiveness to scope as well as in the Diamond and Hausman adding-up test.

The Hicksian WTP measures differences in the 'spacing' of indifference curves (measured in terms of a numeraire good and the non-marketed resource) in monetary terms. This can be appreciated when the WTP to obtain the change is written as equation (6.11), (i.e., with the initial income m_0, an unchanged price vector, and improved q_1, a higher utility level, u_1 can be realized). This equation leads to the informal characterization of WTP as a monetization of the change in utility from u_0 to u_1.

$$\text{WTP} = e(p, q_1, u_1) - e\,(p, q_1, u_0) \qquad (6.11)$$

Measures for WTP require that we specify the relationship between changes in *q*, income, *and* the spacing in these indifference curves. Normally we describe these as akin to substitution and income effects, but in fact they are interrelated. Thus, Diamond and Hausman's argument that concavity alone implies the 'adding up' condition, or Diamond's suggestion that income effects play a small role in his restrictive scope bound miss this point. Unless we select specifications for preferences that impose specific constraints (e.g., quasi-linearity) we can expect that the curvature and spacing (or substitution and income effects) appear separate only at a point. Their interrelationship changes as we change either the level of the environmental resource or the level of well-being. When the specification is simplified to abstract from the role of the income-utility link, it has implications for the role of substitution.

This can be seen in an example developed with Laura Osborne that changes the perfect substitution assumption and examines its role for both tests. Without this perfect substitution assumption all we can expect from a scope test is what the Arrow–Solow Panel proposed – a large amount of the same object should have a greater measured WTP than a smaller amount (provided they are perceived this way by the respondents involved, see Smith and Osborne (1996)). Equally important, the ratio of the sum of the WTPs associated with each of the components of a Δq change to the WTP for the full Δq can be substantially different from unity (unity is the value required by the adding-up test), depending, again, on this substitution elasticity (see Kopp and Smith, forthcoming).

I believe most environmental economists would agree on a few general responses to the four criteria for reliability of CV estimates based on the evidence to date. First, the scope test is not as big a 'hurdle' for CV estimates as originally anticipated (i.e., several old and new CV studies have 'passed' the NOAA Panel's standard).[35] Some recent examples illustrate the evidence for this conclusion. Laura Osborne and I performed a meta analysis (Smith and Osborne, 1996) of CV studies of visibility changes at national parks, including early and recent work. The variation across studies (and sub-samples in some individual cases) in the proposed visibility changes provide sufficient variation in the object of choice across independent sub-samples to develop a test. The estimates confirm statistically significant responsiveness in estimated WTP to the size of the visibility change. A study more specifically responsive to the Arrow–Solow Panel is Carson *et al.* (1996). Using in-person interviews and a CV design adhering to the NOAA guidelines, this study documents unambiguous responsiveness to the scope of the injuries explained to respondents. The choices of independent samples at each stated payment were significantly different for plans to accelerate the recovery of two different injury conditions. The estimated WTP for the plans were also significantly different. These findings are especially relevant to criticisms of CV because in contrast to much of the earlier evidence of responsiveness to scope, the object of choice in this study is unlikely to involve appreciable use-values.

Even with modest sample sizes and a fairly complex specification for the attributes of environmental quality, CV estimates are consistent with responsiveness to scope. One example supporting this conclusion is a case where the object of choice was cleaning up marine debris on recreational beaches. Xiaolong Zhang, Ray Palmquist, and I used four independent samples with different photos to characterize debris levels and found significant differences in choices for control programmes (see Smith, Zhang and Palmquist (forthcoming)). In these cases, the levels of p-values for the tests are not as convincing as in the case of the Carson *et al.* (1996) study where nearly 3000 households were interviewed. Nonetheless, even CV's critics now acknowledge the evidence of responsiveness in WTP to the 'size' of the object of choice. The disagreement arises over what constitutes 'adequate' responsiveness to scope and whether it can be documented in cases where primarily non-use values would be provided by the environmental resources being evaluated.

Second, the adding-up test is, for practical purposes, infeasible and unlikely (for the reasons I cited earlier) to be informative. It requires a clear-cut quantitative metric for measuring the amount of the environment resource that is also understood by respondents in a way that is consistent with analyst's needs. These requirements imply that the framing task must convey reasons why the object of choice is partitioned in components.

Third, the Kahneman–Ritov condition seems hard to evaluate because it requires a clear-cut and uniformly shared standard (by respondents) for what are important versus trivial objects of choice. I have conducted one experiment (Smith, 1996) that indicates CV surveys can discriminate between different public goods. However, the direction of the distinction as to which object of choice was important was mine. I believe it would be accepted by a number of others judging the two programmes. Nonetheless, there is nothing in economic theory that requires that people evaluate the personal importance of public goods the same way. This is one of the key difficulties in their proposal. Finally, most of the large-scale (and many of the more limited) CV studies have reported choices (or WTP estimates) consistent with construct validity tests.

Overall, this record appears reasonably positive. Nonetheless, I do not feel this view is widely accepted among economists. Indeed, there is a curious dichotomy in the research using CV for non-market valuation. Environmental economists actively engaged in non-market valuation continue to pursue very technical implementation or estimation issues while the economics profession as a whole seems to regard the method as seriously flawed when compared with the indirect methods. They would no doubt regard this further technical research as foolish in light of what they judge to be serious problems with the method.

The overview in this section was intended to document reasons why the judgement of the profession at large does not seem to be consistent with the 'realities' of using the indirect approaches for non-market valuation. Based on the evidence to date, CV and the indirect methods remain, in my judgement, on an equal footing.

CALIBRATION AND CONJOINT ANALYSIS

Background

While non-market valuation sometimes seems like a fairly new area of economic inquiry to economists in general, most environmental economists recognize that both the travel cost and contingent valuation methods were proposed 50 years ago. Indeed, there has been some empirical experience with most of the methods for about 30 years.

By contrast, the two topics discussed in this section are quite new, and as a result evidence on their performance and advantages in comparison to traditional methods more limited. It is not clear at this stage that either of these proposals will actually advance the practice of non-market valuation. Each seems to offer a promising line for future research.

Calibration – Theory and Practice

The term calibration implies that it is possible to adjust a measuring technique to a standard. As a rule we would expect this to mean the true value of the desired variable is known in at least one situation. Moreover, we must also have the information available to estimate this variable. Under these conditions, calibration calls for using the measuring technique (e.g., a hedonic property value model or CV survey) and typical information to estimate the value for this unknown variable. Because the 'truth' is known, it becomes possible to adjust the method based on the discrepancies between its estimate and the true value. The reason for conducting the exercise is a presumption that some adjustment procedure can be developed that would be useful in situations where the true value is *not* known. Based on common dictionary definitions for calibration, the logic seems to arise from the calibration of scientific instruments. I am not sure when the proposal to calibrate CV estimates was first made. Shortly after the Exxon-sponsored symposium on contingent valuation (see Hausman, 1993) it was suggested that results from stated preference surveys in marketing research analyses were routinely calibrated to other information before they are used to project the demands for new products.

From these hazy beginnings, a number of participants in the activities associated with natural resource damage assessments sought to identify calibrating factors to adjust CV-based WTP estimates.[36] NOAA's 1994 proposed regulations for damage assessment under the Oil Pollution Act 1990 (OPA) further heightened interest in the factor by posting a 'target' calibration factor of *50 per cent*. The draft regulations suggested that:

> Estimates of hypothetical willingness-to-pay (WTP) may incorporate biases in opposite directions. On the one hand, the appropriate measure of damages is willingness-to-accept (WTA) not WTP, ... There are theoretical arguments for why WTA may exceed WTP by a substantial margin in a natural resource context with relatively few substitutes ... . On the other hand, several experimental studies (of lower quality survey design than proposed in this rule) suggest that stated intentions of WTP in CV surveys exceed observed responses in simulated markets ... . *Because of the various possible biases a discount factor is included in the proposed rule to apply to estimated WTP. The proposed rule gives a default factor of fifty percent for the purposes of soliciting comment. However, the trustee(s) may adopt a different calibration factor if it can be shown that a different factor is appropriate for a specific application of CV.* (NOAA, 1994, p. 1140, emphasis added)

Until the complete change in NOAA's position, displayed in the final regulations for damage assessment under OPA issued in January 1996, this proposal further heightened interest in calibration.

Parallel to this discussion, Cameron (1992) and Morikawa (1989) (see also Morikawa, Ben-Akiva and McFadden, 1990) proposed different types of joint estimation combining the models developed from information about actual behaviour with CV responses, when both sets of information were available for the same respondents.[37] This research will be the primary focus of my discussion of calibration.[38]

Cameron assumed a quadratic direct utility function in deriving a travel cost demand model for sport fishing and providing the behavioural framework to interpret CV responses. The key question included in her analysis was structured to consider the maximum *total* expenditures on fishing trips an individual would be willing to incur in a season before stopping fishing. Her approach uses Roy's identity (as given in the first row of Table 6.1) and the indirect utility function (derived from this quadratic specification) to provide parametric restrictions *across the two models*. The restrictions for parameters shared between the two models mutually calibrates the two sources of information on recreation demand. Recently, Chapman, Hanemann and Kanninen (1996) have extended this logic to contingent behaviour models (see also Englin and Cameron, 1996).

By contrast, behavioural models (as a source of parametric restrictions) do not serve a central role in the Morikawa, Ben-Akiva and McFadden framework. In this case the two data sets (one stated and one actual choices) permit estimation of the relative scale factors associated with the errors from two discrete choice models, provided the other parameters are restricted to be equal. Thus, they assume identical behavioural functions for the stated and actual choices. The specification of the characteristics of each mode is assumed to be complete.

Several recent studies have replicated the basic logic of these two initial pioneering approaches. For example, Englin and Cameron (1996) use the initial Cameron logic to combine responses to repeated contingent behaviour questions (i.e., how respondents indicate their recreation trips would change with several percentage increases in travel cost per trip) with an individual's actual trips. The responses are treated as a panel on each recreationist with the actual and stated responses assumed to arise from a common data generating behavioural framework.

Adamowicz, Louviere and Williams (1994) extend the Morikawa *et al.* logic to a RUM framework where the focus is on site choice. Considering actual and stated site decisions for recreational fishing, they restrict the preference parameters for variables measured in the two samples to be equal. This assumption allows the combined estimator to identify a relative scale factor (i.e., the ratio of the scale parameters for each error). Before turning to some further extensions to this calibration framework, some potentially important 'details' in the models should be noted.

First, I believe that tasks associated with combining revealed and stated preference information increase the need to understand how respondents will interpret the questions posed in stated preference surveys. To illustrate this point, consider Cameron's question (1992, p. 305, the $A corresponds to a specified dollar amount): 'If the total cost of all your saltwater fishing last year was $A more, would you have quit fishing completely?' Her analysis assumes that people's answers to this question are based on a decision framework in which the number of trips can be altered in response to the proposed additional fixed charge. Whether this is correct depends on how respondents interpreted the conditioning phrase – 'all your saltwater fishing last year'. Another view of the question being posed is that the individual is being asked to assume he (or she) will take *the same* number of trips in the proposed new situation. This distinction changes the link between the indirect utility function governing the response to this question and the travel cost demand.[39] A similar issue arises in the Englin–Cameron application which asks about the number of fishing trips that would have been taken if the cost were higher. Englin and Cameron *assumed* the cost corresponded to the *travel cost* for the average observed trip. Respondents could have interpreted cost as expenditures (i.e., travel cost times number of trips, with the number corresponding to the season the survey had just asked about). In this case the interpretation of the percentage increment as an increase in the unit price would be incorrect and the model used to link their responses would change.

A more general concern arises if we assume that there is some uncertainty at the time recreationists plan their trips. This formulation would imply a distinction between *ex-ante* plans and *ex-post* behaviour.[40] It is not clear how respondents would interpret contingent questions under these conditions.

A third type of concern arises with the data collection strategy used in Adamowicz, Louviere and Williams (1994). Responses to multiple-choice questions asked of the same respondent (64 sets of three alternative choices) are treated as independent in the statistical analysis. Moreover, in their case a data collection problem (see 1994, note 5) required that they assume the revealed (RP) and stated preference (SP) responses are not correlated for each respondent. Cameron did not make this assumption. Nonetheless, arguments can be made to support either position when the data includes *past* (from the respondent's perspective) revealed preference information and *current* stated preference information. The Adamowicz *et al.* assumption of independence across stated choices seems less subject to debate and therefore more questionable.

The Adamowicz *et al.* approach is an example of a much larger set of research outside applications to the valuation of environmental resources. This other research seeks to combine RP and SP data for predicting choice or market shares (see Louviere, 1996a and b). In these other applications a common preference structure is assumed. The role of stated costs, partial attribute lists, and other distinctions between actual and stated choices is not explicitly considered. The primary goal is to estimate the relative scale parameter to adjust predictions about choices or to gauge the reliability of the types of data. Little attention is given to the behavioural foundations for the nonstochastic component of the models used in the analysis.

Three recent extensions to the Cameron proposal have been developed. The first of these by Young Sook Eom and I (Eom and Smith, 1994) focuses on using joint estimates to combine people's actual responses to an unobservable quality dimension of a commodity with their stated choices for variations in this attribute. The specific application involves the health risks associated with pesticide residues on fresh produce. Taking advantage of Viscusi's (1989) prospective reference theory which assumes Bayesian updating of subjective probabilities, our model considers how consumers respond to proposed increments in *their* (unobservable) baseline perceived health risks given specific product choices (fresh produce with and without pesticide residues). The model also uses a different approach to describe consumer preferences. After isolating a demand model that offers a good description of consumer demand for an aggregate of fresh produce (based on their actual purchases) we use the corresponding quasi-indirect utility function (adapted for the uncertainty in the choice process) to describe consumer preferences for the stated choices.

Finally, our analysis considered the influence of how consumers interpret the pricing condition. It poses a contingent choice question (between two types of produce) with a different price per unit for each produce variety in two different ways (one with a specific commodity identified and a second described as most frequently purchased). The demand model treats this as a component of a fixed weight aggregate demand for produce and evaluates the effects of different price descriptions across independent sub-samples. Our results suggest differences in how respondents answered the questions. Unfortunately, this effect could not be separated from the difference in definitions for the commodity price associated with each formulation. Thus, as Englin and Cameron's study, these respondent interpretations appear important to the form and plausibility of the behavioural restrictions in calibrated models.

Larson, Loomis and Chien (1983) considered a different modelling strategy. Based on the expenditure function corresponding to an Almost Ideal Demand System (Deaton and Muellbauer, 1980), they use a composite model to estimate the total value of a resource enhancement, recognizing the use and non-use values. The resource change involves increases in the grey whale population off California. Because the annual migration of this species supports a significant amount of recreation (e.g., whale-watching), the decision to travel to locations that provide opportunities for viewing the annual offshore migration, is analysed jointly with responses to a CV question offering to clean coastal waters, purchase additional calving habitat areas, and other interventions intended to increase the population. By recognizing the potential for differences in how individuals who participate in whale-watching vs. non-participants would respond to an open-ended CV question, Larson *et al.* were able to formulate a joint model linking the expenditure equation for whale-watching recreation with the WTP function for enhancements in the population. The link is different for users and non-users. Non-users may have a positive value for enhancements in the population but their WTP is not influenced by the terms of use. By estimating these models jointly, with an identification of users vs. non-users, it is possible to adjust the models for each situation.

Xiaolong Zhang and I (Zhang and Smith, 1996) have used their basic logic to consider a more general formulation with variations in the pricing, type of resource, and respondent behaviour in the joint estimation of the value of proposed changes in environmental quality. Our application involves marine debris as a source of quality deterioration for coastal resources. The design altered the types of resources (some available for beach recreation and others providing exclusively habitat for marine species), the proposed terms of payment for the plans to provide the improvement (i.e., lump sum payments vs. beach access fees where total cost to the individual depends on his(her) level of use), and questions intended to identify whether respondents used the resources affected by the proposed plan. The framework and survey design offer multiple ways for the behaviour described in use and non-use values to be 'observed'. For the most part, these variations affect the type of CV question asked as independently assigned design points across the respondents in our sample. Information about their actual recreational behaviour was also collected and combined with responses to discrete choice questions.

A behavioural model recognizing the non-separabilities between environmental quality (i.e., debris) and beach recreation, as well as the separable contribution associated with the non-use values provides the overall framework for joint estimation. Zhang (1995) reports the results from a linearized version of the model that offers preliminary support for joint estimation of economic values that embody both use and non-use dimensions.

All of the approaches I discussed as calibrated methods could also be described as convergent estimates. This terminology would parallel the use of convergent validity criteria in evaluating CV. Regardless of terminology, the frameworks developed here do not regard one approach as the true values and the other as estimates to be adjusted. Instead, they acknowledge a common unknown behavioural process should provide the basis for the choices that comprise each data type. Distinctions must be built into the description of the data generation process for each approach (i.e., indirect and CV). Thus, each study summarized here offers a variation on a joint or multiple equation estimator where a mix of a priori restrictions to preferences and the specific formulation of an individual's time and income constraints provide the basis for the cross equation parameter restrictions. To implement these methods, the data available must include information about multiple types of choices (motivated by a common behavioural framework) from each individual.

At several points in the earlier discussion of travel cost models, less formal approaches for using different benefit measures were introduced as calibrating adjustments. Indeed, the CV literature has a variety of proposals for using the results from laboratory experiments, theory, or both to adjust CV estimates (see Fox *et al.*, 1994; Cummings, Harrison and Rotström, 1995; Bjornstad, Cummings and Osborne, 1996). The distinction between these proposals and the methods described here is that in the approaches described above a consistent behavioural model provides the basis for the restrictions used in estimating these models. They are applied to the multiple types of behaviour observed from a *common set of individuals*. The other methods do not have a common behavioural framework that is used to derive their proposed adjustments.

Similarly, adjustments to benefit measures in the literature based on meta analyses or other procedures (e.g., Walsh, Johnson and McKean, 1992) have similar problems in that they do not have a direct link to a model of individual behaviour.

This is not intended as an argument that they are inappropriate. Rather, the point is simple – we have no basis for concluding (without experience and evaluation) that they will improve the properties of the resulting benefit estimates. By contrast, parametric calibration, as developed from Cameron's general logic, can be treated as a set of prior restrictions that offer the potential for improving the efficiency of the estimates. They have the potential for introducing bias should the restrictions be incorrect.[41] Thus, the general strategy can then be evaluated by considering how prior and sample information contribute to the properties of an econometric estimator.

Conjoint Analysis

The prospects for using conjoint analysis in non-market valuation has attracted considerable attention among environmental economists.[42] The term actually refers to an array of methods that, as Louviere (1988) notes in his early review, focus on using individual evaluations constructed by a sample of respondents for a specified set of multi-attribute alternatives to measure 'part-worth utilities'. In our terminology, the focus seems to be on methods for eliciting marginal WTP (or marginal rates of substitution) for specified changes in the characteristics of heterogeneous commodities.

Some of the earliest applications in environmental economics were associated with risk. Viscusi, Magat and Huber (1991), for example, used risk-risk trade-offs to construct measures of the marginal WTP for changes in the risk of chronic bronchitis. Their approach considered pairwise comparisons and changes in different elements in economic lotteries (i.e., combinations of probabilities and stated outcomes with hypothesized implications for individual well-being) to isolate points of *ex-ante* indifference for each respondent.

Two aspects of their strategy distinguish it from both open-ended and discrete choice CV questions. First, a specific reference situation is given and often the adjustments are made to non-monetary components of each lottery. For example, an individual would be asked to consider living in a community with a specified risk of being killed in an automobile accident and a risk of chronic bronchitis due to air pollution vs. another community with a different set of risks for each outcome (these scenarios would be structured so that the probability of a different outcome was lowest in each community). Respondents would then be asked to rank the two situations, based on where they would prefer to live. In the next stage of what is usually a computer-based interview, they are asked to adjust a pre-specified variable (in this example one of the risks for one community) until they would be indifferent between the two communities.

The second distinction arises from using a model of how the indifference judgement is made to recover measures of economic value. That is, the interview process yields an 'equivalence relationship' (given we accept conventional expected utility theory, as well as a variety of simplifying assumptions) between the health outcome (in my example chronic bronchitis) and an individual's evaluation of risks to his (or her) survival.[43] This link is then used with estimates of people's willingness to accept risks in the workplace (i.e., values of statistical lives, see Viscusi (1993) (to estimate the *ex-ante* monetary value of compensation for chronic bronchitis (based on the derived equivalence relationship).

The Adamowicz *et al.* calibration study relied on conjoint methods to develop the stated preference component of their sample. Multiple differentiated situations as sets of three alternatives were presented to each respondent and, as I noted, they were asked for a choice. This strategy is consistent with a RUM framework and appears to be the most active area of current research (see Louviere, 1996b; Adamowicz, Louviere and Williams, 1994).

Alternatively, the elicitation process can present pairs of alternatives and seek a rating of the degree of preference. In this case an ordered probit (or logit) model based on utility differences assumed to arise from attribute differences would be estimated (see, as recent examples, Johnson *et al.*, 1995; Desvousges *et al.*, 1996).

It is too early to compare the performance of conjoint strategies with CV. More experience is needed for non-market objects of choice before an evaluation of this questioning mode for environmental resources can be developed. This qualification is important because some practitioners are concluding based on experience in marketing research that the method avoids (or substantially mitigates) the problems argued to be present with CV. There is no basis for this conclusion. Indeed, there are at least two issues that suggest caution in assuming the record of positive performance is relevant.

The first arises from the design of most conjoint methods. If the experience of double-bounded CV questions offers any guide to how individuals react to sequences of questions, then all conjoint studies, whether trade-off adjustment, choice, or ratings, face problems. This conclusion follows because they rely on collecting multiple answers from each respondent. That is, sets of alternatives are presented to each individual and analysed *as if* they were independent responses. The double-bounded estimator as proposed by Hanemann, Loomis and Kanninen (1991) assumes a 'perfect' correlation between responses to two discrete choice CV questions to develop interval estimates. Tests with several different applications suggest a high degree of consistency in the stochastic process generating the responses but sufficient differences to reject 'perfect' correlation (see Hanemann and Kanninen, forthcoming). To my knowledge, no one has considered the potential bias from assuming the question sequence presented to each individual in a conjoint study can be treated as a panel of uncorrelated responses.

A second, equally difficult, issue concerns the theoretical consistency of what is estimated. Rating and trade-off models provide estimates of *marginal* WTP (or the marginal rate of substitution based on commodity to commodity comparisons). These are *not* measures of total WTP for a change in q, as defined by equation (6.2). The information recovered does not permit estimation of the WTP function without further a priori restrictions (including independence of the responses to the question sequence). Moreover, even the choice based conjoint models face a significant conceptual problem in measuring Hicksian WTP. They rely on the prior specification of a choice set for each respondent. IIA allows estimation of the parameters of simple RUM specifications, but *not* welfare measurement (see Kaoru, Smith and Liu (1995) for discussion of the role of the full choice set for the definition of welfare measures in the context of travel cost models).

DISCUSSION

My title was selected to catch the reader's attention. However, it was not exclusively an effort to 'sell' this review of where we stand in non-market valuation. It has another purpose as well – to call attention to the project orientation of most applied studies associated with one of the valuation methods. This orientation contrasts with the policy needs for what are often described as 'transferable' benefit estimates or benefit functions.

There have been efforts to compare results from specific methods (travel cost, hedonic, and CV) using standardized benefit measures such as consumer surplus per trip or the marginal WTP to a comparable change in air quality. Neither measure is a 'price' in the usual sense. Indeed, as Morey (1994) has documented for the case of using consumer surplus per trip measures to compare travel cost demand and RUM estimates, there are significant theoretical problems.

Nonetheless, the needs for benefit measures are increasingly expressed in terms of some type of unit value. To meet these needs, future research must begin to adopt strategies that parallel the theoretical and practical research that served to enhance the development of price indexes for marketed goods.

This strategy seems feasible for environmental resources that primarily give rise to use-related values. Nonetheless, to meet this goal requires a change in the focus of research away from specifically defined resources to frameworks that seek to identify the attributes of resources that distinguish their contributions to different use-values. Such a unified structure would be similar to what RUM and hedonic frameworks provide in describing how individuals make choices among sites with different characteristics, and provide links between these characteristics and benefit measures. My suggestion is that such models need to be developed more generally with the goal of consistent unit benefit functions. It implies that estimates will need to be regularly updated *for the same environmental resources*. It is only through this process that we could begin to judge whether environmental resources are in fact becoming more scarce over time.

This overall research strategy seems feasible for use-related benefits because they are associated with goods and services that are exclusive and rival in consumption (i.e., they are more like private than public goods). Non-use values, associated with public goods, are not as readily described as comparable to unit benefit functions.

Addressing the issues associated with the development of unit benefits or benefit indexes for public goods requires theoretical and empirical research. What is known is more limited and therefore further from being able to provide the transferable models (and the quantity measures) that would be required to formulate 'unit benefit measures'. Nonetheless, for an important part of the issues addressed in environmental valuation, (i.e., those associated with use-values). I believe it is possible to develop a new generation of research that parallels price index number development that routinely takes place in statistical bureaux around the world. Perhaps this transformation in our research strategy will be accomplished before non-market valuation celebrates its 75th birthday.

NOTES

1. Thanks are due to Henk Folmer, Per Olov Johansson, Alan Randall and Tom Tietenberg for their most helpful (and rapid) reviews of an earlier draft, and to Paula Rubio for preparing and editing multiple drafts of this paper. Partial support for this research was provided by the UNC Sea Grant Program under project No. R/MRD-32.

2. The first part of my title was selected to try to capture potential readers' attention but is not completely accurate. I will not devote the attention required to describe fully how the methods used to monetize economic values must be adapted to develop virtual prices. See Madden (1991), Morey (1994), Smith (1992) for an outline of the issues, and Espinosa and Smith (1994) for further evaluation of alternate approaches.

3. See Kopp and Smith (1993) for an overview of the statutes and practices of damage assessment as of 1993.

4. This figure has been widely quoted in the national press at the outset of the 1996 summer season in the context of limitations on the National Park Service's resources. More generally see OECD (1991) for a discussion of the importance of domestic tourism in exports of key trading areas.

5. It would be inappropriate to conclude that attention to non-market valuation resulted from a direct realization of the importance of the 'environmental sector' through some systematic process of considering these types of aggregate expenditures. Interest in the US was prompted by requirements to undertake benefit-cost analyses for new major environmental regulations and, in 1989, to valuing the injuries due to releases of oil and hazardous substances. Benefit-cost mandates also prompted interest in other developed countries. Nonetheless, it is also likely that the origin of these mandates and support for continued efforts to maintain and improve environmental resources reflects consumers' preferences.

6. A comparison of the real GDP estimates for those reported in Summers and Heston (1991) for 1988 indicates that 53 of the 62 developing nations in Africa and South America had real GDP under one per cent of the US level. The OECD (1991) reports estimates of pollution control expenditures in the mid-1980s at approximately 1.47 per cent of GDP for the US and with estimates ranging from 0.82 to 1.52 per cent for other member countries (see Table 21,

in OECD (1991)). More recently, Carlin, Scodari and Garver (1992) report annualized estimates of the costs for all US pollution control (in 1986 dollars) at about 2.5 per cent of GNP.

7.   Examples include Just, Hueth and Schmitz (1982), Johansson (1987), Braden and Kolstad (1991) and now the greatly expanded revision by Freeman (1993). Indeed, it may be hard to appreciate the various sources of confusion in the early literature given the existence of these volumes. Morey's (1984) overview, appropriately titled 'Confuser Surplus', provides some perspective on the early confusions in interpreting consumer surplus measures.

8.   This formulation assumes no income changes and is sometimes described as a money metric.

9.   There are actually few direct measures of the quantities of market goods. As a rule, we have measures of prices and expenditures on specific good. These are used to construct price indexes and then quantity indexes as expenditures on a class of commodities relative to the price index developed for that group. See Diewert (1993) for a discussion of the history of the theory and practice of construction of price and quantity indexes.

10.   These concerns were among the early motivations for Waugh's research on hedonic price functions for vegetables. He also conducted an early form of contingent valuation. He concluded his evaluation of both methods noting that: 'It is evident from this discussion that the two methods (surveys of attitudes and preferences and market data on prices and quantitative measures of attributes) supply data of a different nature, and that they supplement rather than duplicate each other ... the ideal study of demand should use both methods.' (Waugh, 1929, p. 108).

11.   Of course, there are situations where problems of quality and quantity measurement do arise. This is especially true for new products or for improvements in the quality of product in the presence of technical change. Here the commodity improves and becomes less expensive over time so relative prices over that time do not provide a basis for gauging the quality differences. The case of microcomputers is one of the best examples of this situation. See Nelson, Tanguay and Patterson (1994) for an example of a hedonic price model used to take account of quality changes in microcomputers.

12.   Conventional economic measures for values cannot be defined where preferences are incompatible with substitution and the associated trade-offs (i.e., in the case of lexiographic preferences). This is not incompatible with complementarity relationships between one (or more) goods and a non-market resource permitting measures of economic value to be recovered from choices. In this case there are substitution relationships being used. The private good(s) included in the composite is (are) assumed to substitute for other private commodities.

13.   Bockstael and McConnell (1993) describe the conditions sufficient to develop this relationship. The non-market resource, q, should be a weak complement to a non-essential private good, say x_i. The non-essential requirement is needed because weak complementarity is imposed when the demand for x_i is zero. In addition they should satisfy the Willig (1978) condition. This corresponds to *any* one of three mutually dependent conditions:

    (a) v_q / v_{p_i} is independent of income;

    (b)   consumer surplus per unit of the associated commodity is independent of

    (c) $v_q / v_{p_i} = \int x_{iq} dp_i / x_i$

For more details on the implications of these conditions see Willig, 1978, pp. 1253–5.

14.   This follows because the arguments in equation (6.2) that are specified to change will be different. For example, the WTP for access to a resource that provides the non-market resource (designated here as $\overline{\text{WTP}}$) would be given as: $\overline{\text{WTP}} = m_0 - e(p^*, q, v(p, q, m_0))$. p^* replaces the element of the price vector corresponding to the good related to q with its choke price. In this case the change in the $\overline{\text{WTP}}$ within q is given as:

$$\frac{\partial \overline{\text{WTP}}}{\partial q} = -\frac{\partial e}{\partial q} - \frac{\partial e}{\partial v} \cdot \frac{\partial v}{\partial q}$$

With weak complementarity between the private good and q, the first term in this expression is zero. See McConnell (1990) for further discussion of other examples.

15. For a summary of the early arguments about the treatment of zonal data, see Bockstael, Hanemann and Strand (1987). More recently, this issue has been discussed for individual observations as an 'excess zero' problem (see Haab and McConnell (1996) and Shonkwiler and Shaw (forthcoming).

16. See Hanemann (1984b), Morey *et al.* (1995) for discussion of the modelling strategies for extreme and generalized corner solution problems.

17. This simple formulation imposes a normalization rule on the scale parameter. See Louviere (1996b) for a discussion of this issue in the context of combining data where the scale parameters are different.

18. Hausman, Leonard and McFadden (1995) suggest that their specification combines a discrete choice model with a utility-consistent count model. In their terms it 'encompasses both the number of trips (purchases) and the sites for each trip (brand choice)' (p. 13). There are two difficulties with their proposed consistent link. The first is unique to the travel cost application and is shared by all the other proposed approaches for consistent links between site choice and seasonal demand. It arises when the travel cost is specified to include a time cost of travel. The model (and their derivation) assumes that the 'prices' of sites are exogeneous. Indeed, time allocation decisions are treated as separable, when in fact most of the evidence suggests this is inappropriate. While Hausman *et al.* offer an imaginative estimate of the opportunity cost of time, using travel mode data this is treated as a per trip decision separable from the allocation of time within a season. Most of the other recreation literature would question this assumption. Of course, to be fair to them, they are not alone in the assumption. Most applications have used a less sophisticated approach. My point is only that the full details of the link between seasonal usage and site choice needs to consider how this opportunity cost of time varies with the level and timing of use over the season.

A more specific concern with the mechanics of their link arises with the quantity measure. They argue that the measured expenditures on fishing trips of an individual when divided by the inclusive value from the RUM specification will be equal to the number of trips. As a rule, this would only be true if the individual visited only one site. Expenditures for fishing trips to K different sites, y_F in the Hausman *et al.* notation, would be the sum of the expenditures on trips to each site as given below.

$$y_F = \sum_j p_{ij} T_j,$$

where p_{ij} is travel and time costs to site j, and T_j is trips to site j. There is no reason to believe that ΣT_j, which is the total trips will be equal to y_F scaled by the inclusive value as they suggest in a key step of their derivation (p. 12), that is:

$$\frac{\sum p_{ij} T_j}{\frac{1}{\gamma} \ln\left(\sum \exp(\gamma p_{ij})\right)} \neq \sum T_j$$

It would seem that the link they propose requires a different measure for the total quantity of use, more consistent with the left side of the above equation as a quantity index for site usage so the product of the price index (the denominator of the left side) and the quantity index equals the relevant total expenditures, y_F.

19. Brown and Mendelsohn (1984) proposed the hedonic travel cost model as a recreation analog to the hedonic property value model. Unfortunately, market equilibrium cannot be relied upon to provide the price (travel cost) function. This conclusion follows because the travel cost is an imputed price that the analyst assumes is perceived by each individual, not one established through market interactions. Smith, Palmquist and Jakus (1991) have suggested an alternative interpretation of the function as a locus describing how individuals conceive of the substitution alternatives available to them. However, there is not a priori basis for evaluating the reliability of this description of how substitution influences people's choices.

20. Vaughan *et al.* (1985) provides to my knowledge first recognition of this possibility and an application.

21. These same types of interconnections could be suggested for hedonic and averting behaviour models where multiple sets of goods are combined to produce amenities. Carol Gilbert and I proposed using such connections along with the durability of the marketed good being used to estimate long-run versus short-run benefits (see Gilbert and Smith, 1985). I am grateful to Alan Randall for making this general point and suggesting the difficulties posed by formulating individual partial models for each type of adjustment when multiple household production processes may be taking place.

22. I will use calibration in several different ways in this discussion. All are intended to imply that estimates are developed from a composite of sources. Later, I discuss proposals for joint estimation. Here a calibrated assessment is intended to mean an evaluation of benefit estimates for the same resource change derived from independent sources, combined with attempts to understand the sources of the differences and develop a 'best' estimate from the process. It can be somewhat informal as in Freeman's (1982) early evaluation of the aggregate benefits of clean air and water programmes, or statistical as in the Banzhaf, Desvousges and Johnson (forthcoming) comparison of methods used to estimate the economic damages from air pollution for social costing of electricity.

23. One interpretation of this process is that it is an attempt to provide a theoretical model to describe relationships one should expect to find in a meta analysis of different approaches (i.e., micro and aggregate) to measuring benefits for a common environmental resource.

24. The record may not be as clear-cut as this comment suggests. Alan Randall, after reviewing an earlier draft of this paper, argued that the evidence for sub-markets has often been imposed on the empirical studies. My own experience is based on a study with Greg Michaels (see Michaels and Smith, 1990) where we found realtors identified sub-markets for suburban Boston and these were confirmed by the differences in the estimates of the hedonic price functions. It is also the case that to my knowledge there have been few studies since the Straszheim (1978) study that tested for market segmentation.

25. As a rule, wage hedonic models have been estimated with national samples and regional dummy variables included to take account of local conditions in each area. Because there is evidence that the model is more effective in recovering the wage-risk trade-off with blue-collar workers (see Viscusi, 1993) where we might expect more limited knowledge of opportunities in other regions, one might also argue that wage models should be evaluated for separate geographic areas as sub-markets. This would parallel the market segmentation in hedonic applications to housing markets. Under these conditions it would be foolish to base the model used in estimating quality of life indexes on a framework that assumes a national market equilibrium.

26. The value of a statistical life is the aggregate willingness to pay to reduce the risk of death. In order to make this measure tangible one must specify the size of the risk change and the number of people over which the individual willingness to pay is being summed. Johansson (1995, p. 61) described the process as aggregate WTP to save b lives by the group (say n individuals who experience the (b/n) risk reduction. This is reported by life saved (i.e., the aggregate divided by b) to be labelled the statistical value of a life.

27. Of course, we assume they recognize these options and make them. If they did not, then there would be no scope for the indirect methods I summarized earlier.

28. This result follows from Smith and Osborne (1996). Equation (6.8) is a generalization to the quasi-linear form they discuss to evaluate expectations for scope effects.

29. The reason for this conclusion is that the need for use of CV is greatest in monetizing non-use values. Because these economic values arise from pure public-good services of environmental resources, it is difficult to envision a situation where an enforceable contract could be offered to participants in an experiment. Once a donation vehicle is used, the link to CV is completely changed. As noted earlier, economic values estimated with CV or any method require choices that connect objects of choice to something that is given up (actual choice) or proposed to be given up (CV). With a donation, people may perceive that the object of choice is available with no trade-off required.

30. More specifically, they conclude that: 'We have re-analyzed perhaps the best known such validation of CV, the Dickie, Fisher, Gerking (1987) paper. We find, using a non-parametric approach, that the hypothetical CV responses significantly overstate the actual market responses, both in terms of consumer demand and in terms of consumer surplus.' (p. 11).

31. This conclusion was based on comparing estimated price and income coefficients using a Poisson count estimator (see Smith, 1994, footnote 28 – printing errors deleted a minus for one of the price coefficients and decimal points for two of the estimated parameters in the models developed with actual sale data). The relevant issue is the degree of consistency that should be expected with micro data and a small sample. Hausman and Leonard impose a stringent standard in their analysis and draw rather general conclusions when it is not satisfied, noting that: 'Our findings suggest that the CV method does not provide a reliable estimate for consumer surplus even in this most ideal of situations. Given such a large upward bias for a familiar market good like strawberries, we find no reason to believe that the performance of CV for unfamiliar environmental goods will be any better' (1992, p. 11).

32. The specific results are given in the table below. When the Cummings, Harrison and Rutström (1995) sample is split, based on those who own calculators vs. those who do not, there is no significant difference in the revealed preference (RP) and stated preference (SP) at the 5 per cent level.

| | Sample (%) | | | |
| | Own calculator | | Do not own a calculator | |
Decision	RP	SP	RP	SP
Purchase	57.1	45.4	8.3	1.6
Not purchase	42.9	54.6	91.7	98.4
P-value				
χ^2		0.529(NR)		0.086(NR)
Fisher-exact		0.712(NR)		0.111(NR)

33. The issue is how one treats individuals who did not return requests in the real and hypothetical samples. If we assume their values are zero then there will be wide discrepancies in the estimated WTP from actual and stated responses. If the analysis is confined to a comparison of the actual and hypothetical responses there is no significant difference based on each sample's estimates for WTP.

34. In a follow-up set of comments, a subset of the original NOAA Panel authors (see Arrow *et al.*, 1994) offered clarifying comments on the meaning of adequate responsiveness to scope. Their comments were prepared in reaction to the scope test in the January 1994 proposed rules. They note that: 'The proposed scope test is built to assure that there is a *statistically detectable* sensitivity to scope. This is, in our opinion, an improper interpretation of the word 'adequately'. Had the panel thought that something as straight-forward as statistical measurability were the proper way to define sensitivity, then we would (or should) have opted for language to that effect. A better word than 'adequate' would have been *'plausible'*. A survey instrument is judged unreliable if it yields estimates which are implausibly unresponsive to the scope of the insult. This, of course, is a judgment call, and cannot be tested in a context-free manner, as would be the case if the proposed scope test were implemented' (Arrow *et al.*, 1994, p. 1).

35. Hanemann (1996), for example, notes that there is extensive evidence of responsiveness to scope. Among the studies he sites is Carson's (1995) review of 27 tests of scope. Overall, he indicates that there have been at least 130 tests of scope. Reviewers more critical of CV have argued that most of these tests involve environmental resources with substantial use-values reflected in the CV responses. In their view, the scope issue remains to be evaluated for cases where WTP is dominated by non-use values.

36. Desvousges, Gable and Johnson (1995) describe four types of calibration relationships:

    1. ratio of average stated to 'actual' values;
    2. ratio of the number of individuals who say they will purchase a commodity at a posted price to the number who actually purchase it at that price;

3. stated and actual demand curves;
4. a function that can be used to adjust CV values depending on the specific parameters of the CV study.

Based on this structure, the first approach is only available in experimental or simulated markets and one can easily question whether the 'actual' value is known for anything used in these experiments (except as a monetary incentive).

37. Cameron's paper (1992) was prepared at about the same time as Morikawa's thesis and had been circulating under a different title since 1988.
38. See Desvousges, Gable and Johnson (1995) and Mansfield (1996) for discussion of the use of simulated market data to develop calibrating functions.
39. The quadratic specification has closed-form expressions for both commodity demand functions and the indirect utility function.
40. I am grateful to Per Olov Johansson for calling this issue to my attention. To some degree, the Eom–Smith (1994) model is forced to deal with the issue because both choices involve decisions that convey commodities and risk of a health effect (i.e., cancer due to exposure to pesticides). We account for changes in beliefs as information evolves using the Viscusi (1989) prospective reference framework. In principle one could use a lottery framework and the actual outcomes to evaluate an *ex-ante – ex-post* distinction.
41. An approach using a consistent behavioural framework is also what Mansfield (1996) has recently suggested for comparing simulated and CV experiments and within different CV surveys for discriminating among proposed data generation processes.
42. It is mentioned in the revised NOAA regulations for damage assessments as a promising approach for estimating habitat equivalency.
43. The approach used in this derivation assumes a simple form for the expected utility model with

$v(b)$ = utility realized with chronic bronchitis, holding all else equal (i.e., an indirect utility function with income and prices fixed)
$v(h)$ = utility realized in a 'healthy' state without chronic bronchitis
$v(d)$ = utility perceived *ex* ante of dying in automobile accident (e.g., altruistic concerns)
π_b^i = stated probability of having chronic bronchitis in community i ($i = 1, 2$)
π_d^i = stated probability of dying in automobile accident in community i.

For an individual to be indifferent between communities 1 and 2, it must be that:

$$\pi_b^1 v(b) + \pi_d^1 v(d) + (1 - \pi_b^1 - \pi_d^1) v(h) = \pi_b^2 v(b) + \pi_d^2 v(d) + (1 - \pi_b^2 - \pi_d^2) v(h).$$

Rearranging terms we can express $v(b)$ in terms of the standard gamble associated with decisions involving risks to life as:

$$v(b) = \frac{\left(\pi_d^2 - \pi_d^1\right)}{\left(\pi_b^1 - \pi_b^2\right)} v(d) + \left[1 - \frac{\left(\pi_d^2 - \pi_d^1\right)}{\left(\pi_b^1 - \pi_b^2\right)}\right] v(h)$$

For more details see Viscusi, Magat and Huber (1991).

REFERENCES

Adamowicz, W., J. Louviere and M. Williams (1994), 'Combining Revealed and Stated Preference Methods for Valuing Environmental Amenities', *Journal of Environmental Economics and Management*, **26**, 271–92.

Anderson, S.P., A. de Palma and J. Thisse (1987), 'The CES is a Discrete Choice Model?', *Economics Letters*, **24**, 139–40.

Anderson, S.P., A. de Palma and J. Thisse (1988), 'A Representative Consumer Theory of the Logit Model', *International Economic Review*, **29**, 461–6.

Anderson, S.P., A. de Palma and J. Thisse (1992), *Discrete Choice Theory of Product Differentiation*, Cambridge, The MIT Press.

Arrow, K., R. Solow, P.R. Portney, E.E. Leamer, R. Radner and H. Schuman (1993), 'Report of the NOAA Panel on Contingent Valuation', *Federal Register* **58**(10), 4601–14.

Arrow, K., R. Solow, E.E. Leamer, R. Radner and H. Schuman (1994), 'Comment on NOAA Proposed Rule on Natural Resource Damage Assessments', ANPNM, Comment No. 69, 7 January.

Banzhaf, H.S., W.H. Desvousges and F.R. Johnson (forthcoming), 'Assessing the Externalities of Electricity Generation in the Midwest', *Resource and Energy Economics*, Special Issue on Environmental Costing and Electricity.

Bartik, T.J. (1987), 'The Estimation of Demand Parameters in Hedonic Price Models', *Journal of Political Economy*, **95**(2), 81–8.

Bishop, R. and T. Heberlein (1979), 'Measuring Values of Extra-Market Goods, Are Indirect Measures Biased?', *American Journal of Agricultural Economics*, **61**(8), 926–30.

Bjornstad, D., R. Cummings and L. Osborne (1996), 'Real Responses to Hypothetical Valuation Questions, A Learning Design for the Contingent Valuation Methods', unpublished paper, Georgia State University, 1 June.

Blomquist, G.C., M.C. Berger and J.P. Hoehn (1988), 'New Estimates of Quality of Life in Urban Areas', *American Economic Review*, **78**(3), 89–107.

Bockstael, N.B., W.H. Hanemann and I.E. Strand Jr. (1987), *Measuring the Benefits of Water Quality Improvements Using Recreation Demand Models*, Vol. II, final report to US Environmental Protection Agency, Department of Agricultural and Resource Economics, University of Maryland.

Bockstael, N.B. and K.E. McConnell (1993), 'Public Goods as Characteristics of Nonmarket Commodities', *Economic Journal*, **103**(3), 1244–57.

Braden, J.B. and C.D. Kolstad (eds), (1991), *Measuring the Demand for Environmental Quality*, Amsterdam: North Holland.

Brookshire, D.S., M.A. Thayer, W.D. Schulze and R.C. d'Arge (1982), 'Valuing Public Goods, A Comparison of Survey and Hedonic Approaches', *American Economic Review*, **72**(1), 165–77.

Brown, G.M., Jr. and R. Mendelsohn (1984), 'The Hedonic Travel Cost Method', *Review of Economics and Statistics*, **66**(3), 427–33.

Brown, T.C., P.A. Champ, R.C. Bishop and D.W. McCollum (1996), 'Response Formats and Public Good Donations', *Land Economics*, **72**(2), 152–66.

Cameron, T.A. (1992), 'Combining Contingent Valuation and Travel Cost Data for the Valuation of Nonmarket Goods', *Land Economics*, **68**(3), 302–17.

Cameron, T.A. and M.D. James (1987), 'Efficient Estimation Methods for Closed Ended Contingent Valuation Surveys', *Review of Economics and Statistics*, **69**(5), 269–76.

Carlin, A., P.F. Scodari and D.H. Garver (1992), 'Environmental Investments, The Cost of Cleaning Up.' *Environment*, **34**(2), 12–20, 38–44.

Carson, R.T. (1995), 'Contingent Valuation Surveys and Tests of Insensitivity to Scope', discussion paper 95–05, Department of Economics, University of California, San Diego, February.

Carson, R.T., R.C. Mitchell, W.M. Hanemann, R.J. Kopp, S. Presser and P.A. Ruud (1992), 'A Contingent Valuation Study of Lost Passive Use Values Resulting From the Exxon Valdez Oil Spill', unpublished report to Attorney General of the State of Alaska, 10 November, La Jolla, Calif. NRDA, Inc.

Carson, R.T., W.M. Hanemann, R.J. Kopp, J.A. Krosnick, R.C. Mitchell, S. Presser, P.A. Ruud, V.K. Smith, with M. Conaway and K. Martin (1996), 'Was the NOAA Panel Correct About Contingent Valuation', discussion paper 96–20, Quality of the Environment Division, Resources for the Future, May.

Chapman, D.J., W.M. Hanemann and B.J. Kanninen (1996), 'Non-Market Valuation Using Contingent Behavior: Model Specifications and Consistency Tests', presented at AERE Workshop, Lake Tahoe Co., 2–4 June.

Clark, D.E. and J.R. Kahn (1989), 'The Two-Stage Hedonic Wage Approach, A Methodology for the Valuation of Environmental Amenities', *Journal of Environmental Economics and Management*, **16**(2), 106–21.

Cummings, R.G., G.W. Harrison and E.E. Rutström (1995), 'Homegrown Values and Hypothetical Surveys, In the Dichotomous-Choice Approach Incentive-Compatible', *American Economic Review*, **85**(1), 260–66.

Deaton, A. and J. Muellbauer (1980), 'An Almost Ideal Demand System', *American Economic Review*, **70**(1), 312–26.

Desvousges, W.H., F.R. Johnson, R.W. Dunford, K.J. Boyle, S.P. Hudson, K.N. Wilson (1993), 'Measuring Natural Resource Damages With Contingent Valuation Tests of Validity and Reliability', in J.A. Hausman, *Contingent Valuation, A Critical Assessment*, Amsterdam: North Holland.

Desvousges, W.H., A.R. Gable and F.R. Johnson (1995), 'Calibrating Contingent Valuation Estimates, A Review of the Literature and Suggestions for Future Research', Triangle Economic Research, Durham, NC, December.

Desvousges, W.H., F.R. Johnson, S.P. Hudson, A.R. Gable and N.C. Ruby (1996), 'Using Conjoint Analysis and Health State Classifications to Estimate the Value of Health Effects of Air Pollution: Pilot Test Results and Implications', draft report, Triangle Economic Research for Environment Canada, Health Canada, Ontario Hydro and others, Durham, NC, 6 June.

Diamond, P.A. (1996), 'Testing the Internal Consistency of Contingent Valuation Surveys', *Journal of Environmental Economics and Management*, **30**(3), 337–47.

Diamond, P.A. and J.A. Hausman (1994), 'Contingent Valuation, Is Some Number Better Than No Number', *Journal of Economic Perspectives*, **8** (Autumn), 45–64.

Dickie, M., A. Fisher and S. Gerking (1987), 'Market Transactions and Hypothetical Demand Data, A Comparative Study', *Journal of the American Statistical Association*, **87**(1) 69–75.

Diewert, W.E. (1993), 'The Early History of Price Index Research' in W.E. Diewert and A.O. Nakamura (eds.), *Essays in Index Number Theory*, Vol. I, Amsterdam, North Holland.

Duffield, J.W. and D.A. Patterson (1992), 'Field Testing Existence Values, An Instream Flow Trust Fund for Montana Rivers', paper presented to W–133 Meetings, 14th Interim Report, edited by R.B. Rettig, Department of Agricultural and Resource Economics, Oregon State University.

Englin, J. and T.A. Cameron (1996), 'Augmenting Travel Cost Models with Contingent Behavior Data', *Environmental and Resource Economics*, **7**(2), 133–47.

Eom, Y. S. and V.K. Smith (1994), 'Calibrated Non-Market Valuation', unpublished paper, Center for Environmental and Resource Economics, Duke University, August.

Epple, D. (1987), 'Hedonic Prices and Implicit Markets, Estimating Demand and Supply Functions for Differentiated Goods', *Journal of Political Economy*, **95**(1), 59–80.

Espinosa, J.A. and V.K. Smith (1994), 'Implementing Thatcher's Full Repairing Lease, Properties of Virtual Price Indexes for Environmental Resources', unpublished paper, Center for Environmental and Resource Economics, Duke University, March.

Feather, P.M. (1994), 'Sampling and Aggregation Issues in Random Utility Model Estimation', *American Journal of Agricultural Economics*, **76**(4), 772–80.

Feather, P.M., D. Hellerstein and T. Tomasi (1995), 'A Discrete-Count Model of Recreation Demand', *Journal of Environmental Economics and Management* **29**(4), 214–27.

Fox, J.A., J.F. Shogren, D.J. Hayes and J.B. Kliebenstein (1994), 'CVM–X, Calibrating Contingent Values with Experimental Auction Markets', Iowa Agriculture and Home Economics Experiment Station, Iowa State University.

Freeman, A.M., III (1979), *The Benefits of Environmental Improvement, Theory and Practice*, Baltimore: Johns Hopkins.

Freeman, A.M., III (1982), *Air and Water Pollution Control, A Benefit-Cost Assessment*, New York: John Wiley.

Freeman, A.M., III (1993), *The Measurement of Environmental and Resource Values, Theory and Methods*, Washington, DC: Resources for the Future.

Gilbert, C.S. (1985), 'Household Adjustment and the Measurement of Benefits from Environmental Quality Improvement', unpublished PhD dissertation. University of North Carolina at Chapel Hill, Chapel Hill, NC.

Gilbert, C.S. and V.K. Smith (1985), 'The Role of Economic Adjustment for Environmental Benefit Analysis', unpublished paper, Department of Economics and Business Administration, Vanderbilt University, 10 December.

Graham, D.A. (1992), 'Public Expenditures under Uncertainty, The Net Benefits Criteria', *American Economic Review*, **82**(5), 882–946.

Graves, P.E. and D.M. Waldman (1991), 'Multimarket Amenity Compensation and the Behavior of the Elderly', *American Economic Review*, **81**(5), 1374–81.

Haab, T.C. and K.E. McConnell (1996), 'Count Data Models and the Problem of Zeros in Recreation Demand Analysis', *American Journal of Agricultural Economics*, **78**(1), 89–102.

Hanemann, W.M. (1984a), 'Discrete/Continuous Models of Consumer Demand', *Econometrica*, **52**(3), 541–63.

Hanemann, W.M. (1984b), 'Welfare Evaluations in Contingent Valuation Experiments with Discrete Responses', *American Journal of Agricultural Economics*, **66**(3), 332–41.

Hanemann, W.M. (1996), 'Theory Versus Data in the Contingent Valuation Debate', in D.J. Bjornstad and J.R. Kahn (eds.), *The Contingent Valuation of Environmental Resources*, Cheltenham, UK: Edward Elgar.

Hanemann, W.M. and B. Kanninen (forthcoming), 'The Statistical Analysis of Discrete-Response CV Data' in I.J. Bateman and K.G. Willis (eds), *Valuing Environmental Preferences, Theory and Practice of Contingent Valuation Method in the U.S., E.C. and Developing Countries*, Oxford: Oxford University Press.

Hanemann, W.M., J.B. Loomis and B. Kanninen (1991), 'Statistical Efficiency of Double Bounded Dichotomous Choice Contingent Valuation', *American Journal of Agricultural Economics*, **73**(4), 1255–63.

Harrington, W. and P.R. Portney (1987), 'Valuing the Benefits of Health and Safety Regulations', *Journal of Urban Economics*, **22**(1), 101–12.

Hausman, J.A., (1981), 'Exact Consumer's Surplus and Deadweight Loss', *American Economic Review*, **71**, 662–76.

Hausman, J.A. (ed.) (1993), *Contingent Valuation, A Critical Assessment*, Amsterdam: North Holland.

Hausman, J.A. and G.K. Leonard (1992), 'Contingent Valuation and the Value of Marketed Commodities', unpublished paper, Department of Economics, MIT, 24 July.

Hausman, J.A., G.K. Leonard and D. McFadden (1995), 'A Utility-Consistent, Combined Discrete Choice and Count Data Model, Assessing Recreational Use Losses Due to Natural Resource Damage', *Journal of Public Economics*, **56**(1), 1–30.

Hotelling, H. (1947), Letter to National Park Service in *American Economic Study of the Monetary Evaluation of Recreation in National Parks*, US Department of the Interior, National Park Service and Recreation Planning Division, 1949.

Jakus, P.M. (1994), 'Averting Behavior in the Presence of Public Spillovers, Household Control of Nuisance Pests', *Land Economics*, **70**(3), 273–85.

Johansson, P. (1987), *The Economic Theory and Measurement of Environmental Benefits*, Cambridge: Cambridge University Press.

Johansson, P. (1995), *Evaluating Health Risks, An Economic Approach*, New York: Cambridge University Press.

Johnson, F.R., W.H. Desvousges, E.E. Fries and L.L. Wood (1995), 'Conjoint Analyses of Individual and Aggregate Environmental Preferences', Triangle Economic Research, Durham, NC, working paper T–9502, March.

Just, R., D. Hueth and A. Schmitz, (1982), *Applied Welfare Economics and Public Policy*, Englewood Cliffs, NJ: Prentice Hall.

Kahneman, D. and I. Ritov (1994), 'Determinants of Stated Willingness to Pay for Public Goods, A Study in the Headline Method', *Journal of Risk and Uncertainty*, **9** (July), 5–38.

Kaoru, Y. (1995), 'Measuring Marine Recreation Benefits of Water Quality Improvements by the Nested Random Utility Model', *Resource and Energy Economics*, **17**(2), 119–36.

Kaoru, Y., V.K. Smith and J.L. Liu (1995), 'Using Random Utility Models to Estimate the Recreational Value of Estuarine Resources', *American Journal of Agricultural Economics*, **77**(1), 141–51.

Kiel, K.A. (1995), 'Measuring the Impact of the Discovery and Cleaning of Identified Hazardous Waste Sites on House Values', *Land Economics*, **71**(4), 428–36.

Kiel, K. and K. McClain (1995), 'Housing Prices During Siting Decision Stages, The Case of an Incinerator from Rumor through Operation', *Journal of Environmental Economics and Management*, **28**(3), 241–55.

Kling, C.L. and J.A. Herriges (1995), 'An Empirical Investigation of the Consistency of Nested Logit Models With Utility Maximization', *American Journal of Agricultural Economics*, **77** (November), 875–84.

Kling, C.L. and C.J. Thompson (1996), 'The Implications of Model Specification for Welfare Estimation in Nested Logit Models', *American Journal of Agricultural Economics*, **78**(1), 103–14.

Kolhase, J.E. (1991), 'The Impact of Toxic Waste Sites on Housing Values', *Journal of Urban Economics*, **30**(1), 1–26.

Kopp, R.J. and V.K. Smith (eds) (1993), *Valuing Natural Assets, The Economics of Natural Resource Damage Assessment*, Washington, DC: Resources for the Future.

Kopp, R.J. and V.K. Smith (eds) (forthcoming), 'Constructing Measures of Economic Value', in R.J. Kopp, W. Pommerhne and N. Schwarz (eds), *Determining the Value of Non-Marketed Goods, Economic, Psychological and Policy Relevant Aspects of Contingent Valuation*, Boston: Kluwer Nijhoff.

Kriesel, W., A. Randall and F. Lichtkoppler (1993), 'Estimating the Benefits of Shore Erosion Protection in Ohio's Lake Erie Housing Market', *Water Resources Research*, **29**(4), 795–801.

Larson, D.M., J.B. Loomis and Y.L. Chien (1983), 'Combining Behavioral and Conversational Approaches to Value Amenities, An Application to Gray Whale Population Enhancement', paper presented to American Agricultural Economics Association, August.

Liu, J.L. (1995), *Essays on the Valuation of Marine Recreational Fishing Along Coastal North Carolina*, North Carolina State University, unpublished PhD thesis.

Liu, J.L. and V.K. Smith, (1996), 'Household Production, Recreation Index Numbers and Site Quality Differentials', paper under revision, Center for Environmental and Resource Economics, Duke University.

Louviere, J.L. (1988), *Decision Making: Metric Conjoint Analysis*, Sage University Paper No. 67, Newbury Park: Beverly Hills Co.

Louviere, J.L. (1996a), 'Relating Stated Preference Measures and Models to Choices in Real Markets, Calibration of CV Responses', in D.J. Bjornstad and J.R. Kahn (eds.), *The Contingent Valuation of Environmental Resources*, Cheltenham: UK: Edward Elgar.

Louviere, J.L. (1996b), 'Combining Revealed and Stated Preference Data, The Rescaling Revolution', paper presented to 1996 AERE Workshop, Lake Tahoe, CA, 2 June.

Madden, P. (1991), 'A Generalization of Hicksian Q Substitutes and Complements with Applications to Demand Rationing', *Econometrica*, **59**(5), 1497–508.

Mäler, K.G. (1985), 'Welfare Economics and the Environment', in A.V. Kneese and J.L. Sweeney (eds.), *Handbook of Natural Resources and Energy Economics*, Vol. I, Amsterdam: North Holland.

Mansfield, C. (1996), 'A Consistent Method for Calibrating Contingent Value Survey Data', Nicholas School of Environmental, Duke University, unpublished paper.

Math-Tech Inc. (1982), 'Benefits Analysis of Alternative Secondary National Ambient Air Quality Standards for Sulfur Dioxide and Total Suspended Particulates', Vol. II, report to US Environmental Protection Agency, Research Triangle Park, NC: Office of Air Quality Planning and Standards, US EPA, August.

McConnell, K.E. (1990), 'Models for Referendum Data, The Structure of Discrete Choice Models for Contingent Valuation', *Journal of Environmental Economics and Management*, **18**(1), 19–34.

McConnell, K.E. and T.T. Phipps (1987), 'Identification of Preference Parameters in Hedonic Models, Consumer Demands with Nonlinear Budgets', *Journal of Urban Economics*, **22**(1), 35–52.

McConnell, K.E., I.E. Strand and L. Blake-Hedges (1991), 'Random Utility Models of Recreational Fishing, Catching Fish with a Poisson Process', unpublished paper, Department of Agricultural and Resource Economics, University of Maryland.

McFadden, D. (1974), 'Conditional Logit Analysis of Qualitative Choice Behavior', in P. Zarembka (ed.), *Frontiers in Econometrics*, New York: Academic Press, 105–42.

McFadden, D. (1994), 'Contingent Valuation and Social Choice', *American Journal of Agricultural Economics*, **76**(4), 689–708.

Michaels, R.G. and V.K. Smith (1990), 'Market Segmentation and Valuing Amenities with Hedonic Models: The Case of Hazardous Waste Sites', *Journal of Urban Economics*, **28**, 223–42.

Mitchell, R.C. and R.T. Carson (1989), *Using Surveys to Value Public Goods, The Contingent Valuation Method*, Washington, DC: Resources for the Future.

Morey, E.R. (1984), 'Confuser Surplus', *American Economic Review*, **64**(1), 163–73.

Morey, E.R. (1994), 'What is Consumer's Surplus Per Day of Use, When is it a Constant Independent of the Number of Days of Use and What Does it Tell us about Consumer's Surplus', *Journal of Environmental Economics and Management*, **26**(3), 257–70.

Morey, E.R., D. Shaw and M. Watson (1993), 'A Repeated Nested Logit Model of Atlantic Salmon Fishing', *American Journal of Agricultural Economics*, **75** (August), 578–92.

Morey, E.R., D. Shaw and R. Rowe (1991), 'A Discrete Choice Model of Recreation Participation, Set Choicem and Activity Valuation When Complete Trip Data are Not Available', *Journal of Environmental Economics and Management*, **20** (March), 181–201.

Morey, E.R., D. Waldman, D. Assane and D. Shaw (1995), 'Searching for a Model of Multiple Site Recreation Demand that Admits Interior and Boundary Solutions', *American Journal of Agricultural Economics*, **77**(1), 129–40.

Morikawa, T. (1989), *Incorporating Stated Preferences Data In Travel Demand Analysis*, unpublished PhD thesis, Department of Civil Engineering, MIT.

Morikawa, T., M. Ben-Akiva and D. McFadden (1990), 'Incorporating Psychometric Data in Econometric Travel Demand Models' presented at Banff Symposium on Consumer Decision Making and Choice Behavior, May.

National Oceanic and Atmospheric Administration (1994), Natural Resource Damage Assessments, Proposed Rulemaking for Oil Pollution Act of 1990, *Federal Register*, **59**(5(1)), 1062–190.

National Oceanic and Atmospheric Administration (1996), Natural Resource Damage Assessments Final Rule for Oil Pollution Act of 1990, *Federal Register*, **61**(4), 440–510.

Nelson, R.A., T.L. Tanguay and C.D. Patterson (1994), 'A Quality Adjusted Price Index for Personal Computers', *Journal of Business and Economic Statistics*, **12**(1), 23–32.

Oates, W.E. (1969), 'The Effects of Property Taxes and Local Public Spending on Property Values, An Empirical Study of Tax Capitalization and the Tiebout Hypothesis', *Journal of Political Economy*, **77**(5), 957–71.

OECD (1991), *The State of the Environment* (Paris, Organization for Economic Co-operation and Development).

Palmquist, R.B. (1991), 'Hedonic Methods', in J.B. Braden and C.D. Kolstad (eds), *Measuring the Demand for Environmental Quality*, Amsterdam: North Holland.

Palmquist, R.B., F.M. Roka and T. Vakim (forthcoming), 'The Effect of Environmental Impacts from Swine Operations on Surrounding Residential Property Values', *Land Economics*.

Parsons, G.R. (1991), 'A Nested Sequential Logit Model of Recreation Demand', College of Marine Resources, University of Delaware, unpublished.

Parsons, G.R. and A.B. Hauber (1996), 'Choice Set Boundaries in a Random Utility Model of Recreation Demand', discussion paper 96–3, Department of Economics, University of Delaware, March.

Parsons, G.R. and J.J. Kealy (1992), 'Randomly Drawn Opportunity Sets in a Random Utility Model of Lake Recreation', *Land Economics* **68**, 93–106.

Parsons, G.R. and M.S. Needelman (1992), 'Site Aggregation in a Random Utility Model of Recreation', *Land Economics*, **68**, 418–33.

Pollak, R.A. and T.J. Wales (1981), 'Demographic Variable in Demand Analysis', *Econometrica*, **49**, 1533–51.

Ridker, R.G. (1967), *Economic Costs of Air Pollution, Studies in Measurement*, New York: Praeger.

Ridker, R. and J. Henning (1967), 'The Determinants of Residential Property Values With Special Reference to Air Pollution', *Review of Economics and Statistics*, **49**(3), 246–57.

Roback, J. (1982), 'Wages Rents and the Quality of Life', *Journal of Political Economy*, **90**(6), 1257–78.

Rosen, S. (1974), 'Hedonic Prices and Implicit Markets, Product Differentiation in Pure Competition', *Journal of Political Economy*, **82**(1), 34–55.

Rosen, S. (1979), 'Wage Based Indexes of Urban Quality of Life', in P. Mieszkowski and M. Straszheim (eds), *Current Issues in Urban Economics*, Baltimore: John Hopkins University Press.

Roy, A.D. (1950), 'The Distribution of Earnings and of Individual Output', *Economic Journal*, **60**, 489–505.

Shapiro, P. and T. Smith (1981), 'Preferences for Non-Market Goods Revealed through Market Demands', in V.K. Smith (ed.), *Advances in Applied Micro Economics*, Vol. I, Greenwich, CT: JAI Press.

Shonkwiler, J.S. and W.D. Shaw (1996), 'A Discrete Choice Model of the Demand for Closely Related Goals, An Application to Recreation Decisions', unpublished paper, Department of Applied Economics and Statistics, University of Nevada, Reno, March.

Shonkwiler, J.S. and W.D. Shaw (forthcoming), 'Hurdle-Count Data Models in Recreation Demand Analyses', *Journal of Agricultural and Resource Economics*.

Smith, V.K. (1989), 'Taking Stock of Progress With Travel Cost Recreation Demand Models, Theory and Implementation', *Marine Resource Economics*, **6**(4), 279–310.

Smith, V.K. (1991), 'Household Production and Environmental Benefit Measurement', in J. Braden and C. Kolstad (eds), *Measuring the Demand for Environmental Improvement*, Amsterdam: North Holland.

Smith, V.K. (1992), 'Environmental Costing for Agriculture, Will it be Standard Fare in the Farm Bill of 2000?', *American Journal of Agricultural Economics*, **74**(5), 1076–88.

Smith, V.K. (1994), 'Lightning Rods, Dart Boards and Contingent Valuation', *Natural Resources Journal*, **34**(1), 121–52.

Smith, V.K. (1996), 'Can Contingent Valuation Distinguish Economic Values for Different Public Goods?', *Land Economics*, **72**(2), 139–51.

Smith, V.K. and W.H. Desvousges (1986a), *Measuring Water Quality Benefits*, Boston: Kluwer Nijhoff.

Smith, V.K. and W.H. Desvousges (1986b), 'Averting Behavior, Does it Exist?', *Economics Letters*, **20**, 291–6.

Smith, V.K. and J.C. Huang (1993), 'Hedonic Models and Air Pollution, Twenty-five years and Counting', *Environmental and Resource Economics*, **3**(4), 381–94.

Smith, V.K. and J.C. Huang (1995), 'Can Markets Value Air Quality? A Meta-Analysis of Hedonic Property Value Models', *Journal of Political Economy*, **103**(1), 209–15.

Smith, V.K. and Y. Kaoru (1990), 'Signals or Noise? Explaining the Variation in Recreation Benefit Estimates', *American Journal of Agricultural Economics*, **72**(2), 419–33.

Smith, V.K., J.L. Liu and R.B. Palmquist (1993), 'Marine Pollution and Sport Fishing Quality, Using Poisson Models as Household Production Functions', *Economics Letters*, **42**, 111–16.

Smith, V.K. and C. Mansfield (1996), 'Buying Time: Real and Contingent Offers', unpublished paper, Center for Environmental and Resource Economics, Duke University, August.

Smith, V.K. and L. Osborne (1996), 'Do Contingent Valuation Estimates Pass a "Scope" Test? A Meta Analysis', *Journal of Environmental Economics and Management*, **31**(3), 287–301.

Smith, V.K., R.B. Palmquist and P. Jakus (1991), 'Combining Farrell Frontier and Hedonic Travel Cost Models for Valuing Estuarine Quality', *Review of Economics and Statistics*, **73**(4), 694–9.

Smith, V.K., X. Zhang and R.B. Palmquist (forthcoming), 'Marine Debris, Beach Quality and Non-Market Values', *Environment and Resource Economics*.

Straszheim, M. (1978), 'Estimation of the Demand for Urban Housing Services from Household Interview Data', *Review of Economics and Statistics* **55**, 1–8.

Summers, R. and A. Heston (1991), 'The Penn World Trade Table (Mark 5), An Expanded Set of International Comparisons, 1950–1988', *Quarterly Journal of Economics*, **106**(2), 327–69.

Tiebout, C. (1956), 'A Pure Theory of Local Expenditures', *Journal of Political Economy*, **64**(3), 416–24.

Tinbergen, J. (1956), 'On the Theory of Income Distribution', *Weltwertshaftliches Archive*, **77**, 489–505.

Van De Verg, E. and L.L. Lent (1994), 'Measuring the Price Effects of Shoreline Erosion on Chesapeake Bay Area Properties Using the Hedonic Price Approach', in *Toward Sustainable Coastal Watershed, The Chesapeake Experiment*, proceedings of a conference, Norfolk, Va., 1–4 June.

Vaughan, W.J., C.M. Paulsen, J.A. Hewitt, and C.S. Russell (1985), *The Estimation of Recreation-Related Water Pollution Control Benefits, Swimming, Boating and Marine Recreational Fishing*, Final Report to US Environmental Protection Agency, Resources for the Future, Washington, DC, August.

Verboven, F. (1996), 'The Nested Logit Model and Representative Consumer Theory', *Economics Letters*, **50**, 57–63.

Viscusi, W.K. (1989), 'Prospective Reference Theory, Toward an Explanation of the Paradoxes', *Journal of Risk and Uncertainty*, **2**(3), 235–64.

Viscusi, W.K. (1993), 'The Value of Risks to Life and Health', *Journal of Economic Literature*, **31**(4), 1912–36.

Viscusi, W.K., W.A. Magat and J. Huber (1991), 'Pricing Environmental Health Risks, Survey Assessments of Risk-Risk and Risk Dollar Tradeoffs for Chronic Bronchitis', *Journal of Environmental Economics and Management*, **21**(1), 32–51.

Walsh, R.G., D.M. Johnson and J.R. McKean (1992), 'Benefit Transfer of Outdoor Recreation Demand Studies, 1968–1988', *Water Resources Research*, **28**(3), 707–13.

Waugh, F.V. (1929), *Quality as a Determinant of Vegetable Prices, Studies in History, Economics and Public Law*, No. 312, first AMS Edition (from the Columbia University 1929 edition), edited by Faculty of Political Science, Columbia University, New York: AMS Press, 1968.

Willig, R.D. (1978), 'Incremental Consumer's Surplus and Hedonic Price Adjustment', *Journal of Economic Theory*, **17**(2), 227–53.

Zabel, J. and K. Kiel (1994), 'Estimating the Demand for Clean Air in Four United States Cities', unpublished paper, Penn State University.

Zhang, X. (1995), 'Integrating Resource Types, Payment Methods and Access Conditions to Model Use and Nonuse Values, Valuing Marine Debris Control', unpublished PhD thesis, North Carolina State University.

Zhang, X. and V.K. Smith (1996), 'Using Theory to Calibrate Nonuse Value Estimates', unpublished paper under revision, Center for Environmental and Resource Economics, Duke University.

7. International trade and the environment: a survey of recent economic analysis[1]

Alistair Ulph

INTRODUCTION – THE ISSUES

There are three main factors linking environmental policies and international trade. First, international trade affects both the extent and the pattern of production and consumption of goods in different countries, so if these activities have detrimental effects on the environment of the countries where consumption and production take place then trade will affect the environment. Equally, policies designed to ameliorate detrimental effects on the environment of production and consumption will affect the pattern of international trade. Second, production and consumption activities in one country could affect the environment of other countries – as in the acid rain problems of Europe and North America. While such transboundary pollution problems could arise in the absence of any trade between countries, if there is trade between the affected countries, then countries may use trade policy as a weapon to reduce their exposure to transboundary pollution. This is related to the third factor: international trade policies may be used to enforce international environmental agreements, not necessarily with a view to directly affecting the pollution generated by that country but simply as part of a package of sanctions for failing to join or comply with an international environmental agreement. In this chapter I will be concerned mainly with the first factor, and will deal briefly with the second factor, but will not discuss the third factor (see Cesar (1993) and Folmer, Mouche and Ragland (1993) for analysis of 'issue linkage' as this factor has come to be called).

The interaction between environmental policy and trade policy has been the focus of considerable debate in recent years, sparked by the moves towards further trade liberalization in the Single European Market, the Uruguay round of GATT, and, particularly, NAFTA (see, for example, the debate between Bhagwati and Daly in the *Scientific American* (1993), and the contributions in Low (1992)). In this debate, a number of environmentalists argued that any gains from trade liberalization would be substantially outweighed by the damage trade liberalization would do to the environment. There were a number of strands to this argument. To the extent that trade liberalization led to an increase in consumption and production this would lead to an increase in associated damage to the environment through pollution and loss of natural resources. A more substantial concern was that in the absence of traditional trade policy instruments governments might seek to distort their environmental policies as a surrogate for trade policy. In the case of environmental damage related to 'production and process methods' (PPM in the language of GATT), governments might be concerned that imposing tough environmental policies could damage their domestic industries, either through loss of market share or by 'flight of capital' to 'pollution havens' abroad. These concerns could lead to 'ecological dumping' where all governments relax their environmental policies in a process of legislative competition.

To counter ecological dumping it was argued that governments should be allowed to intervene in trade, for example by imposing counter-veiling import tariffs on products coming from countries with lower environmental standards as a form of anti-dumping device (see, for example, Arden-Clarke (1991)). The rejection by GATT of such measures in the famous tuna-dolphin case between the US and Mexico reinforced the view of some environmentalists that free trade and environmental policy were incompatible. There have also been suggestions that international bodies should seek to harmonize environmental standards between countries,[2] or at least set minimum environmental standards in the hope that if some countries are forced to raise their standards then others will respond by raising their standards – a kind of ratchet effect.

Most economists have rejected this analysis and the policy proposals that stem from it. The conventional economic argument runs as follows. When there are externalities, then obviously *laissez-faire* is not desirable, and it may be the case that an expansion of exports due to trade liberalization could cause an increase in environmental damage that outweighs the gains from expanded trade (see Pethig (1976) for example). But the theory of policy targeting (e.g. Bhagwati, 1971) tells us that since the environmental damage is due to an uncontrolled externality, not to trade, then the first best policy is to correct that externality through appropriate environmental policies. Provided something close to optimal environmental policies is imposed, then the usual welfare gains from trade will apply (see Dean, 1992; Anderson, 1992; amongst others). Because of differences in resource endowments or preferences there are no reasons to suppose that optimal environmental policies will be the same in each country. Attempts to harmonize environmental standards would deny some countries the ability to exploit their comparative advantage in environmental resources, and can result not just in an inefficient economic outcome but in greater environmental damage (see Dean, 1992; Robertson, 1992).[3] With transboundary pollution, policies which are optimal from an individual country's perspective need not be optimal from a global perspective, so there will need to be international *coordination* of environmental policy, but this need not imply harmonization.

Of course it may be difficult for countries, particularly less developed countries (LDCs), to implement something close to first-best environmental policies, and in the absence of such environmental policies some second-best policies may be required. But these are likely to be production taxes or consumption taxes rather than trade taxes. Trade policies are likely to be third-best policies, and in addition to any economic efficiency losses they may fail even to protect the environment (see Barbier and Rauscher, 1994; Braga, 1992[4]).

The above analysis provides no support for the claim that governments have incentives for 'ecological dumping'. In the 'small country' case, governments have no incentive to distort their environmental policies from the first-best rule (equating marginal damage costs and marginal abatement costs), since by assumption they cannot influence their terms of trade, and failure to internalize environmental externalities is welfare reducing (Markusen, 1975b), Long and Siebert (1991) amongst many). Allowing countries to have market power will give governments an incentive to manipulate terms of trade in their favour, but the first-best policies will again involve trade taxes to manipulate the terms of trade and environmental policies to address the environmental distortion (Markusen, 1975a and b), Panagariya *et al.*, 1993; amongst many). In the absence of trade instruments governments may well use environmental policies to address both sets of distortion, in which case environmental policies will not be set using the simple first-best rule outlined above. But there is no presumption that this will involve *relaxing* environmental policies by all governments. A country which is a net exporter of a good which causes pollution in production will wish to set too tough environmental policies, essentially as a proxy for the optimal export tax; but a country which is a net importer will wish to set too lax an environmental policy in order to encourage domestic production and so reduce its demand for imports and hence the price it pays for the imports.

So the conventional economic analysis, where producers and consumers act competitively while governments may or may not be able to influence world prices, provides no support for the concerns about general relaxation of environmental policies in a liberalized trade regime. But there remains the question of what happens when producers themselves exploit market power, due to significant increasing returns to scale, and governments engage in 'strategic behaviour' to try to shift rents towards their domestic producers. There have been a number of studies recently which have taken the framework of strategic trade theory (see Helpman and Krugman (1989) for a useful summary) and applied it to the analysis of environmental policy. As I shall show, this can produce an argument supporting 'ecological dumping', though as I shall also show this argument is by no means robust. The introduction of strategic behaviour by governments will also allow me to address another claim that emerged in the debate over recent moves towards trade liberalization, a claim that is sometimes associated with the name of Michael Porter (the 'Porter hypothesis (Porter, 1991), namely that far from setting environmental policies which are too lax, governments acting strategically would set policies which are too tough (relative to the first-best rule) as a way of inducing their producers to innovate new 'green technologies' ahead of their rivals and thus gain a long-term competitive advantage, even if this meant a short-term competitive disadvantage. The literature on strategic behaviour by governments in trade and environmental policies provides a framework for assessing this claim too.

In the next section of this chapter I will give a more technical account of the traditional arguments sketched above, and then in the rest of the chapter I will survey the more recent literature which has addressed these questions in the framework of strategic trade theory. I will introduce a basic strategic model which shows that 'ecological dumping' will arise in the equilibrium, and then discuss the robustness of that finding. Then, the basic model is extended to allow for strategic behaviour by firms in two forms – investment in R. & D. and choice of location, which allows me to address issues such as the Porter hypothesis and delocation. Then follows an assessment of the implications of the analysis of strategic environmental policy for the design of international environmental policy. It will be clear that I shall mainly survey recent developments in the theory linking environment and international trade, since I believe that the lack of a clear understanding of the theoretical underpinnings has confused the debate on trade and the environment. I will make some reference to how these theoretical developments impinge on the policy debate, but lack of space regrettably prevents me saying anything about the empirical literature.

SURVEY OF TRADITIONAL ANALYSIS

In this section I shall provide a more technical review of some of the results of the traditional analysis of the interactions between environmental policy and international trade mentioned in the previous section. By traditional analysis I mean that households and firms are all assumed to act competitively, and if there is any market power to be exploited that is done by the government. I shall use the dual approach to international trade theory (see, for example, Dixit and Norman (1980), and the exposition will draw on the very useful papers by Copeland (1994) and Panagariya *et al.* (1993). There are a number of factors which could be taken into account:

(a) whether a country is small or large;
(b) whether environmental damage is purely domestic or there are transboundary spillovers;
(c) whether factors of production are internationally mobile or not; and

(d) whether the government is able to use a full set of policy instruments and whether it is setting its policy instruments at the optimal level or whether it is carrying out a partial policy reform.

For the sake of brevity I will ignore transboundary pollution[5] and assume that factors of production are internationally immobile (see Ulph (1994b) for a fuller survey).

I refer to a typical country, and assume that there are n goods and m pollutants. World prices are denoted by the n-vector p and domestic prices by $q = p + t$ where t is a vector of trade taxes; good 1 will be the numeraire with $q_1 = p_1 = 1$; $t_1 = 0$. Pollution emissions are related solely to the activities of production, and I denote by z the m-vector of emissions associated with domestic production of the n-vector of outputs y; the production feasibility of (y,z) is given by requiring that $(y,z) \in T(v)$ where $T(v)$ is the production possibility set given the endowment vector of factors, v. Letting s denote a vector of emission taxes on the pollutants, z, I shall represent the production side of the economy by the revenue function:

$$R(q, s, v) \equiv \max_{y,z}[(q.v - s.z) \quad s.t \ (y, z) \in T(v)]$$

By the usual duality relationships we have: $y = R_q$; $x = -R_s$. Governments may not use emission taxes as a policy instrument, and may use some form of quantity constraint such as emission standards or tradable emission permits. I shall refer to this approach in shorthand as the use of emission standards, but I shall assume that these are allocated efficiently across individual producers; I model this approach by simply assuming that the authorities set an upper limit on aggregate emissions, say $\bar{z}$, and that producer behaviour can be captured by the *restricted revenue function*:

$$\bar{R}(q, \bar{z}, v) \equiv \max_{y,z}\{q.y \quad s.t. \ (y, z) \in T(v), z \leq \bar{z}\}.$$

Again, $y = \bar{R}q$ while $\bar{R}_{\bar{z}}$ now stands for the marginal cost of reducing emissions, i.e., the *marginal abatement costs*.

I assume that the consumption side of the economy can be represented by a single household. I suppose, without loss of generality, that environmental damage is purely of the 'eyesore' type – i.e. it damages household utility but not production. Pollution damages are purely domestic, and are represented by $d = D(z)$ where $D' > 0$, $D'' > 0$. I represent the household side of the economy by its dual representation in the form of the expenditure function: $E(q, d, u) = \min_c \{q. c \text{ s.t. } u (c, d) \geq u\}$ where c is the n-vector of consumption, and $u(c, d)$

is the household's utility function, with $u_c > 0$; $u_d < 0$. Again there is the usual duality relationship that: $c = E_q$; while E_d represents the household's willingness to pay for reductions in environmental damage (i.e., the marginal damage cost). To complete the description of the economy, I let M denote the vector of net imports to the economy (positive if imports, negative if exports), where $M = E_q - R_q$. Then assuming that the revenues from trade taxes and emission taxes are redistributed to the household as a lump-sum subsidy we can summarize the equilibrium for the economy given any vector of trade taxes t and emission taxes s by:

$$E(q, d, u) = R(q, s, v) + t.M + s.z \qquad (7.1)$$

$$M = E_q(q, d, u) - R_q(q, s, v) \qquad (7.2)$$

$$z = -R_s(q, s, v) \qquad (7.3)$$

In the case where the government uses emission standards, (7.1) will contain no emission tax revenues, and the revenue function is replaced by the restricted revenue function. This completes the notation. I now turn to the results.

The Small Country Case

I now consider first-best policy, where the government is free to vary all its policy instruments, and compare that to second-best policy, where the government is restricted in some way in the policies it can set (these restrictions will take the form of not being able to vary either its trade or its environmental policies).

First-best policy
Total differentiation of (7.1) using (7.2) and (7.3) yields:[6]

$$E_u.du = -[E_d D_z - s]dz + t.dM \qquad (7.4)$$

This tells us that for an optimum the first-best policy involves setting emission taxes equal to marginal damage costs, i.e. $s = E_d.D_z$, which I will refer to as the *first-best* policy rule for setting emission taxes, and setting trade taxes equal to zero ($t = 0$) i.e., the country should pursue free trade. In the case of the use of emissions standards (7.4) becomes:

$$E_u.du = -[E_d D_z - \bar{R}_{\bar{z}}]d\bar{z} + t.dM \qquad (7.4')$$

This has the same interpretation: first-best policy involves setting emission standards so that marginal costs of abatement equal marginal damage costs (the *first-best* rule for emission standards), and no trade taxes (i.e., free trade). Thus with first-best policy emission taxes and emission standards are equivalent. This is a standard result and can be found in Markusen (1975a and b), Long and Siebert (1991), Anderson (1992), and Copeland (1994), among others. Thus, provided countries adopt the appropriate (first-best) environmental policies there is no case for interfering with free trade. Under the assumptions made so far, if all countries follow these policies the resulting resource allocation will be Pareto optimal.

Second-best policy

To derive these policies totally differentiate (7.2) and (7.3) to obtain:

$$dz = -(R_{sq}. dt + R_{ss}. ds) \tag{7.5}$$

$$dM = (E_{qq} - R_{qq}) dt + E_{qd}. D_z dz + E_{qu}.du - R_{qs}.ds \tag{7.6}$$

Define $\Sigma_{qq} \equiv R_{qq} - E_{qq}$, a positive-definite matrix of substitution effects, $m \equiv E_{qu} / E_u$, a vector of marginal propensities to consume, and $\delta \equiv E_d D_z - t.E_{qd}.D_z - s$ a vector which represents a vector of *environmental distortions*, i.e., the difference between emission taxes and the full social costs of additional emissions, which includes not just the direct damage costs to consumers but also the tariff distortion of any additional consumption triggered by additional environmental distortions – e.g. if extra pollution in a country causes households to take more foreign holidays, and these have trade taxes on them, then this will be part of the social costs of pollution. Inserting (7.5) and (7.6) in (7.4) yields a general expression for the welfare effects of a change in trade and emission taxes (see Copeland, 1994):

$$E_u.du (1 - t.m) = (\delta R_{sq} - t. \Sigma_{qq}) dt + (\delta R_{ss} - t.R_{qs})ds \tag{7.7}$$

Assuming that the equilibrium is stable, the term $(1–t.m)$ is positive. The terms in the brackets on the right-hand side of (7.7) shows that the welfare effects of a change in either trade taxes or emission taxes must take account of the existing distortions in both trade taxes and emission taxes. It is easily seen that first-best again requires the imposition of the first-best Pigovian taxes and free trade.[7]

Now suppose that the government uses emission standards for its environmental policy, but trade taxes for its trade policies, then a similar set of calculations to those above yields an equivalent expression to (7.7) for the welfare effects of a change in trade taxes and emission standards:

$$E_u.du (1 - t.m) = -(\bar{\delta} + t.\bar{R}_{qz}) d\bar{z} - t.\Sigma_{qq}dt \tag{7.7'}$$

where $\bar{\delta} \equiv E_d.D_z - t.E_{qd}D_z - \bar{R}_{\bar{z}}$ is again a measure of the distortion of emission standards, taking account of the full social costs of a change in emission standards when there are trade distortions in the economy. While (7.7') has a similar form to (7.7) there is one important difference, namely that the effect of a change in trade taxes has no term for the impact on the environmental distortion; the reason is simple – if environmental policy is implemented through quantity constraints which bite, then a change in trade taxes cannot change the extent of environmental distortion.

Now suppose that the government is not able to set the first-best policies, and in particular that there are fixed, non-zero, environmental distortions. Then we can calculate the second-best trade policies. Thus in (7.7) set $ds = 0$. Then to obtain $du = 0$ we require:

$$t^* \equiv \delta.R_{sq}(\Sigma_{qq})^{-1} \qquad (7.8)$$

assuming that the matrix of substitution terms is of full rank. Equation (7.8) tells us that in the absence of first-best environmental policy there may be a case for deviating from free-trade as a surrogate for not being able to modify environmental policy. Note though that this simple model just assumes that the only other policy instruments are trade taxes; in general the government will have available to it a range of production, consumption and trade taxes, and will want to optimize over whatever instruments are assumed to be available, and it is not obvious that this will require the use of trade taxes. To interpret (7.8) note first that δ is itself a function of t. Suppose that there is only one good, other than the numeraire good, which is subject to both a fixed (perhaps zero) environmental tax and a trade tax; suppose that initially $t = 0$ and $s = 0$, so that $\delta > 0$, i.e. marginal damage cost is above the current emission tax (zero); clearly $R_{sq} < 0$ while the last term in (7.8) is > 0, so for this case what (7.8) tells us is that the optimal policy is for a *subsidy* to imports, for the obvious reason that this will reduce domestic production which is already excessive because the pollution externality has not been internalized (Panagariya *et al.*, 1993).

If emission standards are being used, then the policy prescription is very simple. Set $d\bar{z} = 0$ in (7.7') then the optimal trade policy is free trade ($t = 0$), again for the obvious reason that since the pollution externalities are being controlled by the quantity restrictions then there is no interaction between trade and environmental policy so even if environmental policy is not first-best there is no reason for interfering with free trade.

So far I have considered optimal trade policy given restrictions on environmental policy. I now briefly consider optimal environmental policy in the face of fixed, but non-zero, trade taxes. In both (7.7) and (7.7') set $dt = 0$; optimality of environmental policy requires that the terms multiplying ds in (7.7) and $d\bar{z}$ in (7.7') be zero. The deviations from first-best environmental policies in the cases of emission taxes and emission standards are given by:

$$E_d D_z - s = t.(E_{qd}.D_z + R_{qs}.(R_{ss})^{-1}) \qquad (7.9a)$$

$$E_d D_z - \bar{R}_{\bar{z}} = t.(E_{qd}.D_z - \bar{R}_{q\bar{z}}) \qquad (7.9b)$$

The first term in brackets on the right-hand side of (7.9a) and (7.9b), as already noted, reflects the effect of changes in environmental damage on consumption decisions, while the second terms reflect the impact of environmental policy on firms' output decisions. Since these are both distorted by the trade taxes t this has to be reflected in the setting of environmental policy. The interpretation of (7.9) is straightforward. It will pay to relax environmental policy (have taxes (equal to marginal abatement costs) below marginal damage costs) if that encourages the net imports of goods which have a positive trade tax, since that trade tax means that, in the absence of environmental policy, imports would be too low. Of course if relaxing environmental policy discourage such imports, then (7.9) tells us that governments should set environmental policy to be tougher than first-best.

The Large Country Case

The key difference between this and the small country case is that world prices are now endogenous. I capture this very simply by assuming that the demand for net imports is given by $M = E_q - R_q = \phi(p)$. I therefore write the budget constraint in the cases of emission taxes and emission standards as, respectively:

$$E(q, d, u) = R(q, s, v) + t\phi (p) + sz \qquad (7.10a)$$

$$E(q, d, u) = \bar{R}(q, \bar{z}, v) + t\phi (p) \qquad (7.10b)$$

As before I analyse first-best and second-best policies. In the large country case however it is important to enter the obvious caveat that what is deemed first-best or second-best from the viewpoint of a single country will be suboptimal from a world point of view, since the exploitation of market power leads to a distortion of the worldwide allocation of resources.

First-best policy
Total differentiation of (7.10a) and (7.10b) yield, respectively:

$$E_u.du = (t\phi_p(p) - \phi(p)) dp + (s - E_d.D_z)dz \qquad (7.11a)$$

$$E_u.du = (t\phi_p(p) - \phi(p))\,dp + (\bar{R}_{\bar{z}} - E_d.D_z)d\bar{z} \qquad (7.11b)$$

First-best policy then requires that governments impose first-best environmental policies plus optimal tariffs defined by:

$$t. = \phi(p).[\phi_p(p)]^{-1} \qquad (7.12)$$

In the case where import demand depends only on the own-price of each good, (7.12) is just the familiar optimal tariff rule:

$$\frac{t}{p} = \frac{\phi(p)}{p.\phi'(p)} \qquad (7.13)$$

i.e., the *ad valorem* tariff rate is inversely proportional to the elasticity of net import demand.

Second-best policy

In the case of emission taxes, a complete analysis of second-best policy at the same level of generality as I presented for the small country case becomes rather messy, and would go beyond the scope of this chapter so I shall make two simplifying assumptions: I ignore income effects (i.e., $E_{qu} = 0$) and I assume separability between the externality and consumption demand (i.e., $E_{qd} = 0$; these simplify the interpretation of the policy rules, without affecting the broad message of this section. Furthermore, I consider only the case where the government takes its trade taxes as fixed (i.e., $dt = 0$). Then, totally differentiating (7.3) and the import demand function yields:

$$\phi_p.dp = -\Sigma_{qq}.dp - R_{qs}.ds$$
$$dz = -R_{sq}.dp - R_{ss}.ds$$

Substituting in (7.11a) and rearranging yields:

$$E_u.du = (s - E_d.D_z)B.ds - (t\phi p - \phi).A.R_{qs}ds$$

where

$$A \equiv (\phi_p + \Sigma_{qq})^{-1} \text{ and } B \equiv -(R_{sq}.\,A.R_{qs} + R_{ss})$$

Then the optimal set of environmental taxes are given by:

$$s - E_d.D_z = (t\phi_p - \phi).\,C = (t - \hat{t}(p)).\,\phi_p.\,C \qquad (7.14)$$

where

$$C \equiv A.R_{qs}.\,B^{-1} \text{and } \hat{t}(p) \equiv \phi.(\phi_p)^{-1};$$

$\hat{t}(p)$ is the formula for the optimal tariff. Thus (7.14) says that in this second-best, environmental taxes should differ from marginal damage costs in a way that reflects the deviations of tariffs from their optimal value. To get a bit more intuition for what is implied, suppose that $t = 0$ and consider the case of a single good with a single pollutant. Then it can be shown that C in (7.14) is a positive scalar, and (7.14) says that the government should set its environmental tax above marginal damage cost if the good is a net export and below marginal damage if it is a net import. The rationale is obvious: if the country exports the good then the government wants to exert market power by raising the price its producers set, and it does this by driving up their environmental costs. On the other hand, if the good is an import, then the government wants to expand domestic production of the good in order to drive down import demand and hence import prices, and it does this by relaxing the environmental policy it imposes on its domestic producers (see Markusen, 1975b; Krutilla, 1991; Rauscher, 1993; Long and Siebert, 1991).

In the case of emission standards, analysis is somewhat more straightforward. I define $\theta \equiv (t\phi_p - \phi).A = (t - \hat{t}(p)).\phi_p.A$ as a measure of the distortion of trade taxes away from the optimal tariff. Then a bit of manipulation shows that (7.11b) can be written as:

$$E_u.du\,(1 - \theta.m) = -(\hat{\delta} + \theta.\bar{R}_{qz})d\bar{z} - \theta\Sigma_{qq}.dt \qquad (7.15)$$

where

$$\hat{\delta} = E_d.D_z - \theta E_{qz} - \bar{R}_{\bar{z}}$$

Equation (7.15) is a direct analogue of (7.7') in the small country case, except that θ replaces t as the measure of trade tax distortion and the measure of environmental policy distortion is modified accordingly. Thus much of the discussion of second-best policy in the small country case carries over to the large country case, with the difference that the trade taxes from which distortions are measured are the optimal tariffs, not zero. In particular, it follows that if emission standards are set at a level different from their first-best value, then the optimal trade policy still consists of just setting the optimal tariffs, for the same reason as before, that trade policy does not spillover on to environmental policy as long as environmental emissions are constrained by the emission standards. In the case of fixed trade taxes, the optimal second-best environmental policy is given by:

$$E_d.D_z - \bar{R}_z = \theta. (E_{qz} - \bar{R}_{qz}) \qquad (7.16)$$

Equation (7.16) is again a straightforward analogue of (7.9b) in the small country case, with θ replacing t. To see the relationship with the emission tax case, I impose the same simplifying assumptions as in the emission tax case (no income effects and separability), then (7.16) becomes:

$$\bar{R}_{\bar{z}} - E_d.D_z = (t\phi_p - \phi). \bar{C} = (t - \hat{t}(p)).\phi_p.\bar{C} \qquad (7.16')$$

Equation (7.16') is the analogue of (7.14) and has the same interpretation.

Summary of Traditional Analysis

To summarize the main findings of this section, in the small country case there is no reason for interfering with free trade, provided governments have optimal environmental policies in place; indeed in the case where governments use emission standards, even if environmental policy is not first-best, there is no case for deviating from free trade. In the large country case, there will be standard reasons why individual countries may seek to move away from free trade, but this has nothing to do with environmental factors, and again as long as environmental policy is first-best, trade policy is given by conventional optimal tariff; this remains the optimal policy in the case of emission standards even if these are not first-best. If policy is second-best, then in the absence of optimal first-best emission taxes there is a case for distorting trade taxes as a surrogate for first-best emission taxes, but this is driven by domestic considerations rather than what is happening in other countries. Conversely, if trade policy is not first-best, environmental policy will need to take this into account. But this does not suggest that governments have universal incentives for weakening environmental policies; thus in the large country case a country which sets its export tariff below the optimum should set environmental policy which is tougher than first-best as a means of capturing some additional monopoly profits. Finally, I have noted that with first-best policies there is no difference between policy instruments, provided they are efficiently imposed domestically, but when second-best policies are considered there are important differences, particularly for trade policy.

IMPERFECT COMPETITION AND STRATEGIC ENVIRONMENTAL POLICY – SOME SIMPLE MODELS

While perfect competition may be a plausible description of some markets, many markets for manufactured goods may have significant scale economies in production, so that imperfect competition may be a better characterization of their market structure. In the 1980s a substantial literature explored the implications for trade policy of imperfectly competitive international markets (see Helpman and Krugman, 1989) and more recently this literature has been adapted to explore the implications for environmental policy, especially in regimes where trade policy is outlawed.

One reason why imperfect competition might provide more rationale for governments to engage in ecological dumping is that imperfect competition allows producers to earn rents and provides incentives for governments to try to shift those rents in favour of their domestic producers, by giving their producers a cost advantage through less stringent environmental policies. However, it may be asked why governments need to distort their policies at all if producers are already earning rents. The reason is that governments are presumed to be able to commit themselves to policies prior to the decisions by producers to set output or prices, and it is this ability to *precommit* which allows governments the scope to manipulate markets in a way which is not available to producers themselves. This prior manipulation of markets is referred to as *strategic behaviour.*

In the rest of this chapter I will review this recent literature to assess how far the intuitions sketched above can be supported by economic analysis. As the discussion above of strategic behaviour makes clear, strategic behaviour depends crucially on the structure of moves by different agents. The models I review in this section have a three-stage game structure. In stage 1, governments choose the *form* of environmental policy they will employ. In the second stage, governments choose the *level* at which they set their policy instruments. Finally, in stage 3, producers choose their *market variables* – either output or price. In the rest of this section I develop a particular example: first, the analysis of stages 2 and 3 when the government uses emission taxes; next, the analysis of stages 2 and 3 when the government uses emission standards; and then an analysis of the stage 1 game of the choice of emission standards or emission taxes. Finally, I discuss how the results of this model are modified by changing the basic assumptions. The basic model is similar to those developed by Barrett (1994), Conrad (1993a and b), Kennedy (1994) and Ulph (1996b), and is a variant of the original Brander and Spencer (1985) model.

Suppose there are two firms, each located in a separate country, with the profits of these firms accruing to shareholders located in the same country. There are no consumers of the product located in these countries, so their output is sold to a third group of countries. I assume the two firms and countries are identical. Demand for the product is summarized by the total revenue function of a firm $R(x, y)$ where x is own output and y is the rival firm's output and $R_x > 0$, $R_{xx} < 0$, $R_y < 0$, $R_{xy} < 0$. The firm has total cost function $C(x)$, which has either constant or diminishing returns to scale (there might also be some fixed cost present to help explain why there are only two firms in the market, but I do not model entry explicitly). In the third-stage market, game firms set outputs, i.e., there is Cournot competition. Units of measurement are chosen so that each unit of output produces one unit of pollution, but the firm is able to abate pollution. Letting *a* denote the amount of pollution abated, $A(a)$ is a (convex) total abatement cost curve. Net emissions to the environment by the firm are therefore $e = x - a$. Pollution is entirely domestic, and there is a total damage cost function $D(e)$ which is strictly convex. The government can choose two forms of environmental policy – an emission tax, *t*, or an emission standard *e*, an upper limit on the units of emissions by the firm. Note that with the assumption of a single firm, in the absence of any trade considerations these two forms of environmental policy would be equivalent. Governments maximize welfare which is total revenue minus total social costs (production costs plus abatement costs plus damage costs). I shall use τ and ε to refer to the policy instruments of the rival government. I now calculate a (sub-game perfect) Nash equilibrium of the three-stage game, beginning by solving the stage three and stage two games when the government uses emission taxes and standards respectively.

Emission Taxes

Stage three – market game
The firm takes as given the emission tax, *t*, and the output of the rival firm, *y*, and chooses output, *x*, and abatement, *a,* to maximize:

$$\pi \equiv R(x, y) - C(x) - A(a) - t.(x - a)$$

for which first-order conditions are:

$$R_x - C' - t = 0 \tag{7.17a}$$
$$A'(a) - t = 0 \tag{7.17b}$$

Equation (7.17a) requires that marginal revenue equal marginal cost plus the emission tax, while (7.17b) says that the firm abates pollution to the point where marginal abatement cost equals the emission tax. Equation (7.17b) can be inverted to yield: $a = B(t)$ where $B \equiv (A')^{-1}$ and $B' = (A'')^{-1}$ while (7.17a) can be rewritten as the firm's reaction function, $x = r(y, t)$ where

$$r_1 = \frac{-R_{xy}}{R_{xx} - C''}, -1 < r_1 < 0, \quad r_2 = \frac{1}{R_{xx} - C''} < 0 \tag{7.18}$$

and r_1, r_2 are the derivatives of the reaction function with respect to y and t respectively. Thus reaction functions are downward sloping and stable, and an increase in the emission tax will reduce the domestic firm's output for any given output by the rival, i.e., it shifts downwards the domestic firm's reaction function.

Nash equilibrium is given by solving the reaction functions to yield the *equilibrium* output level:[8]

$$x = r[r(x, \tau), t] \equiv \rho\,(t, \tau) \tag{7.19}$$

where $\rho_1 = r_2/(1 - r_1^2) < 0$ and $\rho_2 = r_1.r_2(1 - r_1^2) > 0$. Equation (7.19) says that an increase in the emission tax will reduce the equilibrium output of the domestic firm and expand the equilibrium output of the rival firm, with the absolute impact on the domestic firm being greater than that on the rival firm.

Stage 2 – choice of emission tax level
The government takes as given the emission tax set by the rival government, τ, and chooses its own emission tax rate, t, to maximize welfare:

$$W(t, \tau) = R(x, y) - C(x) - A(a) - D(x - a)$$

where $x = \rho(t, \tau)$, $y = \rho(\tau, t)$ and $a = B(t)$. The first-order condition is:[9]

$$W_t = (R_x - C' - D')\,\rho_1 + R_y.\rho_2 - (A' - D').\,B' = 0$$

$$t - D' = A' - D' = \frac{R_y.\rho_2}{B' - \rho_1} < 0 \tag{7.20}$$

Equation (7.20) says that the government has an incentive to relax environmental policy (set emission tax below marginal damage cost). The reason is that this shifts out the domestic firm's reaction function, thereby hoping to reduce the rival firm's output level. Note that the incentive for strategic behaviour arises solely because the government thinks it can manipulate the output of the *rival* producer. The domestic producer chooses output to maximize profits taking as given the output of the rival firm; but the government believes that if its domestic producer was to expand output further, then the rival firm would reduce its output.

Equation (7.20) implicitly defines the reaction function for the government. Write this as $t = \Phi(\tau)$. It is straightforward to show that this is upward sloping with slope less than 1 (see Ulph, 1996a). The intuition is as follows. Suppose the foreign government toughens its environmental policy (raises its emission tax); that will reduce the output of the foreign firm, raise the marginal profits of the home firm and encourage the home firm to expand output. If the home government left its emission tax unaltered, that would leave the amount of abatement by the home firm unaltered, and all the extra output of the home firm would take the form of extra pollution, with increasing marginal damage. But that is not the efficient solution from the government's point of view. It would want some of the extra pollution to be abated, and to encourage its domestic firm to do more abatement it has to raise its emission tax. So the home government has to raise its emission tax as well, though not by as much as the foreign government.

To complete the analysis of the second-stage game, we can solve for the pair of government reaction functions, which, given that symmetry implies $t = \tau$, simply means finding the emission tax which solves $t = \Phi(t)$. In equilibrium, both governments (in general all governments of producing governments) will relax their environmental policies in an attempt to increase the market shares of their domestic producers. Note that these attempts to increase the market shares of their domestic producers are doomed, since both governments act in the same way, and, by symmetry, in equilibrium each firm must have an equal share of the market. The net effect is rather to expand industry output, driving down profits of both firms and increasing pollution in both countries, making both governments worse off than if they had followed the first-best policy of setting emission tax equal to marginal damage cost.

In the previous paragraph I compared the outcome when the governments set their emission taxes in a non-cooperative Nash equilibrium with the first-best rule. A further comparison would be to ask what taxes the governments would set if they acted cooperatively. This would be done by choosing t and τ to maximize $W(t, \tau) + W(\tau, t)$. Carrying out the maximization and rearranging the first-order condition as was done in deriving (7.20) yields the following condition for the optimal emission tax in a cooperative equilibrium:

$$t - D' = A' - D' = \frac{R_y(\rho_1 + \rho_2)}{B' - (\rho_1 + \rho_2)} > 0 \qquad (7.21)$$

Thus in a cooperative equilibrium the governments would set emission taxes above marginal damage costs. The reason is that the Cournot equilibrium chosen by firms leaves industry output above the monopoly level, and hence industry profits below the monopoly level, taking account of environmental damage. So governments seek to reduce industry output by setting environmental taxes above marginal damage costs (see Barrett, 1994). This result is the analogue of the result in the traditional analysis that net exporting countries would seek to set environmental policies which were tougher than the first-best rule.

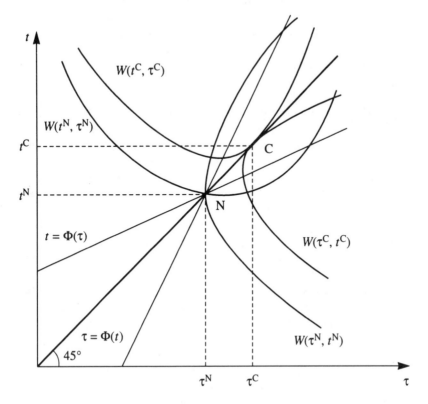

Figure 7.1   Cooperative and non-cooperative equilibria – emission taxes

The comparison between the cooperative and non-cooperative emission taxes is illustrated in Figure 7.1. This shows the iso-welfare contours and the reaction functions for the two countries; the non-cooperative equilibrium is where the reaction functions intersect and the iso-welfare contours are orthogonal to each other; the cooperative equilibrium is where the iso-welfare contours are tangent to each other.[10]

Emission Standards

It is straightforward to conduct a similar analysis for the case where both governments use emission standards as their policy instruments, but due to lack of space the reader is referred to Ulph (1994b) for the details. I begin by simply noting the two main (and closely related) differences that arise when the governments use emission standards:

1. In the stage 3 game of output setting, the reaction function of the firm when the government uses emission standards is shallower than with emission taxes (the domestic producer will increase output more in response to a decrease in rival's output if the government uses taxes than standards). The reason is that when the firm is faced with an emission standard, each additional unit of output it wishes to produce must be matched to an additional unit of abatement, and the marginal cost of abatement is an increasing function of abatement, in general. On the other hand, with an emission tax, the firm believes that each additional unit of production will require it to pay an emission tax on the associated increased unit of pollution, and since the firm takes the emission tax as fixed, the firm believes it faces a constant additional cost of production. A corollary is that an emission tax and emission standard will lead to identical reaction functions if there are constant marginal costs of abatement.

2. In the second-stage game, the government reaction function, $e = \Psi(\varepsilon)$, is downward sloping with slope less than 1 in absolute value. The reason is as follows. Suppose that the foreign government toughens its environmental policy (reduces its emission standard). That will again reduce the foreign firm's output and raise the home firm's marginal profits, encouraging the home firm to expand output. But if the home government keeps its emission standard unaltered, then any increase in output will be matched by an increase in abatement, driving up marginal abatement costs but leaving marginal damage costs unaffected. Again, this is not the efficient solution from the home government's point of view. It would prefer to have some increase in pollution damage in order to save on abatement costs and encourage its domestic firm to expand output a bit more. So the home government will relax its environmental policy in response to a toughening of environmental policy by the foreign government.

Despite these differences, the main results of the analysis using emission taxes carry over to emission standards: when governments act non-cooperatively they set emission standards which are too lenient by comparison with the first-best rule (i.e., they set emission standards such that marginal abatement costs are below marginal damage costs); and they are even more lenient in comparison with the standards they would set if they acted cooperatively, when they would set emission standards so that marginal abatement costs exceed marginal damage costs. The comparison between the cooperative and non-cooperative outcomes are shown in Figure 7.2 which again shows the iso-welfare contours and reaction functions for the two countries and where the non-cooperative equilibrium is where the reaction functions intersect while the cooperative equilibrium is where the iso-welfare contours are tangents.

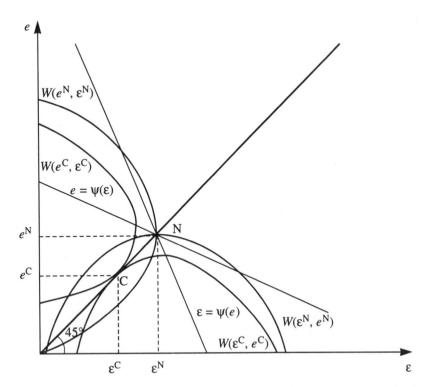

Figure 7.2   Cooperative and non-cooperative equilibria – emission standards

Stage One Game – Choice of Policy Instruments

Much of the literature (Barrett, 1994; Kennedy, 1994; Conrad, 1993a and b) has considered only the first two stages assuming that both governments use either emission taxes (Kennedy and Conrad) or emission standards (Barrett). Ulph (1992, 1996a and b) considered the first-stage game: the choice of policy instruments. I shall not go into details (see Ulph (1994b) for more discussion), but merely note that a range of outcomes are possible. The reason for this range of results is that while the use of emission taxes and standards both lead to ecological dumping by governments, the extent to which governments relax policies from the first-best rule differs between standards and taxes, but not in a consistent way. A key determinant of the extent of strategic behaviour is the nature of the marginal abatement cost curve.

At one extreme, consider the case where abatement is not available (marginal abatement costs are essentially infinite). Then in the stage 3 game, the use of emission standards means that in the stage 3 game, the firm's level of output is determined by the emission standard; this means that a government can precommit the output of its firm, independently of the environmental policy of the rival government. In this case it is clear that if one government uses standards then there is no incentive for the rival government to engage in strategic behaviour, since it cannot shift the rival's output. In particular, if both governments use standards then there will be no strategic behaviour. On the other hand, if both governments use taxes, the output of both firms still depends on the emission taxes set by both governments, and so both governments will act strategically. Since we know that strategic behaviour by *both* governments is actually self-defeating, i.e., both governments are worse off than if they had not acted strategically, it follows that both governments are better off using standards than taxes. Moreover, if one government uses taxes and the other standards, the one using taxes engages in no strategic behaviour, while the one using standards will engage in strategic behaviour. The use of strategic behaviour by one government, *in the absence of any strategic behaviour by its rival*, makes that government better off, so the government using standards will be better off than the government using taxes. In short, for this special case, the use of standards is a dominant strategy. This was the case analysed in Ulph (1992).

However, it is possible to construct other examples, e.g. where marginal abatement costs are linear, where the use of taxes gives a greater market share to the domestic firm than the use of standards, so that the use of taxes becomes a dominant strategy (see Ulph, 1996a and b). In this case the choice of policy instruments is a Prisoner's dilemma since the use of taxes results in greater strategic behaviour by producers, resulting in greater output and pollution than would be the case if both governments selected emission standards. In this case there is a double set of Prisoner's Dilemmas: governments would be better off if they could commit to using standards rather than taxes; but they would be even better off to commit to not distorting their environmental policies at all.

Extensions

It is clear that the model I have used is very simple – deliberately so since I wanted to highlight the nature of the purely strategic incentives for distorting environmental policy. The question I address in the rest of this section is how robust are the conclusions to six variants of the simplifying assumptions.

Other instruments

The results above arise because governments use a single policy instrument to achieve both environmental and trade targets. As Barrett (1994) has shown, if governments can also use trade policy instruments (e.g. a production subsidy) then there is no longer any need to distort environmental policy. Even if the government has two environmental policy instruments (say an emission tax and a subsidy to pollution abatement), Conrad (1993a) has shown that this will restore the efficiency of environmental policy. This is very much in line with the conclusion of the traditional analysis where distortions to environmental policy arose solely from inability to set appropriate trade policy.

Other kinds of environmental policies

Verdier (1993) considers the choice between emission standards and the use of 'design standards' where firms are required to invest in particular technologies for pollution abatement or carry out prescribed minimum amounts of emission reduction (the BATNEEC policies in the UK could be of this type). Unlike the policies I have discussed, there is an inherent inefficiency in the use of design standards (since they prevent firm's making the cost-minimizing choice between abating pollution and cutting output). But he shows that there can be incentives for governments to use design standards as a strategic device to try to help their domestic producers to gain a larger market share. The results are consistent with the broad findings set out above, although Verdier does not address the question of the *level* of policy instruments since he assumes pre-specified targets for emissions.

Number of firms

Suppose there is more than one firm in each country. Because they compete with each other, as well as with foreign producers, for any given output by foreign rivals, the domestic firms produce too much output – they would be better off colluding and acting like a single firm. This means the government has two conflicting incentives. It still has the rent-shifting incentive for *relaxing* policy, but, as with the traditional analysis it also has an incentive for *toughening* environmental policy to get domestic firms to cut their output. Again, if environmental policy is the only instrument it can use to achieve these goals it is not obvious which of these two conflicting incentives will be stronger, so it is not clear whether the net effect will be to have too lax or too tough environmental policy. As Barrett (1994) shows, not surprisingly the larger is the number of firms the stronger is the second incentive for toughening environmental policy, and so the more likely it is that the net effect will be a tougher policy; in the limit as the number of firms gets very large we just get back to the competitive model of the previous section, for which we know the incentive is for too tough a policy.

Form of competition

In the model outlined above, it was assumed that the third-stage game involved Cournot competition in which firms set output levels. An alternative assumption is that firms set prices (Bertrand competition). As Barrett (1994) and D. Ulph (1994) have shown, this makes a substantial difference to the results derived above. First, governments now have an incentive to set environmental policy that is tougher than the first-best. The reason is straightforward. When firms set their prices they assume that other producers keep their prices fixed, and so are reluctant to raise their prices. However, reaction functions are upward-sloping in Bertrand competition. Governments recognize this when setting their environmental policies, and so try to induce their domestic firms to raise prices, since they know this will lead rival producers to raise their prices as well. They do this by forcing up the domestic firm's costs by setting tougher than first-best environmental policies. D. Ulph (1994) also shows that in a model which, under Cournot competition, would have the use of emission taxes resulting in greater distortion than the use of emission standards the reverse is true under Bertrand competition.

Domestic consumers
I have assumed that the countries producing the good did not also consume the good. How does introducing domestic consumers affect the argument? Governments now have to take account of the fact that while raising prices and restricting output may be beneficial for producers, it is damaging to consumers. Even in a closed economy, if the government has only one instrument to deal with both pollution and imperfect competition, then the government may set environmental taxes below first-best Pigovian level to reflect the fact that output under imperfect competition is too low. The same argument applies here. Introducing consumers only reinforces the incentive for relaxing environmental policy in the case of Cournot competition, though it could mitigate the argument for toughening environmental policy under Bertrand competition (see Conrad (1993b) for a discussion in the case of Cournot competition).

Transboundary pollution
With transboundary pollution policies which are first-best from a single country's perspective when it is acting non-co-operatively will not be first-best from an international perspective. Thus any relaxation of environmental policy from a purely domestic first-best is an even greater distortion from the global first-best. I shall stick to non-cooperative behaviour. As Kennedy (1994) shows, in a model of Cournot competition, transboundary pollution *increases* the incentive for switching production to domestic firms – namely that it reduces foreign production and hence any associated transboundary pollution. Thus transboundary pollution would reinforce ecological dumping.

STRATEGIC BEHAVIOUR BY PRODUCERS

The models surveyed in the last section assumed that producers only set either prices or output, and all the strategic behaviour was done by governments. In this section I review some models where producers also take strategic actions, such as investing in capital or R. & D. designed to reduce their costs in the market game, or locating their products in characteristics or physical space to increase the demand for their products. One reason for being interested in this extension is that it raises the question whether strategic behaviour by producers eliminates, or at least reduces, the need for governments to act strategically. As I shall show, the answer to this question is mixed. A second reason is that the strategic behaviour of producers raises issues of interest in their own right. I shall consider two examples of producer strategic behaviour-investment in R. & D. and choice of location. The first allows me to address the Porter hypothesis that governments have an incentive to set too tough an environmental policy in order to encourage their producers to engage in more 'green' R. & D. and hence gain a long-term competitive advantage. The second allows me to assess the issue of capital flight in response to environmental policy.

To introduce strategic behaviour by producers requires that an extra stage be added to the three-stage games considered in the last section. The structure I will consider, following much of the literature, is: stage 1 – governments choose environmental policy instruments; stage 2 – governments choose levels of environmental policy instruments; stage 3 – producers choose investments in R. & D. or plant location; stage 4 – producers choose either prices or outputs. Note that this sequence implies that governments are able to commit to environmental policies which last as long as a new innovation or plant location, and it is not obvious that this is appropriate. An alternative ordering would be to interchange stages 2 and 3, so that producers would choose R. & D. prior to governments choosing levels of environmental policies. Perhaps the most appropriate model would be to have a sequence of moves by governments and producers. However, I do not have space to pursue this issue.

Investment in R. & D.

To give a flavour of the issues, I will sketch the results of the model developed in Ulph and Ulph (1996) which is the most general model I am aware of. More details can be found in the surveys by Ecchia and Mariotti (1994) and Ulph (1994c). The model is essentially the same as in the last section except that it is assumed that there is no abatement technology, but the two firms can invest in R. & D., which can be used to both reduce the costs of production (process R. & D.) or reduce the emissions per unit of output (environmental R. & D.). This corresponds to the situation where pollution cannot be reduced by 'end-of-pipe' treatments, but only by introducing new production processes. I shall consider only the case where governments use emission taxes.

The stage 4 (market) game is essentially as before, allowing for the fact that there is no abatement. The interest is in stages 2 and 3. In the stage 3 game, firms choose their investment in R. & D. There are three key points to note:

1. Firms allocate any given total expenditure on R. & D. between process and environmental R. & D. efficiently; that is they allocate R. & D. expenditure to minimize the total costs of production, including the cost of the emission tax, which is affected by the emission/output ratio.
2. Strategic R. & D. competition between the firms leads them to overinvest in R. & D., i.e. to invest beyond the point where the marginal reduction in production costs equals the marginal cost of R. & D. This is because if firm 1 reduces its costs of production through R. & D. that will reduce its rival's output in equilibrium and hence benefit firm 1.
3. The solution of the stage 3 game will determine equilibrium investments in R. & D. as a function of the emission taxes set by the two governments, and the important question, in terms of the Porter hypothesis, is how the emission tax set by the domestic government affects a firm's investment in R. & D. It turns out that this is ambiguous, because there are two factors at work. First, the convexity of costs means that a higher emission tax reduces the effect of a unit reduction in costs on profits. This means that higher emission taxes discourage domestic R. & D. But the higher tax also means that a given amount of environmental R. & D. will have a larger impact in lowering the firm's costs, so the *effectiveness* of environmental R. & D. goes up. This will increase the incentives to do R. & D. So the net effect of an emission tax on R. & D. is ambiguous. This is an important finding for the Porter hypothesis, since implicit in that hypothesis is the belief that an increase in emission taxes by one government will induce producers in that country to increase R. & D. investment, particularly environmental R. & D.

Finally, I consider the stage 2 game, where governments choose their emission taxes.

Recall that we are interested in two questions – does strategic behaviour by producers reduce the need for strategic environmental policy by governments, and does the Porter hypothesis hold? Neither question has a clear-cut answer. To see why note that there are two factors affecting governments environmental policy setting: the *direct rent-shifting* effect which is the same as before, and unambiguously leads governments to relax environmental policy; and the *indirect strategic investment effect* where governments try to manipulate the R. & D. decisions of the producers. This latter effect is in general ambiguous, because the effects of a tax on R. & D. are ambiguous. Where a higher emission tax discourages domestic R. & D. and encourages foreign R. & D. this effect increases incentives for relaxing environmental policy; if higher taxes encourage domestic R. & D. and discourage foreign R. & D. then governments will want to raise environmental taxes. The net effect in terms of the overall direction of environmental policy is thus ambiguous.

I make three comments:

1. When both the direct and indirect effects go in the direction of governments relaxing environmental policy, it might be thought that this would imply that the distortion to environmental policy will be greater when the strategic behaviour of producers is allowed for than when it is not (as in the previous section). This need not be the case. In a particular model where there is only process R. & D., Ulph (1996b) showed that the direct effect is *smaller* when producers act strategically than when they do not, and that this reduction in the direct effect outweighs the indirect effect. So, for this model, the distortion to government environmental policy is indeed smaller when producers act strategically.
2. In relation to the Porter hypothesis it is clear that there is no general presumption that governments will want to set environmental policies tougher than first best, for two reasons. First, raising environmental taxes may well discourage domestic R. & D. and encourage foreign R. & D. – the opposite of what was presumed by Porter (see D. Ulph (1994)). Second, even if the effects of emission taxes on R. & D. go in the direction presumed by Porter, while that gives *one* factor which goes in the direction of wanting to raise environmental taxes there is still the other direct factor which acts to lower emission taxes, so there is still ambiguity about the overall sign of the distortion to environmental policy.
3. The model set out here assumed Cournot competition. Using Bertrand competition again affects the analysis considerably (see Ulph (1996d) for details), but does not change the basic conclusions above that there can be no general presumption either that allowing for strategic behaviour by producers reduces the extent of strategic behaviour by governments or that the Porter hypothesis must hold.

Choice of Location

In the models reviewed so far, the location of production has been fixed, so while tough environmental policies set by one government might reduce the market shares of domestic producers, it would require quite marked asymmetries in policies to shut down domestic production altogether since that would require policy to drive firms' profits to zero. It might be thought that allowing plants to relocate would increase the pressure on governments to relax their environmental policies, since even if plants were making positive profits at home they may decide to locate abroad to earn even higher profits. However, that raises the important question of why governments should care about where firms locate, which requires a more careful specification of what happens to profits.

Again, lack of space prevents a comprehensive treatment of this issue (see Rauscher (1994) for an excellent survey), so to focus on the essentials I shall sketch the main results using a neat model due to Hoel (1994).

Suppose there is a single firm producing a product. There are fixed costs of setting up a plant, but constant unit operating costs and no transport costs; so this firm will only operate one plant to serve the entire world market. Suppose that each unit of output produces one unit of pollution, and there is no abatement technology. Pollution affects only the country in which the plant is located, and the government in that country imposes an emission tax. To establish some notation, suppose t is the emission tax faced by the firm. Let $q(t)$ be the optimal output produced by the firm, where $q'(t) < 0$; let T be the level of emission tax at which it would pay the firm to shut down production (this effectively acts as an upper limit on the tax rates we need consider). Let $V(t)$ be the corresponding world consumer surplus, $\pi(t)$ the optimal level of the firm's (monopoly) profits, $R(t) = t.q(t)$ the level of government emission tax revenue (with $R(0) = 0$), and $D(q(t))$ the level of environmental damage cost, where D is assumed to be strictly convex with $D(0) = 0$. Note that $V(t) < 0$, $\pi'(t) = -q(t) < 0$; R will be initially increasing and then decreasing, while D will be a decreasing function of t. Suppose that there are only two possible countries in which the firm can locate a plant, although there may be other countries in the world in which either consumers or shareholders live. The structure of the moves will be that the two countries first commit themselves to a level of emission tax; then the firm chooses where to locate to maximize profits; in this simple model this is trivial – the firm locates in the country with the lower emission tax; finally, the firm chooses the optimal level of output given the emission tax.

I begin by asking what would happen if the firm was located in one of the two countries and had no opportunity of relocating. Suppose that a fraction $\sigma \leq 1$ of the world market of consumers lives in that country, and the country retains a fraction $\alpha \leq 1$ of the profits (either through a profits tax or shareholding), then the country will set a *non-strategic* tax t^* to maximize welfare defined as: $W(t, 1) = \sigma V(t) + \alpha \pi(t) + R(t) - D(q(t))$ where the argument 1 in the welfare function denotes the fact that the firm is located in that country. The first-order condition (assuming an interior solution) is:

$$t^* - D' = -\frac{\sigma V' + (1-\alpha)q}{q'} \qquad (7.22)$$

It is clear from (7.22) that there are three factors affecting the non-strategic tax:

1. If $\alpha = 1$, $\sigma = 0$, then the optimal tax is just equal to marginal damage cost. This is because the firm, as a monopolist, is doing all that can be done to maximize profits and the government has no need to worry about loss of consumer surplus (since $\sigma = 0$ there are no domestic consumers to suffer from the deadweight monopoly), so the only reason for the government to intervene is to correct the externality.
2. If $\alpha < 1$ but $\sigma = 0$, then the government will want to set t^* above marginal damage costs, essentially as a way of taxing some of the profits that leave the country.
3. If $\alpha = 1$ but $\sigma > 0$ then the government will set t^* below marginal damage costs since it trades off a bit more pollution damage against a reduction in lost consumer surplus.

This is all consistent with the traditional analysis of the second section (pp. 208). Notice one important point. Unless $\alpha = \sigma = 1$, t^* must be *above* the emission tax which would maximize world welfare, or even the welfare of the two countries in which the firm could locate, since in choosing t^* the country has ignored the negative impact which its emission tax has on consumers or shareholders located in other countries.

Now consider what happens when the firm can choose where to locate so there is strategic interaction between the two countries. For simplicity assume the two countries are identical (they have the same value of α and σ). Define $S(t) = R(t) - D(q(t))$ as the *environmental surplus* which a country gets from having a plant located in its country – i.e., the difference between emission tax revenue and environmental damage; note that $S(0) = 0$, and S will be initially increasing; it may or may not become positive and may or may not decrease before t reaches the maximum value T; if there is a value of $t < T$ such that $t = D'(q(t))$ then S must be positive at that value of t (by convexity of D marginal damage cost exceeds average damage cost). Then we can define the welfare of the countries with and without the plant as $W(t, 1)$ and $W(t, 0)$ respectively, where

$$W(t, 1) = W(t, 0) + S(t) \tag{7.23}$$

There are then three possible outcomes, depending on the level of environmental damage costs, as shown in Figure 7.3.

1. Suppose that environmental damage costs are relatively low so that $S(t^*) > 0$, i.e., at the optimal non-strategic tax there is a positive environmental surplus. Then, as Figure 7.3(a) shows, the unique Nash equilibrium in emission taxes involves the two countries setting the same tax $\hat{t} < t^*$ such

that $W(\hat{t}, 1) = W(\hat{t}, 0)$, i.e., $S(\hat{t}) = 0$. The positive surplus induces the countries to compete to get the plant by cutting their emission taxes below the non-strategic level. As long as $W(t, 1) > W(t, 0)$ it will pay the country without the plant to undercut the country with the plant. On the other hand, if $W(t, 1) < W(t, 0)$ it would pay the country with the plant to raise its tax in order to lose the plant. So the only equilibrium is where $W(t, 1) = W(t, 0)$. While the Nash equilibrium tax is below the non-strategic tax, since t^* may be above marginal damage costs (since $\alpha < 1$ by symmetry of the two countries), it is not clear whether the Nash equilibrium tax is above or below marginal damage costs. Similarly, we know that t^* is above the cooperative tax, i.e., the tax which would maximize the aggregate welfare of the two countries, so, since the non-cooperative tax, $\hat{t}$, is less than t^*, we cannot tell in general whether the non-cooperative tax is above or below the cooperative tax rate.

2. Suppose the level of damage costs is intermediate, so that $S(t^*) < 0$. Then as Figure 7.3(b) shows, the Nash equilibrium involves the country with the plant setting the non-strategic tax t^*, while the country without the plant sets a tax at least as great as t' where $W(t^*, 1) = W(t', 0)$. The rationale is as follows. If the country with the plant sets the tax t^* which maximizes its welfare, conditional on having the plant, it will be worse off than the country without the plant, if it set the same tax rate. So, since there will be no competition to attract the plant, the country with the plant may as well set the tax t^*. To ensure an equilibrium, it is necessary that the country with the plant has no incentive to raise its tax in order to get rid of the plant. To ensure this, the country without the plant must commit itself to setting a significantly higher tax, t', such that if the country with the plant sought to set an even higher tax in order to lose the plant, it would end up worse off than keeping the plant. So in this case there is no undercutting relative to the non-strategic tax. Again, it is not possible to say whether this is above or below marginal damage costs. But, by the argument given earlier, the tax the two countries would set if they were acting cooperatively would be below the non-cooperative tax level.

3. Finally, if damage costs are sufficiently high that $S(t) < 0$ for all t, then, as Figure 7.3(c) shows, the only equilibrium involves both countries setting emission taxes at or above T. No country wants the plant, so they commit themselves to setting such high taxes that the firm just closes down. Note that if the two countries act cooperatively, it may well pay to have the plant set up, because although the negative environmental surplus is greater than the profits and consumer surplus of a single country, it is less than the consumer surplus and profits of the two countries. This is referred to as the NIMBY equilibrium.

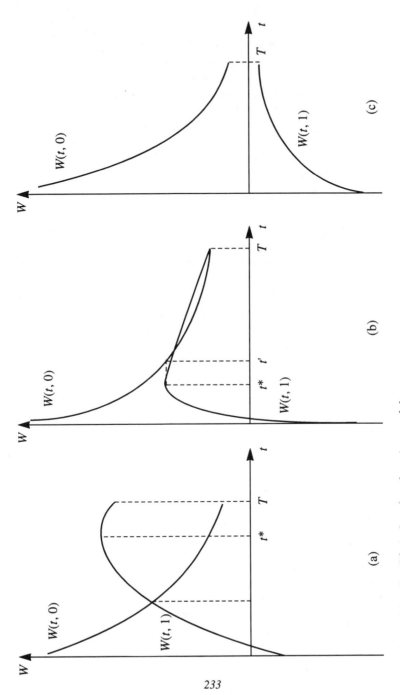

Figure 7.3 Equilibria for plant location model

233

It is clear then that even in the simplest model of plant location there is no general presumption that governments will set emission taxes which are below marginal damage costs or below the level that would be set if the countries acted collusively. This conclusion remains true if the model is extended, by having more than one firm, by introducing transport costs, so that firms may wish to have more than one plant, by having asymmetries between countries, and by introducing inter-sectoral linkages between industries (see Hoel, 1994; Markusen, Morey and Olewiler, 1992 and 1995; Motta and Thisse, 1993b; Rauscher, 1994; Ulph, 1994a; Ulph and Valentini, 1994; Venables, 1994).

POLICY IMPLICATIONS OF STRATEGIC ENVIRONMENTAL POLICY

In this section I discuss briefly some issues of international policy (for more detailed discussions see Pearce (1992), Pethig (1996), Tudini (1993), Ulph (1996c) among others). The kind of questions to be addressed are the following:

1. In the European Union the subsidiarity principle implies that responsibility for dealing with a particular issue should be delegated to the lowest level of jurisdiction unless a case can be made for passing it to a higher level; what does this imply for environmental policy?
2. Under GATT rules countries are allowed to impose regulations on the imports of *products* which might damage the environment of the importing country (i.e., pollution is related to consumption of the product) provided this is done in a non-discriminatory way (as between domestic and foreign sources, or between different foreign sources). Should this be extended to *production and process methods* (PPM), i.e., to allow countries to regulate or tax imports whose production has taken place under less stringent environmental controls than in the importing country?

As I noted in the Introduction the answers given to such questions based on traditional analysis would be that:

(a) Subsidiarity should mean that member states should be allowed to deal with their own purely domestic pollution problems and the only role for the EU would be in dealing with transboundary pollution or representing the EU in international environmental agreements (see, for example Siebert, 1991); prima facie this would suggest that, for example, the European Drinking Water Directive violated the subsidiarity principle (CEPR, 1993).

(b)   There is no case for extending GATT rules on products to PPM since this
      would deny countries the opportunity to exploit comparative advantage in
      environmental resources.

The question I now address is whether the possibility of governments setting
their environmental policies for strategic trade reasons challenges the above
traditional conclusions, and if so what does this imply for policy? One obvious
difficulty which the two previous sections of this chapter should have made clear
is that there are no robust conclusions about even the direction in which
governments would seek to distort their environmental policies for strategic
reasons. Suppose we ignore this difficulty, and use the simple models in the earlier
section which predicted that governments would set environmental policies which
were too lax, with respect to both the first-best rule and the cooperative
equilibrium. What could we conclude about policy? The discussion below
draws on Ulph (1996a).

The first point to make is that the analysis in the previous two sections
provides no support for some of the policy proposals being made, such as
harmonization of environmental policies or the setting of minimum standards.[11]
Harmonization is neither necessary nor sufficient to ensure the absence of
distortions to policy. It is not sufficient because, as shown earlier, if all countries
were identical they would all impose the same environmental tax or standard
but that would still differ from either the first-best or the cooperative level of
emission tax or standard. It is not necessary because if countries differ in
marginal damage costs or marginal abatement costs then first-best or cooperative
environmental policies should differ between countries. Indeed, if countries differ
significantly, then harmonization cannot achieve even a Pareto improvement over
the non-cooperative outcome. This is illustrated in Figure 7.4 which is a
modification of Figure 7.2 to allow for asymmetries in damage costs between
the two countries. Figure 7.4 shows the reaction functions for the 'home'
country, $e = \psi(\varepsilon)$, and the reaction function of the 'foreign' country, $\varepsilon = \psi(e)$.
It also shows the iso-welfare contour for the home country corresponding to the
non-cooperative equilibrium. Figure 7.4 is drawn on the assumption that the home
country has lower damage costs than the foreign country, and so in the non-
cooperative equilibrium in emission standards, point N with emission standards
in the home and foreign country (e^N, ε^N), emission standards in the home
country are laxer (higher) than emission standards in the foreign country.
Harmonization would involve setting equal emission standards for both countries,
a point on the 45° line, and as can be seen from the diagram any such point would
make the home country worse off than at point N. The reason is obvious.
Harmonization involves two aspects. It attempts to reduce total emissions, and
since the non-cooperative equilibrium involves total emissions which are too
high in terms of the total welfare of the two countries such a move will in general

make countries better off. But it also involves changing market shares, with the high emissions country losing market share to the low emission country. This harms the high emission country, and if countries are sufficiently different, this second effect outweighs the first. As shown in Ulph (1996a), countries would only have to differ by about 50 per cent in damage costs for harmonization not to yield a Pareto improvement over the non-cooperative equilibrium.

While it is obvious that with sufficient asymmetries between countries, harmonization of environmental policies will not work, it is sometimes thought that a policy of minimum environmental standards would be desirable, on the grounds that it would raise environmental standards in countries which fell below the minimum standard, and if other countries chose to respond by also raising their standards it would only be because they were better off by doing so. But this argument also fails to deliver a Pareto improvement over the non-cooperative equilibrium, as shown in Figure 7.4. If the home country was compelled to set an emission standard below the level e^N but above $\tilde{e}$, this would leave the

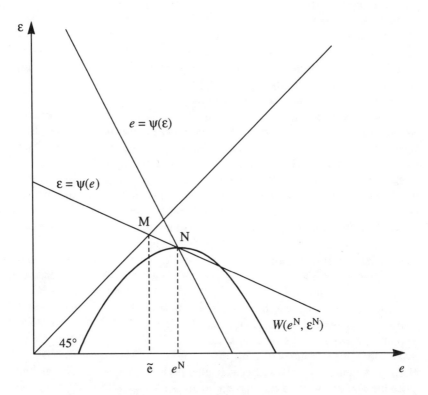

Figure 7.4   Harmonization and minimum standards

foreign country to respond by *raising* its emission standard to a point on its reaction function between N and M. This clearly makes the home country worse off. Any minimum standard tougher than (i.e., lower than) $\tilde{e}$ would be equivalent to harmonization. The reason minimum standards fails is that government reaction functions are downward sloping, so when the country with the laxest environmental policy is forced to toughen its policy, the other country can respond by relaxing its policy. It will be recalled, as discussed earlier, that in the case of emission taxes, reaction functions slope upward, and so setting minimum emission taxes can effect a Pareto improvement, though not a very significant one (see Ulph (1996a) for details; see also Kanbur, Keen and van Wijnbergen (1994) for a model of mobile capital where minimum environmental standards also work because government reaction functions slope upwards).

Thus neither of the policies frequently discussed – harmonization or minimum standards – are appropriate for dealing with national governments that engage in ecological dumping. The obvious policy advice that follows from the analysis of the previous two sections is that what a supra-national agency, like the EU or WTO, should do is to calculate environmental policies which correspond to a cooperative equilibrium. That raises two questions. Would the EU, say, have enough information to calculate such an equilibrium, and could it enforce it? The former question was analysed in Ulph (1996a) which assumed that damage costs were private information to national governments, so that any set of environmental policies imposed on national governments would need to satisfy incentive compatibility constraints. The obvious constraint here is to prevent countries with high damage costs pretending to be low damage cost countries in order to be allowed to set lax environmental policies and hence obtain larger market shares. As Ulph (1996a) showed this can lead to environmental policies in countries which have different damage costs being much more similar to each other than would be the case with full information. The reason is simply that the need to satisfy the incentive compatibility constraint means that countries with high damage costs have to be rewarded for revealing that information by being allowed to produce more output, and pollution, than would be the case with full information. However this falls short of full harmonization.

I have touched on some of the policy issues raised by the analysis of strategic environmental policy, but as this section shows the literature on this topic is in its infancy.

CONCLUSIONS

In this chapter I have surveyed a number of recent studies examining the link between environmental policy and international trade. The literature has been timely in that the issue has been one of considerable public debate, and the literature has been well placed to address some of the issues raised by that debate, since the literature has focused on imperfect competition and the potential scope for governments to manipulate environmental policy for strategic reasons. I have shown that this recent analysis is capable of providing starkly different predictions about environmental policy under liberalized trade regimes from those derived from the traditional trade and environmental literature, but that there is a severe problem of non-robustness of results. This is especially problematic when it comes to trying to draw policy conclusions from this new literature, although the analysis does not support some of the policy prescription discussed in popular debates.

For future research I think the main priorities are to establish better empirical results, so that a judgement can be reached whether any of these strategic trade effects on environmental policy are likely to be quantitatively very significant. If these turn out to be significant, then more work needs to be done on appropriate policy design.

NOTES

1. I am grateful to Henk Folmer and Scott Barrett for helpful suggestions for improving the exposition in this chapter. Remaining errors are my own.
2. For example, recent EU treaties with countries such as Poland include references to harmonization of environmental policies.
3. Suppose environmental policies in a 'lax' country are raised to the same level as in a 'tough' country, and this displaces production activity from the lax to the tough country; the improvement to the environment in the 'lax' country could easily be outweighed by the deterioration in the tough country, since that is why the environmental policies differed in the first place.
4. Braga provides an example where policies restricting exports of timber from Indonesia led to the expansion of local production of timber-based products which was far less efficient than foreign producers, resulting in an expansion of logging activity and further deterioration in the environment.
5. In the conventional analysis, transboundary pollution has the usual implication that countries acting non-cooperatively will ignore the impact of their pollution on other countries and so will set environmental policies which are too lax relative to policies derived by maximizing world welfare.
6. Total differentiation yields: $E_q dt + E_u du + E_d D_z dz = R_q dt + R_s ds + M dt + t dM + s dz + z ds$. Using (7.2) and (7.3) simplifies this to equation (7.4).
7. If $t = 0$ and $s = E_d D_z$ then $\delta = 0$, and so the right-handside of (7.7) is zero, and so we have the optimal first-best level of welfare.
8. To see the derivation of the partial derivative of ρ with respect to t, differentiate (7.19) with respect to t to get:

$$\frac{\partial x}{\partial t} = r_1 . r_1 . \frac{\partial x}{\partial t} + r_2 \Rightarrow \frac{\partial x}{\partial t} = \frac{r_2}{\left(1 - r_1^2\right)}.$$

Similarly for the other partial derivative.

9. To see the derivation of (7.20) recall that both x and y depend on t and that from (7.17a) and (7.17b) $R_x - C' = t = A'$.
10. This follows from the first-order condition for maximizing the sum of the welfare in the two countries.
11. The discussion of harmonization and minimum standards in this section is very limited. In particular, I emphasize that the discussion relates to production-related pollution. The case for harmonization or minimum standards is different for consumption-related pollution, where different standards may be covert forms of trade barriers and where issues such as interconnection externalities may arise. My critique of harmonization also ignores other aspects, such as transaction costs of monitoring environmental policies, although the discussion below of informational constraints could be related to transactions costs. I am grateful to Scott Barrett for his comments on this point.

REFERENCES

Anderson, K. (1992), 'The Standard Welfare Economics of Policies Affecting Trade and the Environment', in Anderson and Blackhurst (eds), *The Greening of World Trade*, Hemel Hempstead: Harvester Wheatsheaf.

Anderson, K. and R. Blackhurst (eds) (1992), *The Greening of World Trade*, Hemel Hempstead: Harvester Wheatsheaf.

Arden-Clarke, C. (1991), *The General Agreement on Tariffs and Trade, Environmental Protection and Sustainable Development*, Gland, Switzerland: World Wildlife Fund for Nature.

Barbier, E. and M. Rauscher (1994), 'Trade, Deforestation and Policy Interventions', in C. Carraro (ed.), *Trade, Innovation, Environment*, Dordrecht: Kluwer, 55–74.

Barrett, S. (1994), 'Strategic Environmental Policy and International Trade', *Journal of Public Economics*, **54**(3), 325–38.

Bhagwati, J. (1971), 'The Generalised Theory of Distortions and Welfare', in J. Bhagwati *et al.* (eds), *Trade, Balance of Payments and Growth*, Amsterdam: North-Holland.

Bhagwati, J. and H. Daly (1993), 'Debate: Does Free Trade Harm the Environment?', *Scientific American*, November, 17–29.

Braga, C. (1992), 'Tropical Forests and Trade Policy: The Case of Indonesia and Brazil', in P. Low (ed.), *International Trade and the Environment*, World Bank Discussion Papers, 159, 173–94.

Brander, J. and B. Spencer (1985), 'Export Subsidies and International Market Share Rivalry', *Journal of International Economics*, **18**, 83–100.

CEPR (1993), 'Making Sense of Subsidiarity', CEPR Annual Report, Monitoring European Integration 4.

Cesar, H. (1993), 'The Comedy and Tragedy of the Commons', PhD thesis, Florence: EUI.

Conrad, K. (1993a), 'Taxes and Subsidies for Pollution-Intensive Industries as Trade Policy', *Journal of Environmental Economics and Management*, **25**, 121–35.

Conrad, K. (1993b), 'Optimal Environmental Policy for Oligopolistic Industries in an Open Economy', Department of Economics Discussion Paper 476–93, University of Mannheim.

Copeland, B.R. (1994), 'International Trade and the Environment: Policy Reform in a Polluted Small Open Economy', *Journal of Environmental Economics and Management*, **26**, 44–65.

Dean, J. (1992), 'Trade and Environment: A Survey of the Literature', in P. Low (ed.), *International Trade and the Environment*, Washington, DC: World Bank.

Dixit, A. and V. Norman (1980), *Theory of International Trade*, Cambridge, UK: Cambridge University Press.

Ecchia, G. and M. Mariotti (1994), 'A Survey on Environmental Policy: Technological Innovation and Strategic Issues', *Nota di Lavoro* 44.94, Milan: FEEM.

Folmer, H.P., V. Mouche and S. Ragland (1993), 'Interconnected Games and International Environmental Problems', *Environmental and Resource Economics,* **3**, 313–36.

Helpman, E. and P. Krugman (1989), *Trade Policy and Market Structure*, Cambridge, Mass.: MIT Press.

Hoel, M. (1994), 'Environmental Policy as a Game between Governments when Plant Locations are Endogenous', paper presented to 21st Annual EARIE Conference, Crete, 4–6 September.

Hoeller, P., A. Dean and J. Nicolaisen (1991), 'Macroeconomic Implications of Reducing Greenhouse Gas Emissions: A Survey of Empirical Studies', *OECD Economic Studies*, **16**, 45–78.

Kanbur, R., M. Keen and S. van Wijnbergen (1995), 'Industrial Competitiveness, Environmental Regulation and Direct Foreign Investment', in I. Goldin and A. Winters (eds), *The Economics of Sustainable Development*, Cambridge, UK: Cambridge University Press, 289–301.

Kennedy, P.W. (1994), 'Equilibrium Pollution Taxes in Open Economies with Imperfect Competition', *Journal of Environmental Economics and Management,* **27**, 49–63.

Krutilla, K. (1991), 'Environmental Regulation in an Open Economy', *Journal of Environmental Economics and Management*, **20**, 127–42.

Long, N.V. and H. Siebert (1991), 'Institutional Competition versus ex-ante Harmonisation – the Case of Environmental Policy', *Journal of Institutional and Theoretical Economics*, **147**, 296–312.

Low, P. (ed.) (1992), *International Trade and the Environment*, Washington, DC: World Bank.

Markusen, J. (1975a), 'Cooperative Control of International Pollution and Common Property Resources', *Quarterly Journal of Economics*, **89**, 618–32.

Markusen, J. (1975b), 'International Externalities and Optimal Tax Structures', *Journal of International Economics*, **5**, 15–29.

Markusen, J., E. Morey and N. Olewiler (1992), 'Noncooperative Equilibria in Regional Environmental Policies when Plant Locations are Endogenous', NBER Working Paper 4051.

Markusen, J., E. Morey and N. Olewiler (1993), 'Environmental Policy when Market Structure and Plant Location are Endogenous', *Journal of Environmental Economics and Management*, **24**, 69–86.

Motta, M. and J.-F. Thisse (1993a), 'Minimum Quality Standard as an Environmental Policy: Domestic and International Effects', *Nota di Lavora* 20.93, Milan: FEEM.

Motta, M. and J.-F. Thisse (1993b), 'Does Environmental Dumping Lead to Delocation?', *Nota di Lavoro* 77.93, Milan: FEEM.

Panagariya, A., K. Palmer, W. Oates and A. Krupnick (1993), 'Toward an Integrated Theory of Open Economy Environmental and Trade Policy', Working Paper No. 93–8, Department of Economics, University of Maryland.

Pearce, D. (1992), 'Should the GATT be Reformed for Environmental Reasons?', CSERGE Working Paper GEC 92–06.

Pethig, R. (1976), 'Pollution, Welfare and Environmental Policy in the Theory of Comparative Advantage', *Journal of Environmental Economics and Management*, **2**, 160–9.

Pethig, R. (1996), 'Noncooperative National Environmental Policies and Capital Mobility', in J. Braden, H. Folmer and T. Ulen (eds), *Environmental Policy with Economic and Political Integration: The European Community and the United States*, Cheltenham: Edward Elgar.

Porter, M. (1991), 'America's Green Strategy', *Scientific American*, p. 168.

Rauscher, M. (1993), 'Environmental Regulation and International Capital Allocation', *Nota di Lavoro* 79.93, Milan: FEEM.

Rauscher, M. (1994), 'On Ecological Dumping', *Oxford Economic Papers*, **46**, 822–40.

Robertson, D. (1992), 'Trade and the Environment: Harmonisation and Technical Standards', in P. Low (ed.), *International Trade and the Environment*, Washington, DC: World Bank.

Runge, C.F. (1996) 'Economic Trade and Environmental Protection', in J. Braden, H. Folmer and T. Ulen (eds), *Environmental Policy with Economic and Political Integration: The European Community and the United States*, Cheltenham: Edward Elgar.

Siebert, H. (1991), 'Europe, '92. Decentralising Environmental Policy in the Single Market', *Environmental and Resource Economics*, **1**, 271–88.

Tudini, A. (1993), 'Trade and Environment: The Issue of Process and Production Methods', *Nota di Lavoro* 7.93, Milan: FEEM.

Ulph, A. (1992), 'The Choice of Environmental Policy Instruments and Strategic International Trade', in R. Pethig (ed.), *Conflicts and Cooperation in Managing Environmental Resources*, Berlin: Springer-Verlag.

Ulph, A. (1994a), 'Environmental Policy, Plant Location and Government Protection', in C. Carraro (ed.), *Trade, Innovation and the Environment*, Dordrecht: Kluwer, 123–166.

Ulph, A. (1994b), 'Environmental Policy and International Trade – A Survey of Recent Economic Analysis', Southampton Discussion Paper in Economics and Econometrics, 9423, to appear in C. Carraro and D. Siniscalco (eds), *New Directions in the Economic Theory of the Environment*, Cambridge University Press.

Ulph, A. (1994c), 'Strategic Environmental Policy and International Competitiveness', in H. Siebert (ed.), *Elements of a Rational Environmental Policy*, Tübingen: J.C.B. Mohr.

Ulph, A. (1996a), 'Environmental Policy Instruments and Imperfectly Competitive International Trade', *Environmental and Resource Economics*, **7**(4), 333–55.

Ulph, A. (1996b), 'Environmental Policy and International Trade when Governments and Producers Act Strategically', *Journal of Environmental Economics and Management*, **30**(3), 265–81.

Ulph, A. (1996c), 'Strategic Environmental Policy, International Trade and the Single European Market', in J. Braden, H. Folmer and T. Ulen (eds), *Environmental Policy with Economic and Political Integration: The European Community and the United States*, Cheltenham: Edward Elgar, 235–56.

Ulph, A. (1996d) 'Strategic Environmental Policy and International Trade – The Role of Market Conduct', in C. Carraro, Y. Katsoulacos and A. Xepapadeas (eds), *Environmental Policy and Market Structure*, Dordrecht: Kluwer, 99–130.

Ulph, D. (1994), 'Strategic Innovation and Strategic Environmental Policy', in C. Carraro (ed.), *Trade Innovation, Environment*, Dordrecht: Kluwer, 205–28.

Ulph, A. and D. Ulph (1996), 'Trade, Strategic Innovation and Strategic Environmental Policy – A General Analysis', in C. Carraro, Y. Katsoulacos and A. Xepapadeas (eds), *Environmental Policy and Market Structure*, Dordrecht: Kluwer, 181–208.

Ulph, A. and L. Valentini (1996), 'Plant Location and Strategic Environmental Policy with Inter-Sectoral Linkages', Southampton Discussion Paper in Economics and Econometrics 9623, to appear in *Resource and Energy Economics*.

Venables, A. (1944), 'Economic Policy and the Manufacturing Base – Hysteresis in Location', Paper presented to CEPR workshop on Environmental Policy, International Agreements and International Trade, London.

Verdier, T. (1993), 'Strategic Trade and the Regulation of Pollution by Performance or Design Standard', *Nota di Lavoro* 58.93, Milan: FEEM.

Index

243